VOYAGE OF GRACE

VOYAGE OF GRACE

From the End of the Road
to the Ends of the Earth

Norbert Bauer

WWW.VOYAGEOFGRACE.COM

Artwork and cover design: Björn Bauer, www.bjornbauerart.com

ISBN: 978-91-981661-0-1

Typesetting services by BOOKOW.COM

For Cathy, my special gift from God, who always trusted and believed in what I perceived to be God's leading, no matter how far-out it seemed at the time.

Thank you for sharing this voyage with me!

And for Stina, Karin and Bosse who showed me God's love in a way that I could not resist. Without them this journey would have ended elsewhere.

Preface

The idea for this book started many years ago. Even as a young man I understood that my story was just a bit out of the ordinary. The first chapters were written many years ago, but then I stopped because I realized I had to wait for the story to evolve some more. I am so glad I did, for back then I could not even have imagined that this ride could get any wilder than it had already been.

Initially, I just wanted to tell the story for my seven children, but then I realized that it might become a blessing for others out there as well. Especially for those who wrestle with their own insecurities and low self-esteem, I trust this story will be an encouragement to you. The words, "I hate my life!" should never pass the lips of any person, least of all a believer in a sovereign God. I was only eighteen when I thought my life was no longer worth living, but then something unbelievably incredible happened! Every life is a gift from God, and as such it is worth living, for He never creates anything without purpose. It is my prayer that even while you read about my journey you would discover more about your own, and your true purpose here in this life.

On this voyage I have crossed paths with far more people than I could ever mention. Maybe you are reading this book because you hope that your name might appear on any page, but chances are that you will not find it. If I had mentioned every single person that played even the tiniest part in this story, then this book would be twice as thick, and no one would like to read it. But be assured of this: I am fully aware that every person I have ever met has in some way contributed to the outcome of this journey. I may have forgotten your name, or even what you look like, but there is Someone who has not, and never will.

Come and join me on a voyage that could have ended in great tragedy, but did not because of something called "grace."

CONTENTS

Childhood

My childhood memories go all the way back to a small wooden house in the town of Bad Mergentheim in Germany, where I spent the first four years of my life. Though my parents, Karl and Anni Bauer originally came from the province of Franconia, they had been driven to Baden Würthemberg through the turmoils of the Second World War. My older sister Monika and I were born there.

My father worked hard as a traveling salesman, putting aside every Deutschmark for a new house someday. I can well remember all the many war stories that he could tell - like the story of being shot in the elbow by a Russian sniper just a few miles outside Moscow. Whenever he told that story he would pull up the sleeve of his left arm to show us his scars, and my sister and I gaped reverently at the crater in his elbow that had almost severed the arm. He never failed to mention one particular part of the story, which I never forgot. He had led his platoon through a birch forest, his rifle ready for action. Suddenly he felt the urge to turn, just as the sniper in the nearby bushes pulled the trigger. The shot was aimed at his heart, but because of the turn the bullet hit his bent arm instead. He never said that it was God who had protected him that day, but hinted that there must have been some higher power involved. Already back then there was a trace of hope in my heart that there must be some higher being watching over our lives.

My father also told us stories about his hard childhood, and what it was like growing up after the First World War in Germany. He never knew who his real father was, and his mother chased him out of the house when he was a teenager, because she could no longer feed all the younger children. He always wanted for us to have a better life, and, as far as I can look back, we never lacked anything.

My mother was always very quiet and withdrawn. Her past had not been easy either, having lived through the ordeal of their home being bombed to the ground by the Allied Forces during the final days of the war. She never talked much about it, and gave us children the impression that she could deal with anything in life. She always fulfilled her duties as a mother, but I can hardly remember her demonstrating her love to me, other than in deeds. Physical contact was a rare thing in our family, except for a mandatory good night kiss, and that only applied to Dad.

In 1957, we moved to our newly build double story home with a large garden in the suburbs of Nuremberg in Bavaria. Full of pride, Father pointed out repeatedly that he had never borrowed any money all of his life and even our new house was paid for in cash. It was his life's fulfill-ment. Since house and garden took a considerable amount of time and energy to keep up, my sister and I had to learn early on to do our part, and my chores mainly consisted of gardening. That in itself would not have been so bad, except for the fact that my father always wanted me to help and assist him when he worked in the garden, which was very frequently, considering the size of it. Add to that the fact that one could never please him, and it becomes obvious that it did not take long for me to resent the garden, the house, and even my father. We were never allowed to openly voice any frustration or criticism – we were expected to obey and be quiet, and that applied to Mother as well.

We were kept away from any possible danger, and even things like playing soccer with my friends, or climbing trees were taboo. That in turn affected my relationship with my peers at school who always saw me as the outsider. Father was always very performance oriented. He could be very generous when he was pleased with my progress, but he would get very angry and punitive when he was not pleased, which was mostly the case.

My first few years in school went well, and my grades were above average. Meanwhile the fear of my father grew in my heart, and with it the fear to fail. In fourth grade, I once got a negative remark from a teacher in my workbook, since I had forgotten part of my homework. I was so scared to show up with that workbook at home that I hid it in the forest, and told my parents the teacher still had it. Somehow, my father found out about it. I was beaten severely and had to write the whole book again, which killed any free time I might have had for the next few weeks.

This incident was the beginning of a lifestyle of lies and deceit that seemed to pull me deeper and deeper, year after year. After starting high school, my grades were down to 'C's and 'D's, and I had totally lost the favor of my father. I spent all of my time hitting the books when I was not mowing the lawn or cutting hedges. On top of that, I had to get tutoring to bring up my grades. My father threatened to send me to a boarding school for difficult children, and although that threat hung like a black cloud over me, there were times when I wished he had cashed in on his promise.

Spiritually speaking, there was not much going on in our family. Mother had been raised Catholic, but she switched over to the Lutheran church for my father's sake. For her it was important that there hung a crucifix on the wall above my bed, and she taught me a simple child's prayer. On religious holidays, we went to church together, and on Christmas and New Year's Eve there was an occasional prayer offered, which seemed highly awkward and embarrassing to us kids. That kind of behavior totally turned me off towards religion in general, since I was becoming aware that things at home were not right. My parents had started to fight more frequently, and Dad treated Mom brutally, especially when he had been drinking. This happened more and more. Things really took a turn for the worse when my Dad lost his job with the company for which he had been working for many years. In his perfectionism, wanting to supply all the needs of the family, this must have driven him crazy, and often we became the recipients of his frustrations.

Our house had an old-fashioned hot-air heating system that was pow-
ered by a burner that used coal fire. My room was on the top floor, and
the warm air got there through a special shaft that branched off to each
bedroom. Opening or closing a special duct in the wall controlled the
temperature in each room. One side effect of that particular construction was that one could hear what was going on in the other rooms, by
pressing one's ear on the grid of the air-duct. We often used this feature
as an intercom, for example, when Mom wanted to call us for dinner, she
only had to yell into the duct in the dining room, and we could hear her
upstairs. Often my father came home late from a business trip, after I had
gone to bed. In order to find out what kind of mood he was in, I would
open the grid in my room and listen to what was being spoken in the
living room. So I became a witness to many fights between my parents,
and often I could hear the dull thuds of the blows my mother received. It
hurt as if I had received them myself.

My spiritual state in those days was nothing more than the evening
prayer that my mother had taught me, except that I had begun to add
certain requests to it, especially when I was afraid to fail in school. However, I can clearly remember one particular incident. One Easter, my
parents had bought me a new red bicycle, which was about two sizes bigger than the little kid's bike that I had before. I had never been especially
well coordinated, so I had trouble riding it. My parents tried to help me
by holding on to me while pushing me around the front lawn, but as soon
as they would let go, I fell over. The whole thing was quite frustrating for
all of us, and I felt ashamed because of my inability to ride the bike. After
some days, my parents gave up, and put the bike in the garage, waiting
for me to grow up some more.

I was really bothered by this, and that night I added a new line to my
prayers: "… and please, dear God, help me to be able to ride my new
bike."

That night, I had a dream. In my dream, I got up early in the morning,
got dressed, and pulled my bike out of the garage. I held it a bit slanted,

so I could put my right leg over the bar and on to the right pedal. I would then push it down with all my weight, while heaving myself onto the seat. It worked – in my dream I was riding the bike. When I awoke the next morning, I could remember every detail of the dream and got up, took my bike out, and did exactly what I had dreamed. I could ride my bike instantly! For me it was nothing short of a miracle. My faith in God grew greatly that day, but I felt somewhat rotten to only come to him whenever I needed something. Otherwise, I had no relationship with Him.

I managed to have a couple of friends at school, but these relationships were rather short-lived, since I was never allowed to be there when something cool was going on. I did have one real friend, and his name was Günther. We had met when I was in second grade, but he was already in third grade and was six months older. That's the way it was in all things – Günther was always ahead of me. Somehow, that helped me, since I could follow his example, and had something to strive for. However, our relationship was a bit one-sided. He was such a friendly and lovable type, that he always had people around him. Since he was my only friend, I was very jealous when I had to share Günther with others. In a strange way, he had taken on the role of my father, since I could talk with him about everything. He always listened to me and helped whenever he could.

One fine day when I was ten, my parents told me that Mother had to go to the hospital, since she was going to have a baby. For nine long months they had kept it a secret from me, and now they were laughing at me for not knowing! Totally confused, I sought help from Günther who did not laugh at me, but gave me my first lesson in Sex Ed. That was 1963 when my brother Winfried was born.

From then on, many things changed in our house, and of course all the attention went to the new arrival. That was certainly normal, but it did not do much for my growing fear of rejection. Winfried and I always got along well with each other, but because of our age-difference we never had a lot in common.

Günther and I spent much time together. When my father was gone on a business trip, I would spend all my free time at his place. We played a lot of "Indians and Cowboys" together, but I usually lost. Often we would make music on various instruments together, and recorded our creations on an ancient reel-to-reel tape recorder.

Many times we just took a walk in the nearby forest, or lay in the grass to philosophize about the meaning of life, or other deep spiritual topics like UFOs or life on other planets.

Günther's parents were not very religious people, and he was not at all positive about Christianity. Nevertheless, when it came to honesty and integrity, he was far ahead of me. When I told him about my problems at home, and how I tried to get out of trouble by lying, he would look at me with his big brown eyes and say, "You know, lying will not get you any-where – I would never lie to my parents." I was jealous of the relationship he had with his father, who treated him like a buddy and gave him much freedom. I knew he was right, but the growing fear of my father led me deeper and deeper into dishonesty. I realized there were a few things in my life that even Günther could not help me with.

The Wild Years

Adolescence hit me with all its turbulence. I had developed into a very quiet and shy young man. Once again, Günther was way ahead of me. His voice broke almost one whole year before mine, and he had his first girlfriend when he was twelve. From then on we did not get to see each other as much as before, since he was always out socializing with his other friends.

It was during those years that I discovered a great love in my life – aviation. In 1965, I had my first airplane ride, when our family went to Spain on vacation. The absolute highlight of that trip was when I was invited to visit the pilot in the cockpit. I was mesmerized by the green glow of the countless instruments, the exotic sounds of this big machine, and the flair of adventure that seemed to hang in the air. Flying captivated my heart like nothing before. I could not understand much of what the copilot tried to explain to me, but on that day I decided that I wanted nothing else in life than to become an airline pilot. I realized that even as a little boy, I loved planes more than cars, building them out of Lego blocks. Now I devoured aviation books and started building model airplanes of all shapes and sizes.

In our neighborhood lived a paraplegic man whose hobby was to build remote-controlled airplanes, and then fly them in the fields around our village. One day, while working in the garden, I heard the high-pitched sound of a tiny combustion engine, and shortly after that saw a beautiful model glider rise into the sky. I had to go see what this was all about, and so I met Herr Söhnitz. Since the left side of his body was paralyzed, he needed someone to carry his gear and to help him launch his airplanes. That gave me the perfect excuse to leave home in order to help a man in need. I spent countless hours with him in his basement, watching him build his models with a patience and endurance I had never seen before. Now all I wanted was to be able to build my own airplanes, and soon that day would arrive.

My father and my sister had left for the USA for four weeks to visit some of our relatives there, and I could not pass up that opportunity. I went and bought a simple airplane kit with a suitable, tiny engine, and all the other odds and ends needed for that type of venture. Good thing it was summer vacation, because for the next two days I barely left my room. Then it was finished, a beautiful little free-flight model, which means it was not radio controlled, but could fly anywhere the wind would take it until the little engine ran out of gas.

The paint was still wet, but I could not wait any longer, and had to find out if it would fly – and it did! It was not trimmed properly, and did one looping after the other, but to me it was the most beautiful thing I had ever seen. I had obviously put too much gas in the little tank, for it flew and flew until I could barely see it with the naked eye. I got on my bike and tried to keep it in sight, but it disappeared into the woods behind the soccer field. Some of the other boys in the neighborhood came running (except for Günther, who had no time for such childish games). They were attracted by the noise, and no doubt the beautiful sight of my masterpiece disappearing on the horizon. Eventually we found it high up in the crown of a huge pine tree, the type that is hard to climb because it only has branches in the upper third of the trunk. We tried everything, but could not get it to fall to the ground, and since it was getting late we all had to go home – I was devastated. Just before dark, one of my friends rang our doorbell. He had brought his dad who would help us get the plane down. So we trudged back into the woods, and eventually found the right tree. My friend's dad pulled a tree saw out of his bag, took a quick look to the right and to the left to make sure none but us was watching, and simply cut down the tree! However, my joy and excitement was short-lived, as one of the branches landed right on top of my model, crushing it into many pieces.

Through this experience, I learned a few things about my character of which I had not been aware. On one hand, I learned that I was able to accomplish what I had set out to do, but, on the other hand I discovered an impulsive behavior that easily led to recklessness. When I stood there ready to launch my model airplane, I did not think about the possible consequences, but only wanted to see a result. This particular weakness would become the reason for many painful experiences in the future, but I also experienced many times how God would use this for his purposes. Later in life, this kind of irresponsible behavior developed into a childlike trust to face challenges by faith, making decisions whose outcome could not be calculated by logic and reason alone - but that was not to happen for a long time.

$$* * *$$

Günther and I grew apart more and more, and it seemed like every time I saw him he had another girlfriend. He only talked about parties, sexual encounters, and things I could not identify with, and it seemed like we had nothing in common anymore. Physically, we also developed quite differently from each other. The hippie-wave had hit Germany, and Günther let his hair grow long and wore jackets with fringes, and other exotic pieces of clothing. I could not compete, since my father had no tolerance whatsoever for things like that. So in the end, I had no other choice but to find some other friends. There was Frank, for example. Coming from a wealthy family with a rather perverted imagination, he was not a good influence on me. Occasionally, he would talk me into playing hooky, and we hung out in cafés, arcades, or the movies, meeting other school kids who had decided not to show up for classes that day. That in turn did not help my grades at school, and that led to more lies at home.

Even though I had panic fear of my father finding out about my episodes, I could not resist further temptations. By now we not only skipped certain classes, but sometimes did not show up several days in a row for school. We would get drunk and then prove our courage to each other by committing petty theft. I was caught up in a vortex that pulled me deeper and deeper into a bondage from which I could no longer escape.

My greatest horror were the annual parent-teacher conferences at school. There was one in particular I will never forget! We had skipped many days of school by now, and had signed the excuse slips ourselves. My grades were the worst ever, and I knew my Dad would not miss the upcoming opportunity to talk to my teachers. Somehow, I had to keep him from going, and I asked one of my so-called friends what it would take to keep our Volkswagen from starting the next morning. "Hmm" – he thought for a minute, "oh I know, pour some water in the distributor, or remove some of the fuses in the fuse box, that ought to do the trick." That night, when my parents were asleep, I sneaked out into the garage, opened the engine compartment of Dad's white VW hatchback, removed the distributor cap and poured one cup of water into the distributor. Then I replaced some of the fuses with old, fried ones, and retreated back into my room.

The next morning, still in bed, I heard the car engine crank but failing to start. So I turned over one more time to catch some more sleep. Shortly after that I heard voices, and recognized the voice of one of our neighbors, Herr Janitz, and my heart sank. That man could fix anything, and it did not take him long to locate the faulty fuses and replace them with good ones. And then – to my amazement and absolute horror – my dad tried again, and the engine caught and purred like a kitten. I decided that day I did not like Volkswagen!

What happened next, I won't describe in detail. The first teacher my dad talked to was very concerned about my health and my grades, after having missed so many days of school. My dad did "go ballistic," as some would say, and whatever sliver of freedom I thought I had vanished that day. Somehow, I made it through the rest of the school year without having to repeat it, but my motivation to finish school was at an all-time low.

*** * ***

There were other tensions in our family during those years. My older sister Monika was already a young lady, looking for serious relationships, which always caused tensions at home. As far as I was concerned, she was already an adult, and we had very little contact with each other. I admired her courage to stand up to my father, but he was not the kind of man who would accept opposition without retaliation. Since I had developed into the black sheep of the family, I ended up on the receiving end of his anger and frustrations. He would lecture me for hours about all his life's achievements, and at one such occasion he revealed to me that one of my uncles from my mother's side was a convicted criminal. I obviously had inherited these genes, and there was not much hope for me. He knew about my dream of becoming a pilot, and he told me more than once that I might as well forget about that. This message of hopelessness filled me with panic fear of the future. I knew that I could not continue on like this, and had vowed many times to change, but had to come to the realization that I was not capable of doing that. Obviously, my father was right, and there really was no hope for me to ever succeed in anything in my life.

More and more I withdrew into my shell, built my model airplanes, and had lost faith in a life and future worth living for. I felt extremely lonely and longed for deep and meaningful relationships, but I could not find any. I was not very successful with the girls either. After all, who wants to hang out with a guy that cannot open his mouth and is obviously depressed? Besides I was always very picky in my choice of friends. When I was 16 and 17, I was allowed to go to some birthday parties of my "friends" from school, but I could not really connect with anyone. I usually ended up drunk, sitting in a corner by myself.

Ah yes, there is still the story with the motorcycle. In those days, you were allowed to drive a certain type of light motorcycle at the age of 16.

The maximum engine size of these bikes was 50 cubic centimeters, which is very small, but the manufacturers had figured out a way to make them quite snappy, and some of them would go 100 km/h, or more. Most of my friends had one of those and drove it to school, including Günther. I should have known better, but I still tried to talk my parents into letting me have one of those bikes. There was no way my dad would agree to that, saying, it is too dangerous, and bad for your health, and that was that. I tried to bargain by offering to work all summer, and even being content with a much slower scooter or moped, but the answer was always a firm "no way."

I was not ready to give up that easily, and was ready to fight for what I thought was my right, even if I had to use illegal means to get what I wanted. One day I heard from one of my classmates that his brother was selling an old motorcycle very cheap. It was an ancient, black "Zündapp 200" with individual tractor seats on springs – a rare beauty. After a short test drive, I knew I wanted that bike more than anything, and had just enough money to buy it. Again, I had acted on impulse without thinking of the possible consequences. You had to be 18 years of age to drive a bike that size and have a special driver's license which, of course, I did not possess. On top of that, the bike was neither inspected, registered, nor insured. I parked it at a public parking lot near our house, left our house each morning to walk to the bus stop, but instead of taking the bus I drove the 10 km to school on my Zündapp.

Of course, the whole thing was quite scary, especially, when I saw a police car nearby. But then I had this grand idea. Back then we had many thousand U.S. troops stationed all over Germany, and there were several barracks in my hometown of Nürnberg. Their vehicles had special green plates that immediately identified them as U.S. forces. I had heard that the German police usually left them alone, since they had their own military police to look after them. So I swiped the green plate of a huge Cadillac parked in our neighborhood, and attached it to my bike – so there. Then I went to one of the popular U.S. Army surplus stores, and bought some army boots, a green parka, and best of all, a motorcycle helmet with a full visor that made it impossible to see the driver's face. Thus camouflaged, I drove my bike for almost 6 months without any incident.

To this day, I can't figure out why none of the teachers at school ever wondered about this kid on a big bike with U.S. Army plates. For a change, I had become somewhat of a hero in my class, at least in the eyes of some. Others, especially some of the older students, thought I was totally crazy, but nobody said anything to the teachers. One day, my luck ran out. I had been cruising through some of our neighboring villages, when I set off a speed trap, going way over the speed limit. A bit further down the road I saw a police car, and the police man stood by the road making it very obvious that he wanted me to pull over. Oh dear – many pictures flashed through my mind – none of them pretty, and I knew this was the end! Or maybe not… as I slowed down to stop behind the police car, I totally panicked, twisted the throttle, and took off with a roar. I could not hear the "halt" shouts over the noise of my engine, but in my rear view mirror I could see a very animated police officer jump behind the wheel of his Volkswagen van to give chase, with blinking lights and siren blaring.

This was getting worse and worse, and by now I was acting on adrenaline alone, overriding any sense or caution I might have had left. I knew I had gone way too far with this, and had to put an end to this episode without my father finding out. And there it came - another brilliant idea. I slowed down enough to make a 90-degree turn onto a dirt path between two fields, leading straight for a patch of forest less than half a kilometer away. The police officer had the good sense not to try and follow me, but by now I was beyond scared. In my mind I saw flashes of pictures of me on my bike on the front page of every local newspaper. I raced through the woods like a maniac, and when I thought I was safe I hid the bike in some bushes and ran all the way home. By the time I got home, a plan had formed in my mind. It was time for another night-time action…

I knew I had to get rid of both the evidence and the temptation of ever driving that bike again, knowing the police were surely looking for this pseudo soldier on an ancient Zündapp. So I sneaked out late at night, walked back several kilometers to where I had ditched the bike, and started it up for one final drive. Right through the center of our village flows a man-made waterway called the Rhine-Main-Danube Canal. It was built back in 1846 in an attempt to connect the North Sea with the Black Sea, by connecting the three main rivers. This particular stretch of the canal was no longer used by ships, but it was still divided into segments that were sealed off by gates to compensate for the changing altitude of the landscape. As I drove along the canal, I was looking for a good place to permanently dispatch of the bike, and found the perfect spot. I drove right up on one of the water gates, revved up the engine, popped the clutch and let the bike jump out from between my legs. It was soon airborne, and then dove five or six meters down into the basin, where it hit with a mighty splash. As I looked over the edge, I could see it sink lower and lower, the lights still glowing eerily, but fading rapidly as it hit the bottom where it has lain ever since (or so I hope…).

I was relieved that this whole escapade ended without any major disaster, but on the walk home that night I realized that I had become scared of myself. It seemed like someone was possessing me to engage in these crazy and dangerous acts that were so unlike my shy and fearful personality. I had a strong sense that someone was out to kill me, or at least ruin my life. As it turns out, I had hit much closer to the truth than I could possibly have imagined.

* * *

The only thing I still enjoyed was my music. When I was six, my father had asked me if I wanted to learn an instrument. I had been fooling around on a toy accordion, and some people thought I had musical talent. So for the next four years I had accordion lessons every week, and had to practice one hour every day. Now that was only fun for the first month, after that, it became a burden and a chore. But my dad had bought me a "real" accordion, and did not let me back out of my commitment. I guess I have been blessed with a musical ear, for I was able to make my teacher believe I could actually read music, when in reality I could play almost anything by ear if I had heard it once. After four years of what I considered unbearable torture, my dad let me off the hook, and I could quit the lessons and the practice. But it did not take me long to pick up my instrument and start playing the kind of music I wanted to play, just for fun! But somehow, playing Beatles songs on an accordion just did not sound right. Since I was one of the taller boys in my class, our music teacher asked me if I wanted to play the upright bass for the school orchestra. I did that for a while and then switched to the electric bass. When I was 17, I played in a blues band. We never really performed anywhere, but used to spend every Friday evening in a cottage, just playing the blues and improvising for hours. That fit my melancholic phase quite well, and I felt accepted by the other musicians, even though I was the youngest.

After some time, even that fell apart, just as everything else in my life threatened to fall apart. My father had been an avid marksman, and I joined him for a few years at his gun club shooting air rifles in competitions. At one point I had gotten pretty good and there are still a few trophies hanging on the wall in our old house, but as my life got more and more complicated, I became too nervous, and could no longer concentrate enough to score high.

* * *

New Year's Eve 1970 turned into a nightmare I will never forget. We had spent the evening as a family in front of the TV, and my dad had been drinking too much. I can't remember what set him off, but he started venting his anger on me by yelling at me, and reminding me of all my failures and offenses. I did not say a word, but just looked at him, and that just made him even madder. I had let my hair grow a tiny bit beyond his acceptable limit, and he just now seemed to notice it. He screamed, "I will not tolerate any hippies in my house," ran into the kitchen to get some scissors, and then butchered my hair in the most terrible way. I still did not say anything, or react in any way, for by that time I was petrified. After that he kept raging through the house, yelling about this and that. After a while he came back into the dining room with his rifle aimed at me. He was calm and quiet, and his voice was dripping with contempt when he said, "One of us has to go – either you or me!" I was totally paralyzed by fear, and even my mother and Winfried did not dare to say or do anything, for fear they could upset my father even more. All of a sudden he turned around and staggered out of the room, climbing the stairs to the second floor. Before any of us could react we heard the shot go off, and then the thump of a falling body. A terrible pain shot through my heart, and we all raced upstairs fearing to find my father lying in a pool of blood. But all we found was a bullet hole in the ceiling, and my father passed out on the floor. Never one word was spoken about that incident, but for me it marked the beginning of the most terrible phase of my life.

* * *

The pressure at school became unbearable. I had changed to another high school with a more science-oriented track that would enable me to finish school after the 12th grade rather than the ordinary 13 years. Regarding my dream to become a pilot, I had decided to join the German Air Force after school and become a fighter pilot. That required a 12-year commitment, and the contract was lying on my desk at home. My father welcomed the idea, thinking the Air Force would give me the discipline I lacked. But by now I had totally lost faith in myself and my dream. Since I had skipped so many lessons in the past, I was not well prepared for all the scientific subjects, and soon lost the connection.

The day came when I had to acknowledge that I was not going to be able to finish my last year of school. Looking back I am sure I could have made it, but I had no more fight left in me, and had given up in my heart. Nothing seemed important anymore; I had failed and I saw no hope for the future. My father wanted to see a diploma, and I could not deliver. I had maneuvered myself into a dead end, and I saw no way out. The next report card would show the truth, and I lived under a mantel of fear of that day. I was having anxiety attacks, and did not sleep well. The night became my closest friend. I somehow made it through the day longing for the night time when I could escape reality in my dreams. So often I went to bed wishing I would never wake up again, but there was always tomorrow with more disappointments, hurts and fears.

After my 18th birthday, the depression had become so intense that I began to entertain thoughts of suicide. I would lay awake at night trying to imagine what it would be like to die. Was there a life after death, or not? If there was, then I could not imagine it to be any worse than what I was experiencing right now. I had stopped praying to God many years ago, and had hardly been to church since my confirmation in the Lutheran church. I did remember the stories about hell we were told as children, but could anything be worse than this?

I arrived at the conclusion that the easiest thing would be to simply take an overdose of sleeping pills, and fall asleep forever. That thought actually gave me some hope, and looked like the only alternative. So I went and bought a package of sleeping pills. They came in a metal tube of 20 tablets, and I figured they would do the trick. I carried that tube in my pocket wherever I went out, and it became a symbol of hope to me. Whenever things got really bad I held that tube real tight, and it actually made me feel better. Deep down I knew that this was only a temporary respite, and that the day would come when there was no turning back.

ESCAPE

And then it came – the day when my world collapsed. We had received our report cards for the first semester, and mine did not look good at all. It projected that I was not going to pass my finals, at least not in that year. I carried the report card around with me for a few days without showing it at home, but I knew that I could hold back disaster for only a few more days.

On top of that, there had been one further disappointment. I had met this girl, Petra, and I thought I was falling in love with her. We had been at a party recently, and I had gotten drunk as usual, and had tried some clumsy advance to get her attention, which had backfired. A few days later, I went to see her at home to apologize, and we had a good talk during which she made it clear that we could never be more than just friends. That rejection gave me the rest. One of the reasons why I had been so attracted to her was the fact that she seemed so happy and carefree, and when I was around her, I could forget about the dark clouds over me. Now this straw was gone as well, and I knew what I had to do.

February 15, 1972 was a day I will never forget. That evening I had gone to my room, as usual. I straightened out the room, and then wrote a farewell-letter to my parents. In it I tried to explain why I had decided to take this radical step. I did not accuse them in any way, but made it clear that my biggest problem was my inability to change myself. I did not really believe that they would understand, but I had to at least give it a try.

Then I filled a glass of water and sat down at my desk, opening the tube with the sleeping pills. It was all scratched and the writing had been worn off by the constant handling in my pocket. A sense of calm came over me and I felt no fear, but there was that nagging uncertainty of what would happen once my heart had stopped beating.

As I held the first pill in my hand and was meditating about life and death, something very strange happened. It seemed like deep from within my heart a thought rose to the surface. It was so absurd that I tried to push it back down, since I knew there was no way that such a thought could have come from my own heart, but it just kept resurfacing. Oh, how I fought that thought and tried to drive it away through logic and reasoning, but it would not budge. On the contrary, very slowly this thought morphed first into a tiny spark of hope, then a bright flame of hope, until it erupted into an absolute certainty that screamed in my heart:

"You don't have to kill yourself – there is a chance to start a brand-new life!"

My whole being became engulfed by this truth, as if I had always known and believed it. I tried to imagine the consequences of that truth and was rewarded with a powerful sense of expectation of good things to come. My whole room was filled with a peaceful atmosphere, a sense of a holy presence that I should soon meet again.

I laid aside the pills and began to pace up and down my room. Somehow I knew that I could trust that voice in my heart. It had been too sudden and powerful that I could ignore it. A new life – exactly what I had dreamed about! Though I now believed that this was a real possibility, I had no idea how that could become a reality in my life.

One thing I did know: even though I would not try to kill myself, I still had to leave this old life somehow. Just thinking about my current troubles at school and at home threatened to dissolve this newfound hope like snow in the sun. I had to get away from here, as soon and as far away as possible, but where could I go? I pulled my old school atlas from the shelf and opened up a map of Europe. I had about 600 Marks left from working during the last summer break, so a trip overseas was out of the question. My parents and I had been on vacation in several countries around the Mediterranean Sea, and somehow I had no desire to go there. That only left the North. Maybe England – no, that was not far enough. I glanced at Scandinavia and considered Sweden or Finland, though there was no valid reason for it, since I had never been there before and did not know one living soul there. Maybe it was the fact that I had heard rumors that there was more freedom and tolerance in those nations. In the end I did not really know why, but I decided to head in that direction.

That, however, needed some good planning, since I knew my father would never let me go. Though I was already 18 he would not trust me to live my own life, and in those days the legal age was still 21. The worst thing I could imagine was to be picked up by the police just to be brought home. So the time had come for another covert activity, and just the thought of it made be shudder with apprehension. The step I was about to take was so finite and irrevocable, and if it had not been for that new-found revelation in my heart, I would not have had the strength to follow through.

The following day, I pretended to go to school, but instead went to the train station, and bought a one-way ticket to Stockholm. I wanted to take a look at Sweden first, and then maybe continue to Helsinki, Finland. Then I went to buy a duffel bag and down sleeping bag from the army surplus store. I spoke with no one about my plans, not even Günther, realizing that this was something I had to do all on my own, and I did not want to have to listen to the advice of others. I did not think that anyone could fully comprehend what had happened to me the night before.

The night before my escape, I deposited my packed duffel bag behind some bushes, so that I could easily retrieve it over the fence without being seen from the windows of our house. I was totally on edge and worried that someone in my family would notice that I was up to something. Having destroyed my first letter to my parents, I wrote a second one with similar content, but urging them not to worry about me. To this day I don't know how I found any sleep that last night at home.

At six o'clock the next morning, my mom woke me up as usual, and I got ready for "school." I could barely get down any breakfast. I had sworn myself to never come back home again, and now that the moment had come, I did feel an unexpected sadness. My mother had always tried to help me as much as she could, and I started feeling sorry for her. Would I ever see my brother Winfried again? Because of our ten-year age difference, we had never become real close, and for many years my role had been that of a baby sitter rather than a brother. I hoped with all my heart that my escape would make things somewhat easier for him. My sister Monika was married by now and no longer lived at home. Her husband Gerhard was an electrical engineer and I liked him a lot because he always took the time to talk to me, but we did not get to see each other very often.

Under the table sat our old dachshund lady "Rixi," who had been my silent companion. I had shared many of my troubles with her, and she always looked at me with those intelligent, brown eyes as if she understood every word I said. Her I would indeed never see again.

"Bye, I'll be home at two," I lied with a lump in my throat, while I took my briefcase and quickly walked out the door. Sheltered by the big blue spruce tree in front of our house, I switched my brief case with the duffel bag, and headed for the bus station. There, I waited for a later bus than usually, since I wanted to escape the curious looks of my neighbors and school mates. What could I have told them? I just wanted to get away as quickly as possible, without having to answer any embarrassing questions.

When I walked through the main train station, looking for the right track, I had that strange feeling that everyone was staring at me. Surly, I must have looked suspicious with my green duffel bag, blue ski jacket, and half-high suede boots with fringes over tight corduroy jeans. Surely everyone would know that I was about to run away from home! I was so tense, and my senses were so sharpened that I was intensely aware of my surroundings. There was the strange smell of steel and oil mixed with the asbestos of hot brakes. The smell of the stale air in smoke-filled waiting launches, mixed with the sound backdrop of many busy feet, the blaring announcements from the cone speakers, and the pained screeching of engine brakes. I could feel the occasional vibrations in the floor, every time a train made its entrance. I climbed aboard.

Deep in thought, I sat back in my compartment, as if it was all but a dream. Then reality would set in, and I was gripped by panic fear to be found out. Germany flew by my window as I looked out – Würzburg, Kassel, Göttingen, Hanover, and Hamburg. By now I should have been home, and I was wondering what my parents were thinking. Had they already discovered my letter, or the briefcase behind the bushes? How would they react, and what would my father do next? Surely he would call the police and have them search for me.

We had passed the border and were on the car ferry from Puttgarten to the coast of Denmark. I had sweat with fear when the German border police came into our compartment to check everyone's passports. The officer gave me this suspicious look as he scrutinized mine. Surely an announcement about this missing young man had been passed to all border crossings, and I would be taken into custody. But then he just turned away from me and moved on to the next compartment. Now, in the safety of the big ship I stood in the bow letting the ice-cold wind whip my face – maybe all would turn out well after all.

The trip through Denmark went quite swiftly, and by now it was dark outside. The passengers in my compartment kept changing constantly. Some stayed with me for several hours, others just for a few stations. By now there were very few people speaking German, but mainly Scandinavian languages which I had never heard before. All of a sudden it occurred to me that this was the first time that I was in a foreign country by myself, totally on my own. For my age I was quite immature and not very independent at all. I started feeling all alone and helpless. I realized that there were many aspects of my operation that I had not thought through at all, but now there was no turning back.

We had to get on another ferry-boat, the only connection between Denmark and Sweden at that time. By now it was late in the evening, and I was feeling exhausted after all the stress of that day. While the Intercity train sped through the south of Sweden, my eyelids became heavy, and I started dosing off. Occasionally I awoke from my restless sleep and gazed at the snow-covered fields of Småland with only a few houses here and there. It was then I noticed that the windows were not covered by heavy shutters as in Germany, or even drapes or curtains. Instead they had little lamps hanging in the windows that made the houses look so cozy and inviting. I remember thinking then that the people living there must be very hospitable, which turned out to be absolutely true. It made me long for the warmth and comfort of a home, and I began to wonder how I was ever going to become part of such a home, not knowing a single person out there.

Twenty-four hours after leaving Nürnberg, we pulled into the Central Train Station in Stockholm – I had made it! But what now? I had absolutely no idea. Sometime during the night a Japanese student had come into the compartment who obviously could read my mind. As we arrived, he asked me in English if I already had a place to stay in the city? Even though I had studied English for six years in school, I was barely able to carry on a conversation. Somehow I was able to let him know that I would be thankful for any assistance he could give me. So I followed him down the long escalator to the subway called, "Tunnelbana" and I was so glad to have someone who could help me take these first steps in a foreign land. We traveled the two stations to a part of the city called "Slussen," and I was impressed by the speed of the subway, but even more by the sight that greeted us as we came out of the tunnel into the bright morning light. Stockholm is built on many islands and is called the Venice of the North for a reason. Everywhere in the city one can see the canals, fjords and waterways. The main islands representing the city are connected by gigantic bridges, and some of these islands are high cliffs with buildings rising like fortresses. Still today I think Stockholm is the most beautiful city of the world, and I instantly fell in love with her.

My Japanese guide showed me a youth hostel near the old city, "Gamla Stan," and let me know that this was one of the cheapest places in town. I thanked him for his help, and I never saw him again. He had given me one more piece of advice: if I wanted to meet other young people I should go and hang out at the city library. Well, the youth hostel was much more expensive than I had expected, and I realized that I had to find an even cheaper alternative rather quickly. After walking aimlessly through the city for many hours, I retreated to my dorm at the hostel to spend my first night in this foreign place. So many questions tortured my mind that night without finding any answers, but somehow I felt that I would find a home in this place.

SVARTENSGATAN 6

The morning sun shone brightly in the streets of Stockholm, but it was freezing cold. This was my second day in the city and I was on my way to the library, following the advice of my Japanese friend. Just to save money, I walked the whole distance, and by the time I arrived there I was frozen through and through. My winter clothing was not quite up to these almost arctic temperatures.

As I walked through the entrance hall, my attention was drawn to a group of young people kneeling in a circle on the carpet. Somehow intrigued I stopped to take a close look. These young people were so-called "Jesus People," but I did not know that back then. The men sported long hair and beards, wearing old and torn jeans. The girls also wore their hair long and either wore jeans, or long skirts, and tops that were either embroidered or tie-died. They sang quietly, and some of them had their hands raised high. I really had no idea what they were doing, but it was obviously something religious, and I thought they were some kind of weirdos. As I stood there watching them, I was overcome by a sense of peace. A pleasant shudder crawled down my back, and I felt a warm, tingling sensation in my hands that I could not explain. Still today I do not know much about the theology of these people, and if I would agree with their lifestyle, but I do know that this was my first concrete exposure to the presence of the Holy Spirit. There was a sense of well-being, and that new found hope in my heart began to rise in my soul.

I sat in the large reading lounge, absent-mindedly flipping through the pages of a magazine. There were many young people in the hall, but how should I make contact with any of them? I was too shy to just approach a complete stranger, and everyone seemed to be so self-absorbed.

"Hi there – what are you doing?" The voice came from a girl who sat down next to me on the couch without me realizing it. Her name was Dorothy, and she was from the UK. She wore her long, red hair in a big braid, and her round face was covered with freckles. Though I had a hard time understanding her British accent, we were actually having a conversation, albeit Dorothy did most of the talking. She had been in Sweden for six months already, working in a local family, and she was here to wait for her boyfriend. I did not tell her my whole story, but I did mention that I was alone here and was looking for a place to stay. While we kept talking, a young man approached us and gave Dorothy a hug while throwing a suspicious glance in my direction.

"Johan," said Dorothy and pointed at me, "this is Norbert from Germany, and he does not know anyone here and needs a place to stay temporarily. Could he not crash at your place for a while?"

Johan did not seem too excited about that prospect, and did not strike me as the friendliest type. He was about one meter ninety tall and very skinny. His narrow face and his shoulder-length stringy hair seemed to emphasize that fact. He had a scraggly beard that reminded me of a goat, and his dark, piercing eyes were underscored by dark shadows. He looked sick, and he wore black, shabby clothes, and old boots. I could not figure out what Dorothy saw in him. Johan started rolling his own cigarette while looking me over from top to bottom. After a while he grinned, revealing rows of yellow teeth, and said in heavily accented English, "Maybe not such a bad idea… I could use someone helping me with my business."

I was not crazy about moving in with Johan, and I could just imagine what kind of business deals he was involved it. On the other hand I knew that I could not afford to stay at the hostel much longer.

It turned out that his one-room flat was not too far from my hostel, in an area called "Södermalm," which turned out not to be the prettiest part of town. Johan's tiny flat was on the ground floor on "Svartensgatan 6." The only room had a low ceiling and one single window facing the street. It was a mess and had obviously not been cleaned in ages.

"By the way," said Johan with a certain glee in his eyes, "you'll have to sleep on the floor, since I only have one bed as you can see."

When I rolled out my sleeping bag on the hard floor that night, I realized how well I had lived at home, and a trace of homesickness tried to settle in, but I quickly pushed away those thoughts.

Living with Johan was anything but easy. He had some strange habits that I struggled with, like sleeping with the light and radio on all night. I also needed to adjust to his eating habits. Johan claimed to be Buddhist, but the only way he expressed that was by not eating any meat. For the first time in my life I ate noodles with ketchup, and that almost daily. Occasionally we ate fish that we had swiped at the supermarket, for we were both running out of money. On top of that he was a chain smoker, and I discovered eventually that his cigarettes were made of more than tobacco and paper.

Otherwise, our relationship was quite relaxed. Johan talked a lot, late into the nights, of his past in Finland, where he deserted from the army and was wanted by the police, as well as his business ideas which were as unrealistic as many other things in his life. I had not seen anything of his "business," until an Indian man and two other guys from England visited us one evening. They had just smuggled a large amount of drugs to Sweden, and Johan was one of their dealers here. They kept talking about different kind of drugs that I knew nothing about. Then they produced small packets with tiny pills that were counted one by one. Since I lived with Johan they seemed to trust me, but they were appalled when they found out that I had never been on a "trip" before. They offered me one of those tiny brown pills the size of a pinhead saying it was a really cool "double trip" which I must try out. I declined, knowing deep inside that this was not the answer to my problems, and they kept making fun of me. I found out later that they wanted me to get hooked, and when I was not watching one of them dropped one of these pills into my tea. That particular night I will never forget…

I had just fallen asleep on my sleeping bag on the floor, when I awoke suddenly and could no longer remember where I was. Since I was not even aware of the fact that I had been drugged, I thought I had either gone mad, or I had died. My thoughts were jumbled, and my eyes could no longer seem to focus on anything. The things I saw morphed into things and creatures I cannot describe. Then I had this sense that my spirit had left my body, rising to the ceiling, and looking down on my own body. In this haze I tried desperately to re-enter my body, but whenever I thought I was there I was being pulled up again by unseen hands. Panic fear gripped my heart thinking I could never return to my body. I felt like I had become a toy for the forces of darkness, and I heard strange voices mocking me, and saw ugly faces all around me laughing as they watched my struggle. It was absolute horror, worse than anything I had ever experienced before and since. On top of that, my head started pounding with the worst kind of headache threatening to steal what little sense I had left.

For one whole week, I felt the effect of that drug, and had given up all hope of ever becoming normal again. The worst thing was that I could not really talk with anyone about it, and no one seemed to notice what was going on inside of me. I can clearly remember the sensation of going down the stairs to the subway platform thinking that I was floating, since I could not feel my legs. For the life of me I could not understand why nobody else noticed, and everyone walked by me like I was walking normal. Why couldn't they see that I was floating? I had lost all touch with reality. Every day the effect of the trip seemed to lessen a bit, and I had found out by now what had really happened. As far as drugs were concerned, I had lost all curiosity to ever try or experiment any further. I had heard of the word "horror-trip" before, and I now knew what that meant.

My days with Johan were flying by, and there was never a dull moment, but I was anything but happy. Somehow, I had ended up in another dead end again, and I had that strong sense this was not the right path. Eventually I would get in trouble with the law. After that encounter with LSD, I thought of ways to get away from Johan and his "friends," but the truth was I had nowhere else to go. My life seemed to have slipped back into this well-known state of desperation, overshadowed by great fear. It was a fear of failing again, or being picked up by the police and being sent home.

Somehow I knew that my father would do anything in his power to find me, and I always flinched when I saw a police car in the streets. But I did want my parents to know that I was OK, and so I sent a letter to one of Dorothy's friends back in England, asking her to put it in another envelope, and sending it on to my parents in Germany without return address. As I found out later, my Dad had called the police, but they refused to search for me since I had no record, and was over 18 years of age. When my parents got my letter via England, my father instructed the pastor of the Lutheran Church back home to look me up while on vacation in the UK. So my fears were partly justified, but things were about to change real soon.

About three weeks later, Johan and I were walking in downtown Stockholm in the afternoon. I can't quite recall where we were planning to go, but we quite often walked aimlessly around, just looking for opportunities. That particular day was extremely cold, and we were hungry, which seemed to happen more and more. We had just turned into a smaller side street, when Johan stopped in front of an old building with glass doors. Above the massive entrance doors was a sign that said "Fenixpalatset," and it looked like some sort of theater.

"Let's go in there," said Johan. "I've been there before, and they serve free coffee and cookies."

He then mentioned something about a religious cult, and that I should not listen to anyone, since they were all a bit "cuckoo." In the entrance hall was a sign with an arrow pointing down a flight of stairs saying "Agape

Coffee House – welcome."

The place was very cozy, and there were several tables with chairs like in a small restaurant. At the counter you could help yourself to hot drinks and pastries, which we readily took advantage of. We sat there for a while, but did not speak. I watched the people in the room and took in the surroundings, and it became quite obvious to me that there were only two types of people in the room: the staff or volunteers of this "church," or whatever it was, and the guests, which seemed more like victims to me. Apparently, this was some kind of setup to recruit more members, and I smelled a trap. I was not exactly against anything Christian, or religious, but it did remind me of my old life, and that was the last place I expected any kind of help. Then, the inevitable happened: a young woman steered towards our table, and Johan and I looked at each other.

He rolled his eyes, and murmured sarcastically, "Get ready… here it comes!"

"Hi, my name is Stina, said the Swedish woman with a warm and friendly smile.

Since Johan was an old "regular" at that place, and Stina obviously had talked to him before, she turned towards me, wanting to know my name and where I was from. Though I had a pretty good idea where this conversation was headed, and I really was not in the mood for some discussion about religion, I was surprised by her open and honest manner. She did not strike me as someone reciting questions learned at a "how to talk people into believing in God" seminar. What I sensed was a warmth and integrity behind her words that totally disarmed me of all my arguments.

Somewhere during our conversation, Johan cut in, and "reminded" me that we really had to move on now, which obviously was not true, but the last few minutes had made him feel very uncomfortable. When Stina welcomed me to come back anytime, I saw true concern in her eyes, for she obviously knew what Johan was all about, and that hanging out with him was a recipe for disaster.

A few days later, I returned to the Agape by myself. I could not explain why, but I just felt drawn to the place, and did not want Johan with me this time. As I walked down the stairs to the café, I passed by a closed door with the sign "Bönerum" on it, which means prayer room as I should find out shortly. Through the door I could hear strange murmuring sounds, and I had to wonder again what I was dealing with here?

After helping myself freely at the counter, I sat down in a corner and watched the people around me. Stina was there as well and greeted me with a smile. She seemed busy in the kitchen and left me alone which suited me just fine. Through the entrance I could see the door to the mysterious prayer room open and several people step out. Some women went up the stairs, but a middle-aged man walked into the place, looked around and after spotting me steered straight towards my table.

"Hi, my name is Arne", he said with a booming deep voice.

He looked exactly like I always imagined a Viking should look - tall and buff, with blond, almost shoulder-length hair and a big mustache. "All that's missing is the helmet with horns," I thought by myself. It turned out that my first impression was not so far off. He told me of his life as a sailor, of faraway places, bar fights and too much alcohol. It actually sounded quite interesting, if only he had not ended every sentence with "Hallelujah," "Praise the Lord," or "Thank you Jesus." The whole conversation was quite one-sided, and he started to irritate me. With great theatrics he told me about the day when he received Jesus in his heart, and he was set free from all his vices and problems.

Finally he popped the inevitable question: "Don't you want to receive Jesus into your heart as well?"

I was afraid he would ask something like that. His stories had not really impressed me at all, nor did I have any desire for a religious experience, but I was so shy and quite intimidated by his strong personality, so I said with a quiet voice, "Maybe."

He slapped his hand on the table like a thunder-clap, stood up and bellowed, "Did you all hear that? He wants to accept Jesus – hallelujah, praise the Lord!"

Before I knew what was happening, he grabbed my shoulder, literally pulled me out of my chair and pushed me towards the door to the prayer room.

"Come on," he said joyfully, "let's do this the right way!"

The prayer room was much smaller than I had expected. A big and simple cross hung on the wall, there were a few posters and a thick brown carpet on the floor. Other than that, there was no furniture. Two women were kneeling in one corner and looked up curiously when we entered the room.

"Kneel down here," instructed Arne, and I felt like a sheep being led to be slaughtered.

After I knelt down for what must have been the first time in my life, Arne put both hands on my head and began to pray loudly. He prayed in Swedish, and I did not understand much except for "hallelujah," and "tack Jesus," which I knew meant "thank you Jesus." To add more power to his prayer he started shaking my head, and I constantly had to counterbalance in order not to fall over. Occasionally he prayed in another language, which I figured he must have picked up at some jungle tribe, since I had never heard anything like it.

Finally Arne was finished. When I rose he gave me a bear hug and said with great emotion: "Now you are a new creature and a child of God."

He actually had tears in his eyes. The two ladies came over and shook my hand like they were congratulating me for some big achievement, and Stina walked into the room as well and said, "I am glad for you, Norbert."

I had a feeling that she understood that I felt like I had just been hoodwinked, and had no idea what was going on.

I left the building in a bit of a daze, and headed for the subway station. Two blocks from the Agape, I walked by a building with a large hall downstairs, and I could see through the low windows that there were many young people inside. Above the entrance was a sign that said in English, "Children Of God." A young guy about my age came out and began to talk to me in English. He was obviously American, and he invited me in for a cup of tea. I did not really feel like it, but he also was very persuasive, so I followed him inside. We sat at a small table in the corner; he brought me tea and cookies, and before I knew it, I was getting another talk about God and religion. He talked a lot about peace and love and Jesus, but I had a hard time understanding his English since he spoke very fast. I started getting real tired of all this, and told him that I really had to go now.

"Just let me pray for you, brother," he said and gently laid his hand on my shoulder.

Luckily, his prayer was a lot shorter than the previous one, and he did not shake me, for which I was grateful.

For the rest of the way back, I was puzzled about all these crazy and religious people in this place. Now I really had to be careful out there. Two religious encounters in one day was more than enough, and I was afraid I might end up in an orange robe singing "Hare Krishna."

KARIN AND BOSSE

I had not been back to the Agape for several days, but for reasons I could not explain I felt drawn back there by some irresistible force. I was still looking for a way to sever my ties with Johan and his friends. They had become increasingly forceful in trying to persuade me to experiment with some of their drugs, and I was getting very frustrated with their whole lifestyle. So far I had not found an alternative, something that was about to change.

A few days after my "conversion," I was out on my own in a bitterly cold day, and ended up going to the Agape just to warm up. When I entered the café, I was glad to see that I was the only one there, and Stina seemed to be the only staff on duty. She seemed pleased to see me, and sat down at my table.

"I've been worried about you," she said. "This Johan character has been coming here for quite some time now, and he only causes problems. He is not a good influence on you, and I think the police are looking for him."

She should not have said that, because the word "police" made me want to panic.

"But I have no other place to go," was my reply.

"Don't you think it would be better to go home?" asked Stina.

"Oh no, there is no way I am going back." I pretty much told her my whole story, and she listened with great interest. It felt so good to open my heart again after so many years of holding everything inside.

It was getting late, and time for me to go. When I said goodbye to Stina, I felt like I had found a friend I could trust.

Before I left, she asked me, "I have my day off tomorrow and am going to visit my sister. Would like to come with me? You could enjoy a nice meal, and a real bath tub."

In those days I was very skinny, and I had indeed not seen a bath tub in a while. So I readily agreed to meet with her the next day.

We took the subway to "Skärholmen," a southern suburb of Stockholm, and there we switched to a bus. There, on a flat hilltop were several rows of apartment blocks that did not look very inviting.

Karin and Bosse lived on the fifth floor, in a cozy two-bedroom flat. They were both in their late twenties. They had a one-year old daughter by the name of Jenny, and I instantly fell in love with her. Bosse did not come home until later, and so I had a lengthy conversation with the two sisters, who had countless questions, and I ended up repeating part of my story. I certainly was not used to that much attention, but I had a feeling they were genuine in their concerns for me. My earlier fears of being bombarded with further conversion attempts proved unfounded. Oh, they did make it quite clear that they loved and followed Jesus, but they were not being pushy, and I was thankful for that.

After a lovely dinner Stina and I were just getting ready to leave, when I saw Bosse exchange mysterious glances with his wife.

He cleared his throat and said, "Please wait another moment. Karin and I have talked about it; would you like to live with us for a while? We can only offer you Jenny's room, but you could have your own key to the flat and come and go as you like. What do you think?"

What did I think? At first I was so overwhelmed that I did not know what to think. Here I was, a stranger and foreigner with a shady past, and these people invite me into their home after we had just met a couple of hours earlier? I was simply dumbfounded. That just had to be more than just Swedish hospitality. I did not have to think very long, for anything was better than living with Johan. So I accepted with a glad heart and a great sense of expectation.

My dream regarding living in one of those cozy homes that I had seen on my train ride through Sweden had become reality. I would now live in such a home and was totally overwhelmed by this turn of events.

It was not hard living with Karin and Bosse, for they poured all their love on me. They bought me new clothes, and made sure I did not lack anything. More than anything, they were taking me seriously, and made me feel valued. Piece by piece, I began to open my heart towards them, and they showed great interest in anything I was willing to share with them. They had a large circle of friends, and often had friends over for a meal. Those were the times when I chose to withdraw and hide in my room. I felt very insecure in the company of new people, and did not feel comfortable socializing. One reason was that I understood very little of their conversations, and was ashamed when I had to ask anyone to interpret for me.

Karin and Bosse tried very hard to find some kind of work for me, but that proved to be a difficult problem. At that time there was a high unemployment rate in Sweden, and it was very hard for foreigners to get a work permit, unless it was for a highly qualified work. In the meantime, I stayed home a lot, and tried to make myself useful around the apartment.

At one point Karin and Bosse had to go away for the weekend to a church function. I remember that I was bored out of my mind and scoured the hundreds of titles in their huge bookshelf. The problem was that I could not yet read in Swedish, and my English was not that great either, so I looked and looked for anything written in German. Eventually I found two books in German. One was a New Testament, and the other one was "The Cross and the Switchblade" by David Wilkerson. I retreated into my room and started reading them both with a tremendous appetite.

I had read through David Wilkerson's book in less than two days, and had just read through the Gospel of John, when something strange began to happen in my heart.

Turning Point

All of a sudden, things started falling into place for me. Looking back at the last few weeks, I realized that Someone had been orchestrating things for me, and even though it seemed like I was on another road headed for disaster, I now found myself in a place of safety, surrounded by people who obviously loved me. What had I done to deserve this?

Reading through David Wilkerson's book made me aware of the power of God in changing people's lives, and I was reminded that it must have been that same power that kept me from killing myself back in my room. The book described the complete change that happened to people in the streets of New York, whose lives had lost all meaning, being lost in a lifestyle of drug abuse and violence. It portrayed the change that came over them once they had surrendered to Jesus. When I read Jesus' dialogue with Nicodemus in the book of John, I could not believe that my deepest desire of just a few months ago now seemed possible: to start all over again – to be born again.

I had to know for sure now, and I realized that all the events of my life until now had led me to this moment. To say that I believed with all my heart at this point would not be truthful. There were still so many things that I did not understand and know about, but the little I could grasp at that time was enough for a decision that would change my life forever.

Somehow I felt it was the right thing to do, so I knelt down by my bed and folded my hands in prayer. Not quite sure how to approach the matter, I began to talk to God. Instantly, I felt drawn back in time, when I had talked to Him as a young boy, telling Him about my troubles, and asking Him to help me ride my bicycle. It felt like talking to an old friend, and I told Him that I wanted to believe that there was a way to start a new life. I ended my prayer with a promise: "… And if you give me a new life, then I promise that I will live it for you!"

There was no lightning, and no voice from heaven. Actually, I would not describe it as an emotional experience. It was not until a few days later that I noticed any difference at all, and it was very subtle. It started with better sleep at night, and a peacefulness that was totally new to my emotions. That came coupled with a more positive outlook on life, and a sense that things were going to turn out all right after all. An awareness of a destiny began to grow inside me, and I realized that I could never spend my life any other way than serving God. The desire of becoming a pilot had already faded since I did not think that I had what it took academically, but now it seemed like a dream from another life, which indeed it was. I have never lost my love for aviation, and I still enjoy flying as a passenger, but from that day forth I stopped pursuing that dream and surrendered it to the One who had given me a much greater destiny.

Karin had an old classical guitar that hung on the dining room wall, and I had begun to learn some simple chords. On the last night before Karin and Bosse returned, I wrote my first song, describing in simple and faulty English my experiences of the previous weeks. It was to be the first of many songs over the years, most of which were just between Jesus and me, and they never left the realm of my private devotion. Already back then I discovered the joy of worship through music, which still today is my absolute greatest joy in life.

I had always declined when Karin and Bosse asked me if I wanted to go to church with them, but now I felt ready to join them. I was utterly amazed at the difference between what I was experiencing compared to my previous visits to church back in Germany. These people were obviously enjoying to be in church, which became obvious by the enthusiasm with which they sang the songs, and prayed their prayers. Even though

I did not understand much of the sermons preached, it was obvious that the speaker actually believed what he was talking about. And the music – something about the style and harmony of the melodies struck a chord deep inside my heart. Still today I believe that the Christian songs and choruses coming out of Scandinavia are some of the most beautiful in the world.

Sometime during the next weeks, a new acquaintance at church asked me if I would be interested in joining him at a missions conference of another church. Not really knowing what to expect, I agreed to join him, since I had not been successful in finding work, and had nothing better to do. The conference turned out to be a series of meetings where various missionaries from many parts of the world shared stories about the work they were doing, and showing slides. Most of the time I was totally bored with their stories and endless pictures, and I cannot remember any of the content. Yet, something very strategic happened during those three days in my life. For reasons I could not explain, I felt more drawn to the pictures and reports from Asia, than to those from other continents. By the end of the conference, a new dream had begun to form in my heart, like an embryo in a mother's womb: one day I would be a missionary to Asia. Again, there was no supernatural manifestation that accompanied that event, and yet it would take root in my heart, as if I had heard the audible voice of God speaking to me.

The days with Karin and Bosse moved on too slow for my taste, and I started to get restless. By now the cold winds of winter had given way to the first signs of spring, and, with nature awakening, came a great desire of finding deeper meaning in this newly discovered life.

One day, Karin began to talk about the possibility of me joining them on their customary Easter trip to her folks way up in the north of Sweden. Winter had returned, and we almost had to cancel our planned trip, but we decided to brave the lingering blizzards, and drove north in Bosse's Audi to a town called Skellefteå. Here, close to the Arctic Circle, winter still had a strong grip on the land, and we arrived there to plenty of snow and ice.

Karin's parents were wonderful people, and they, too, treated me as part of the family. The next few days were filled with lots of fellowship, church meetings, great food, and some wonderful cross-country skiing adventures. Little did I know that Good Friday 1972 would forever become a special milestone in my life.

We had attended a special church service that morning, and we were enjoying a relaxing afternoon indoors. During the conversation with Karin and her sister Stina, who had travelled together with us, it was discovered that I had lied to Karin about something, and there was no way I could deny the truth at this point. Karin became very sad, and sat down with me for a long talk. All along she was very kind and understanding without trying to hide the fact that what I had done was not only wrong, but was called "sin" in the Bible. In the end she forgave me, and we prayed together, which made me feel wonderfully cleansed inside.

Later that night, I lay on my fold-out bed in the living room, listening to music on the stereo, and reflecting on the happenings of the last 2 months. Without any warning something strange but wonderful began to happen to me. There was this warm feeling swelling inside my heart which caused me to do something I had not done in many years: I began to sob and cry for what seemed like hours. But these were not tears of sadness, but rather of release and joy. This sensation came and went in waves, again and again, intensifying as time went on. I was overwhelmed and shocked at the same time, since I had suppressed all emotions for so long.

"Boys don't cry," had been my father's policy, and I remember one particular time when I was maybe ten or eleven. For reasons I cannot remember, I had begun to cry in the presence of my father, who looked at me with stern eyes, and asked, "Why are you crying?" When I was unable to offer any satisfying explanation, he backhanded me across my face while yelling, "Now you have at least a reason to cry!" I don't think I had shed another tear since that day.

Here I was crying and blubbering for what seemed a really long time, and it felt so good. My only problem with this experience was that I had no idea how to explain and classify what had happened to me. No one had ever told me that the Holy Spirit could have that effect on you, and I could not remember ever reading in the Bible about such an overwhelming show of emotion. So I decided to keep this to myself, and never spoke to anyone about that particular night. It was not until about fifteen years later that the revelation hit me that I had indeed received a mighty baptism of the Father's love, and it was not to be my last!

ALL THINGS NEW

The following day I happened to read in my New Testament about three thousand men who turned to God and were baptized on the day of Pentecost. I had never heard of such a thing. Growing up in the Lutheran church, babies were baptized when they were less than one month old, and I was told that my parents had me baptized as well. Of course I could not remember that. Somehow I felt a desire to be baptized now, since I had just made my life right with God. So I talked with Bosse, and was delighted to hear that they actually baptized adults in their church. It was the logical next step for me, and after a phone call to the pastor, a date was set.

On a Sunday evening in May 1972, I found myself dressed in a white robe ready to be baptized together with two other young people from the church called "Citykyrkan". The pastor's name there was Stanley Sjöberg, but it was one of his associate pastors, Ulf Koppelman, who baptized us. He was very warm and kind as he dunked us one after the other in a special pool that was built right into the stage. Afterwards we were told that the elders would come and pray for us to receive the baptism of the Holy Spirit. I was ready and expectant when they laid their hands on us and prayed. To my great surprise and disappointment, nothing really happened, and I was told that that sometimes it would come later, and that I should come again for more prayer.

For the next few weeks I went up to the altar at every opportunity and was prayed for, but again, nothing happened. When Karin confided in me one day that not all people in church could speak in tongues either,

I felt a bit relieved, for I had seriously thought that there was something wrong with my salvation.

Some weeks later, Karin and Bosse arranged for us to meet with some friends who were interested in hiring me as a domestic helper. We had found out from the immigration authorities that this seemed to be the only line of work that would provide me with a work permit.

So we went to see Leif and Carina and their three small children at their apartment in a part of Stockholm called Bromma. Leif had his own business, and Carina was running their office from home, and it was obvious that she was overwhelmed with all the work, plus household. We talked it over and agreed that they would hire me as domestic helper.

Since it was too far for me to commute there from Karin and Bosse's place, and since they obviously needed their children's room back, it was decided that I would live with Carina's brother, Willis, who had an apartment in the same part of town. As it turned out, Willis was living on the top floor of an old apartment block that was about to be demolished. There had been a fire in the recent past, and the walls in the staircase were completely black with soot. The place itself was quite plain and old-fashioned, with round tiled stoves in each of the two rooms. There was only one toilet, and no bathroom. All the washing up had to be done over the sink in the small kitchen.

Willis was a few years older than me, but a bit shorter. With his blue eyes and dark blond hair, he definitely looked Scandinavian. He was quiet and easy-going, and had a dry humor that took me a while to discover and understand. Even though he was trained as a geodetic engineer, he earned his livelihood through odd-jobs, like delivering newspapers, or driving a taxi.

Without being aware of it, Willis became my mentor in more than one way. Having been a true believer for many years, he was well grounded in matters of faith and the Bible, and we would have many discussions in the months to come. He also was quite an accomplished musician, playing the piano, organ, and the guitar. We would spend many hours together after work, playing, singing, and learning new songs. Most of what I learned on the guitar, I did so by simply watching Willis, and copying him.

Working for Carina and Leif became another learning experience, and a new challenge of a different kind. Though I had always had to help out a lot at home, my responsibilities there were mainly outside, relating to gardening and cleaning jobs. The inside of the house was the women's domain, and all I ever did there was occasionally help dry dishes.

Now I was challenged to clean and vacuum floors, do laundry including ironing and folding, cook meals, plus look after three small children. Playing with Christer, who was a lively four-year old boy seemed the easiest, but feeding and changing diapers on two-year old Nina, and four-months old Anki was something I thought I would never do. My job included going shopping as well, and taking the kids out for walks, or visits to the park. Needless to say, I did many blunders on my road to becoming the world's first male nanny, but Carina was always very patient and graciously taught me how to take care of things.

I worked for them for a bit more than one year, and even though I attended some evening classes in Swedish, it was mainly through my interaction with the kids that I learned this beautiful language. I can't think of a better preparation for what was to happen later in my life. Thank you, Christer, Nina and Anki for letting me practice on you.

Living with Willis opened up a whole new world for me. His parents lived in a small village called Bergshamra, about one hour by car in the north of Stockholm. He usually spent all his weekends there, and he was part of a youth group of a Pentecostal church in the town of Norrtälje.

On that first weekend traveling with Willis, I was simply overwhelmed by the beauty of the place. It was nothing like the mountains of Bavaria, nor the coastlines of northern Germany, or the Mediterranean Sea. The Swedes call it "Skärgården," which means, a garden of 20,000 islands, an archipelago of such serenity and natural rugged beauty, unlike any other place in Europe, and maybe the whole world. Later on I would have the opportunity to explore part of it by boat, and to become king of an island for one day.

During those weekends, we would spend most of our time with various members of "Ungdomsgruppen," the youth group of a church in Norrtälje. The unique thing about this 20 member group was that they were also a youth choir. Everyone in the group sang, and many could play several instruments. So we would spend countless hours at church, practicing songs, followed by going to someone's home for coffee and the famous Swedish pastries and Ginger Snaps. Though I felt like an outsider during those gatherings, they connected me with people my own age. Most of them were from Christian families, and were totally different from the young people I had been around back in Germany. There was no alcohol, no smoking, and certainly no drugs, but we had lots of fun, and I had never laughed so much in my life. Once I became more confident in the language, I could pick up on their incredible sense of humor, and occasionally come out of my shell and join right in.

Though we spent much time just hanging out, there was an underlying, legitimate "right to exist" for our group. Our reason for being went far beyond making music, and having a great time together. Several times during any given weekend we would go out to spread the message of our hope in Jesus with the rest of the world. That range of involvement would span from such extremes as singing at a nursing home, to singing in a discotheque during a dance break. We sang at prisons, hospitals, funerals, country fairs, and on several occasions on the ferry boats going to Finland. In addition, there were numerous invitations from churches all over Sweden. The group had gained quite a reputation, and there were offers from radio stations and Christian concerts. One of the highlights was a short stint as an opening event for a well-known Christian pop singer by the name of Evie Tornquist.

The "Ungdomsgruppen" included me in the group even with my limited skills on the guitar, and that proved to be another learning experience God would use in later years. The relationships in the group were relaxed, but there were also intense times of discussion, especially when it came to planning the outreach events. I was intrigued by their integrity and honesty with each other, and there was real concern when someone in the group faced a crisis or was not doing well spiritually. Quite often we would all end up in the prayer room of the church, or at someone's living room, just to spend time in prayer for one another.

Finally, I felt that I had become part of something meaningful, a place where I could truly be myself. God used them to disciple me in my walk with Him, even though they seemed totally unaware of their role in my life.

During these months, I experienced some sort of renaissance in my life, and I discovered gifting and desires in my life that I had never been aware of previously. I truly came alive in many ways, another proof that I had indeed been given a chance for a new life.

Never before had I enjoyed nature's beauties like now, and I took great pleasure being out in the woods, or watching a breathtaking sunset over the Baltic Sea. When the trees began to bloom in May, it seemed to me like I had never seen that before, and I started to bring home branches of lilac and apple trees, just to decorate our little flat. I had discovered a new love for art, and I experimented painting with oil and acrylic paints on canvas. I never became very good at it, but it felt so good to be unrestrained in my newfound creativity.

As always, when there is a new discovery, there is a tendency to overdo things, and I surely did that when I saw a new shade of purple paint at the hardware store, and began to paint the window and door of my room with that color. To top it off, I rolled my ceiling apple green, and painted a huge flower on top of it. But everybody just smiled at my art, and let me be who I was becoming.

One other source of excitement was the fact that Willis let me drive his 1950s Volvo on our long trips between Stockholm and our destinations up north. Life was as good as it gets – or was it?

BABY STEPS

As much as I enjoyed my new life and surroundings, there were times when I experienced intense times of restlessness considering my future. I was introduced to God training me in the art of patience, and little did I know that there were some very intense lessons waiting for me.

One special Sunday afternoon, some of us ended up in the living room of the home of Catharina and Thomas, who lived with their parents in an apartment adjacent the church building. Some older folks from the congregation were there as well, and we had just enjoyed another round of coffee and cakes, when someone suggested that we should have a time of prayer. So we all went on our knees right where we were, and different ones started leading out in prayer. I was way too shy to open my mouth on occasions like this, but I knelt by a chair and tried to follow what everyone was saying. Completely unexpected, one of the older ladies came over to me, and began to prophesy. This was the first time anyone had ever had a personal message from God for me, and I was simply awestruck.

She went on quite long, and there were parts I did not understand, but one sentence stood out to me, and still rings in my ears today: "If you stay close to Him, you will be the bearer of many spiritual gifts, and you will preach the gospel in a language you have never heard, to a people you have never seen." – Wow! She knew nothing regarding my perceived calling to missions, and yet she did know. I felt humbled, scared and excited all at the same time.

Some time later, I was asked by the youth pastor if I would be willing to tell my story at one of their regular open air meetings in the city park. When I was faced with a response, several conflicting notions shot through my mind. The first was a sense of absolute fear and panic, but at the same time there was this flicker of excitement that God was indeed taking me seriously when I had promised that I wanted to spend my life serving Him. In the end I really had no other choice but to say: "Yes."

The week leading up to that dreaded Sunday was absolute agony for me. I could not sleep well at night, my stomach felt like it was tied in knots, and I had a chronic case of diarrhea. That Sunday turned out to be a turning point and an experience that would shape me for a new season in my life.

When it was my turn to be called up on stage, I was overcome with a sense of reckless abandon, a feeling I recognized from my old life, when I had given in to some crazy notion, like buying a motorcycle I was not allowed to drive. But this time it was different. It was the same urge, and yet it seemed so right. I felt like a little boy being pushed to do an adult thing, and the father saying: "Go for it, son – it's all right!"

Not only was I ready to tell my story, but I felt an unknown courage to go all the way, so I grabbed my guitar and for the first time in my life sang one of my songs in public. When I then told my story in English, while Willis translated for me, I sensed what I now recognize as anointing from God. After stumbling a bit in the beginning, I felt a dam break in my heart, and it became quite easy to share with those listening what God had done for me. I spoke much longer than I had anticipated in my wildest dreams, and surprised myself, as well as my friends, with preaching a simple message of salvation. It was an awesome experience, and from that day onward it was much easier to say "yes" whenever I was asked to say or do something that would normally scare me to death.

It took me a few years to realize what actually had happened that day. Eventually, I began to understand that when we surrender to the lordship of Jesus, he can take the weakest parts of our personality and character and redeem them for Himself. Those very things that used to get us in trouble are used by Him to serve Him in our calling, proving that He delights to take the weak things of the world to build His Kingdom. This shatters any carnal notion that we serve Him out of our own strength and gifting. I would discover later on that He delights in showing strength through weakness not just with individuals, but whole people groups and cultures.

After that historic Sunday, I felt ready to take on the world, but was quickly cooled off by the seeming lack of enthusiasm of others in the church, and even our group. It seemed to me that everyone just pursued their personal career, and in their spare time offered some hours to God. I simply could not understand why we did not all strive to become missionaries, and go out to reach the world for God. There was so much I still had to learn about the ways of God, and how He calls and uses people, and I was in danger of judging even my best friends for not being as radical as I thought all Christians should be.

On the bus and subway traveling to work during the week, I had begun to read a modern translation of the New Testament. I was both intrigued and excited about what I read in the book of Acts regarding the Early Church. When I read about all the demonstrations of God's power in and through the church, I realized that somehow we had come far away from the first century church. I remember distinctly praying to God and asking Him to allow me to witness his power, and to be able to experience all the miracles that I had read about in the Book. Amazingly, God would honor that request in the years to come, but the result of that would be quite different from what I had anticipated. That particular lesson was not to be learned until many years later.

In the meantime, while I loved being in Sweden and enjoyed all my new friends, I had a sense that I would get stuck in a rut if I did not turn the rudder in a different direction. I had heard of a strong missionary movement in the city of Örebro, a few hours away from Stockholm. When I heard that there was going to be a special conference on missions, I talked some of the girls from the youth group into going there with me.

There is not much I remember about that conference, but again, it would become one of those special milestones that you don't see until you have passed them. During one of the evening sessions, we were listening to the speaker who was preaching in English which was still a lot easier for me to understand than Swedish. There were several hundred people listening that night, and I cannot recall the topic at all, but in the middle of it something really weird happened. It seemed like he was pausing in the middle of a sentence, and then he turned his head and stared straight at me as he said, "And if you want to become a missionary, you have to go to a Bible school for at least three years!"

He then turned away from me, and resumed his original thought. What on earth had just happened? How did he know about my plans of becoming a missionary anyway? I knew we had never met, and I was totally unknown there, so what was going on? I gave in to what we call "common sense," and began to rationalize the whole thing away. He probably did not look at me at all when he spoke those words, and besides I had an important call on my life, and did not have three years to waste at some school. Oh, if only I had listened to what the Spirit was trying to tell me.

Some of the speakers at that event were from a missionary organization called OM, or "Operation Mobilization." They had some exciting stories to tell, and I was especially intrigued by their story of a missionary ship called the "Logos." That ship cruised all the seas of the world, calling on many exotic destinations, reaching out to the people of many nations through evangelism and book fairs of Christian literature in each harbor visited.

Now, that seemed right up my alley, and I could see myself in many faraway destinations, especially in Asia. When I talked to one of the leaders about what it took to get on that ship, I was disappointed to find out that you had to have been working with their organization for at least one year. If that is what it took, then so be it. So I began making inquiries about their various teams and programs. I talked mostly with one of their Swedish leaders by the name of Hans Ström, and I would be in regular contact with him from then on.

For quite some time nothing happened, and my life resumed in the same rhythm as in the previous months. My first Christmas away from home was not quite what I had expected. Willis and I visited with his family out in Bergshamra. We were both sick with some kind of flu, and spent most of the holidays in bed. By the time New Year's Eve came around, we felt much better and were able to join a celebration with the whole group in an old chapel. We had a blast, and we welcomed the year 1973 with great expectations. Little did I know that it would even surpass my wildest dreams.

* * *

A few days later, I received a letter from my new friend Hans. He asked me to join a two week intensive training event with OM in Belgium. This was a necessary requirement if I wanted to work with them and eventually join the team on the Logos.

I was as ready as I ever would be, and a few days later took the train to their base in the south of Sweden. From there we embarked on a long drive to Brussels in an ancient Saab. There were five of us, and I had some tense moments when we crossed the border from Denmark into Germany, but all went well. After many hours we arrived at the OM training base in a suburb of Brussels, called Zaventem.

The next two weeks were simply amazing. The program was so intensive that we hardly had any time to ourselves at all. I was excited to be with a large group of mainly young people, who had the same sincere desire to serve God. However, that desire was greatly tested when we were sent out two by two in order to knock on doors and sell Christian books. Most people were very unfriendly. We had doors slammed in our faces, and at one occasion were chased by a huge German Shepherd that the owner had released to chase us off his property.

Back at the base we had great times of fellowship, and a real sense of camaraderie. I was able to make friends with people from the UK, Norway, and such exotic places as the Faroe Islands.

Towards the end of the training, we had individual talks with the team leaders, who tried to determine in which team we were to end up eventually. As it turned out, they needed a young man who could speak German and play the guitar for their street evangelism team in Vienna, Austria, and I was the only one who fit the bill. I was not terribly excited about this prospect, but when they told me that I could apply to join the Logos after one year, I readily agreed, for I really wanted to get on that ship.

I had only four days to get back to Sweden, pack my things, and travel down to Austria, but I did not mind – finally things were moving ahead.

Everyone back in Sweden was so supportive of my plans. Many gave me an envelope with cash in it, and we had a very moving gathering with the youth group the night before my departure, where they prayed for me and also blessed me with some gifts.

Leaving turned out to be much harder than expected, and the whole group, plus Karin and Bosse came to the airport in Stockholm to see me off. Less than one year since my escape from home I was on my way to another adventure. The first time around I had no idea what would happen. This time I thought I knew what to expect, but I could not have been more wrong.

LESSONS

Rather than taking the train south to Austria, I joined a charter flight that was part of a three-day skiing trip. The plan was that I would enjoy a few days of skiing in the Austrian Alps, and then leave the group to move on to Vienna.

We flew to Munich, Germany, and from there were taken by bus to the little town of Söll in beautiful Tyrol. Those of us who did not bring their own equipment were able to rent skis and boots locally, and I went to check out the slopes. I had just learned to ski a few years earlier, but had become fairly good at it. After testing the beginner slopes on the first day, I was ready to try some bigger challenges the next day.

It had snowed all night, and the next day was a beautiful winter day. Instead of moving on to the intermediate slopes, I got in line for the lift that would take me to the very top, and the expert slope. There were some stations along the way, and I was surprised that everyone but me got off before the very top. I was not too worried about that, and enjoyed the beautiful mountain scenery all the way up.

When I finally got off the lift I was the only up there, and the mountain top was covered in a layer of clouds, which made for limited visibility. Well, there was only one way down, and I followed the markers for the expert slope. It started out quite steep, and already after a few minutes I realized that I was in deep trouble!

Whenever I had skied before it had been on slopes that were packed hard and icy. But this slope was virgin powder snow, deep and fluffy, which required a totally different technique, especially when making turns. To keep your speed manageable you are supposed to weave your way down in an endless series of turns. I soon discovered that I was not able to make my turns fast enough and kept on building up speed. Eventually, I shot down straight faster than I had ever skied before.

At this point I realized that I had lost total control, and that I could not keep my balance for much longer. A bump in my path sent me flying, and on impact my two skies wanted to go in different directions, which caused me to fall and cartwheel for hundreds of meters before coming to a stop.

Normally, this would not have cost me more than a few bruises since the snow was deep and soft. However, the automatic binding on my right ski was frozen and did not release the boot as it was supposed to.

I actually heard the crack in my bones before my brain registered the inevitable – I had broken my leg. That was confirmed by one look at my right foot. The ski was still attached to it, and where I expected to see my toes, I saw my heel.

Here I was, all alone on a slope at about 2,000 meters, lying on my back with my head pointed downhill, and even before pain and shock set in, I could hear the cry rising in my heart: "God, how could you let this happen? Don't you know that I am on my way to become your missionary, and now I am going to freeze to death on this stupid mountain!"

The reply came as clear as a bell, "I told you, three years of Bible school, but you did not listen!"

In my mind I replayed the scene at that conference a few months earlier, when I felt that God had spoken to me directly through the speaker. I realized what I had done – God had spoken, and I had disobeyed His voice.

My body temperature was dropping fast, and I knew if I did not get help soon I would die of hypothermia. By now, real pain and shock had set in, and with chattering teeth I spoke a prayer I will never forget: "God – you win! If you get me off this mountain I promise to obey you, and even go to a three-year Bible school."

It seemed like a really long time, but it was probably just a few minutes later that one of the skiers in my group came shooting down the slope and found me. He told me to hang in there while he continued all the way down to the base station to call for help.

Eventually, they came with a snow tractor pulling a stretcher on a sled. The long trip down was pure agony, since I could feel the shattered fragments of my shin bone shift and move at every bump. Right in the center of town they left me by the side of the road, and said the ambulance would be there any moment.

A man in a restaurant across the street saw me through the window, and came out with a hot cup of tea. I would not be surprised if it turns out he was an angel. If not, then I believe the Lord has blessed him for his kindness.

The ambulance took me to the town of Wörgl which had a large Catholic hospital. The X-ray confirmed what I already knew, my right shin was broken in multiple places. They called it a spiral fracture, and it looked like someone had taken a popsicle stick and had turned both ends in opposite directions, which left a puzzle of triangles.

They put me to sleep and set the bone, and when I woke up I found myself in a large hall with 10 beds on either side. On the opposite side were all the thigh and pelvis fractures, and I was on the side for lower leg fractures – everyone a skiing accident.

After one painful week with many a sleepless night, I was put in an ambulance and driven all the way to Munich, where they put me in the first class section of a Scandinavian Airlines jet back to Stockholm. I was so shocked by this development. Apparently, my health insurance in Sweden was still active, and they had arranged for my repatriation without ever asking me.

Before long I found myself in "Karolinska Hospital," surrounded by a group of doctors that looked at my leg and the X-rays, shaking their heads. They then told me that the doctors in Austria did a poor job by not patching my shin up with metal plates and screws. Now it was too late to do that, and though it would heal, it would take a very long time – and that it did.

I celebrated my first anniversary since I left my home and old life in my hospital bed. All my friends came to visit me, and I felt a bit embarrassed by the outcome of my first missionary adventure. Tommy, the smart aleck, wrote with big block letters on my new cast that covered my entire leg from hip to foot: "Had I been a horse they would have shot me."

Two weeks later I was released, after they had taught me how to get around on crutches. The following months I moved around the homes of different friends in both Stockholm and Norrtälje, since it was hard for me to function on my own. Everyone was willing to help out and offered their hospitality.

Every month my cast was changed, since my leg muscles were dwindling away, and the cast could no longer support the leg. After three months, the cast became shorter and ended just below the knee which by now had become stiff, and it took several days of painful exercises to be able to bend it again.

By that time I was able to join the youth group again for their various performances and outreaches, and I balanced on one leg while singing and playing guitar. When I got my shorter cast they put a rubber block on the bottom, and I was able to put some weight on that leg, which made life a lot easier.

There was so much free time that I thought I was going crazy. I spent many hours reading, or playing guitar and piano. Most people in Sweden seemed to have a piano in their home.

I had not forgotten my promise to God and started making inquiries about different Bible colleges. This turned out to be more difficult than I had expected, since there was no such thing as a three year school anywhere in Sweden. Several one, or two year programs, but since God was so specific with His instructions, I did not even consider them. Of course there was always the Lutheran seminary, but that was more than three years, so what should I do?

The City Church, where I had met Stina, was putting on a three week missions course, and I signed up for that since I had the time, and was able to get around on my own by now. It was spring time again, and on rainy days I used to wrap plastic bags around the part of my cast that was not protected by my clothes. I made my way to the church every day by bus and subway to attend the classes and I enjoyed meeting more people that shared my passion for missions. But the course went by and I still had not found any clear answers and directions for the future.

Then one day, out of the blue, the answer came. I had been to a larger evening service in Stockholm when I sat next to an American man and his son. Donny was around 40, and his son maybe 12 years. I had no idea what they were doing in Sweden, and he was obviously divorced from his wife. As we talked about different things, he mentioned this wonderful Bible school in the US he had attended called "Faith School of Theology." My ears perked up and my next question came automatic:

"How long is that school, Donny?"

"Oh, it's only three years, since they don't really believe in degrees of any kind there."

I could barely contain my excitement, and before we parted ways I made sure I got the address from Donny. Anxiously I waited for a reply to my letter that I had sent off the following day, asking for information and an application form from FST.

What happened next was quite strange, but looking back it was obvious that God had His hand in it. The school sent me two separate envelopes. One contained all the papers for the application process, and the other one was a catalogue describing the courses, their statement of faith, and all the practical aspects of the school. Well, I only got the first letter, and I worked right away on filling out the forms and getting all the references they wanted. That second letter got lost in the mail. Actually, I would not be surprised if an angel had pulled it out of the mail bag, for if I had read it I don't think I would have even considered applying for that school.

As I answered all the questions on the application, I was faced with a real dilemma. One of the questions said: "Are you filled with the Holy Spirit?" You had to check "yes" or "no."

I honestly did not know what to put down. The teaching I had received was quite clear on the issue. If you can't speak in tongues, then you are not filled with the Spirit. I was prayed for twenty or so times regarding this matter, I had succumbed to the realization that obviously not every believer was blessed with this gift of the Spirit.

What should I put down? If I put down "yes" there was a good chance that I was lying, though I was not totally convinced of that. If I wrote "no" I might not be accepted, since this was obviously an important requirement for this school. I wrestled with my heart for a while, and then ticked the "yes" box, as I mumbled a prayer of forgiveness, in case I was lying. After all, I had to go to that school, since I had come to the conclusion that this must be the only three year Bible school in the world.

While I was still waiting for the acceptance letter from FST, I made serious plans to leave for the USA. My grandmother on my dad's side had three sisters who had immigrated to America between the First and the Second World War. As a young boy I had met two of them when they came to visit us in Germany. Just about 2 years previously, the daughter of the other sister came to visit Germany with her family. Their daughter Karen was a few years older than I, and we all got along well. So I wrote to my distant relatives in the U.S., asking if I could stay with them while preparing to go to the Bible school in the state of Maine.

One great thing about being on sick leave in Sweden was that the government provided generously. I actually made more money being unable to work, than I had made working for Carina and her family. Since I was living with friends for months I had next to no living expenses either, since nobody accepted any money from me while staying with them. So for the first time in my life, I was able to save up some money which would allow me to fly to the US and cover part of my tuition for the first year of college. God was taking care of me, and I felt certain I was on the right track.

Even after they had taken off my cast, I still had to walk on crutches for several weeks and build up my leg muscles through exercises. By late

June I was officially "well," and declared fit for work. So I had about one month to work and make some more money for my next big adventure. I still had not heard from the school, but I was not worried, since I knew God wanted me there.

So I worked some more for Carina, and looked after the kids while the family was vacationing near Bergshamra. It was a wonderful summer, and I enjoyed taking the boat out on little trips in the archipelago. I also took on an extra job filling in at the local newspaper.

Before leaving Sweden, I felt I needed to connect with my parents, so I had written to them from Sweden, telling them of my plans to go to the US, see our relatives there and then go to college. I was worried how my father would react, but I also knew that it was not right for me to keep hiding from him.

July 21 was another milestone in my life, and my last day in Sweden. I had already said good bye to all my friends in Stockholm, and on that particular Saturday morning I sang with the youth group one last time in front of the supermarket in Norrtällje where we had sung so many times before. After that Willis took half of the group and me in his old Volkswagen van to the airport in Stockholm.

This time it was for real, and I did not expect to live in Sweden again. Another chapter in my life began to open up, and I was on my way to the "New World."

Oh, it would be "new" all right – in more ways than one.

NEW WORLD

After my first exciting flight on a jumbo jet, we landed at J. F. Kennedy airport in New York. My "distant cousin" Karen, her boyfriend, and her parents, Ken and Milly, had come to meet me, and we drove in the biggest car I had ever been in to their home on Long Island.

Everything was so different from Europe. For one it was very hot and humid. What really got me was that everything seemed so much bigger and larger here. The cars, the houses, and especially the supermarkets and malls were unlike anything I had ever laid eyes on.

Staying the first few weeks with my relatives was very exciting at first, but frustrating at the same time. They were nominal Christians, and did not share many of my values, so I felt quite lonely and out of place, after having spent the last year and a half with true believers.

After a few days I received a phone call from my parents, and though it was scary, it went better than expected. My Dad did not seem too angry, and even promised to send me some money to help with college.

During my second week, we took a drive to Philadelphia to meet two of my great aunts. Tante Louise and Tante Mina ("Tante" is the German word for aunt). They lived in a small house in the suburbs of Philadelphia, and they seemed so glad to see me. Karen's folks left me there for a few days, and after they had left, the atmosphere in the house changed immediately. We switched to speaking German which was strange at first, and Louise and Mina were a bit rusty, since they both had left Germany more than 50 years ago. What really made me happy was the fact that they both were "born-again" believers.

They were widows in their eighties and full of life, though Mina was a bit frail, and it became clear that Louise was looking after her sister. Though it was not terribly exciting for me to live with two old ladies, some things did happen there that made me forget that.

The first thing was that I finally received confirmation that I had been accepted at Faith School of Theology, and with that letter came another copy of the school catalogue that I had never seen before. I wish someone could have filmed my face as I read through it for I'm sure my mouth stood open most of the time.

I had a hard time comprehending what I was reading and seeing, for it was so unlike anything I had ever encountered up until that time. There were long lists and descriptions of standards and rules that seemed so extreme to me, and I could not grasp and understand the meaning behind them.

There was the fact that we had to wear a suit and tie to class every day, and the women had to wear uniforms that seemed to me like something out of an old black and white movie. No long hair, no beards, and no jewelry or make up for the girls was allowed. No television, no movies, no bowling or playing pool, and obviously no smoking, alcohol and drugs.

The list went on and on regarding do's and don'ts, and most of them just did not make any sense to me at all. There was one called the "two foot rule," which meant you could never be any closer than two feet to the opposite sex. Huh? Being used to the metric system, I looked down at my feet to get an idea what kind of distance they were talking about.

My problem was that I had never met with these kind of expressions among any of the Christians and churches I had met so far, and I was getting worried that the school was connected to some weird cult. I had invested everything to come to this country and to go to this three-year Bible school, and now I was not sure what to make of things.

Tante Louise encouraged me and thought the statement of faith of the school sounded all right, and she took me shopping for a suit, shirts and ties, the kind of things I had never thought I would buy, let alone wear.

Both sisters ended up paying for most of the things I needed for school, and I was so touched by their love and generosity.

On the last evening before I was to return to Long Island, Louise told me something that totally took me by surprise. She opened up her heart and told me a bit of her story, and I was delighted to hear that she had been the wife of a Pentecostal pastor. She had served most of her life in churches and said that she had always prayed for her son John to become a missionary. But when he had grown up, it became evident that he had other ambitions in life. She had met me once before in Germany when I was a young boy, and the Lord had told her then that I was to be a missionary instead, so she started praying for me every day. Wow – and here I had thought that my becoming a believer, and receiving a call for missions were random events. That night I had my first lesson in beginning to grasp the sovereignty of God. He had my life's circumstances all planned before I even knew him!

That story greatly encouraged me in going on with my plans to attend FST, which meant among other things, a visit to the barber shop. Ken and Milly were so sweet in trying to understand my need to attend such a weird college, and they decided to drive me personally up to Maine, just to make sure I really wanted to stay there.

It was a long and fascinating trip through Connecticut, New Hampshire, Massachusetts up to Maine. I instantly liked Maine, for it reminded me so much of Sweden with its vast forests and rocky shoreline. Even some of the buildings were painted in the typical Swedish style of dark red walls with white doors and window frames.

Finding the little town of Brooklin, Maine, turned out to be quite an adventure, and I was delighted to see that we were on a peninsula that led to an archipelago very much like the one near Stockholm. While Ken and Milly started feeling more and more uneasy about this place, I knew in my heart this was going to be just fine.

The campus of Faith School of Theology did not look like a college campus at all, but more like a beach resort, which indeed it used to be.

When we finally pulled through the entrance, and we stopped in front of one of the many scattered houses, Ken got out of the car, stretched his legs, and started lighting up a cigarette. Out of a trailer a little old man appeared with a very distasteful look on his face, pointed at Ken's cigarette and huffed: "You can't smoke here, this is holy ground!"

Poor Ken all but dropped his smoke from his mouth, and then quickly ground it out while muttering something under his breath that I understood to be something that was also on the "don'ts" list.

They helped me unload my trunk, suitcase and guitar, and before they left, Milly looked at me with worried eyes and said: "Are you sure you want to stay here?"

"I'll be all right, Aunt Milly." I thanked them and hugged them good bye. As their big Chevy slowly pulled away, I could just see them shake their heads, and I saw the dim glow of Ken's lighter, as he lit another cigarette in the safety of his car.

✳ ✳ ✳

The next few days felt like I was on a different planet. Just about everything about FST and the folks there was different from anything I had ever encountered. Since I had arrived a few days before the official start of the semester, I was expected to earn my keep by working eight hours per day by helping with the many renovations and building projects around campus. That in itself was an eye-opening experience, since even though I was no stranger to manual labor, I had never worked in construction before, nor had I ever seen anything built with two-by-fours and dry wall.

Thankfully, there was Jim. He was a returning senior, and he kind of took me under his wings these first few days to help me find my place. He became a sounding board for me, as my heart burned with countless questions regarding the Christian standards held by the school and that particular strand of Christianity.

"So Jim, can you explain to me why we always have to get dressed up for every meeting, and even for classes?"

Jim gave it his best shot and explained: "Well, when we meet together in church we are meeting with Jesus, the king of kings. Wouldn't you get all dressed up if you knew you were going to meet a real king?"

In a way that did make sense to me, and I let it rest, even though it still left some things unanswered for me. We discussed many other things, and I realized that there was a good reason behind each rule and expression of faith. I decided then and there that even though I would keep my own standards, I would obey and submit to the laws and standards of the school for the time I was there. I determined that I would make it through the first year of school, and then reevaluate things.

It did not take me long to learn to love FST and its wonderful people, and all that they stood for. Even though there were certain things I could never fully understand, I was able to see the heart, and the true love for God behind everything, and that made it all right for me.

There were so many lessons to be learned, and many of them were totally cultural in nature. On the day that most students arrived, we did not have to work, but got to enjoy some fellowship time with fun and games. I had decided to join a game of croquet with some of the students and staff. At one point in the game, I totally missed the ball on an easy shot, and in my frustration I blurted out the "s" word. In Sweden we had used it all the time (the Swedish equivalent of it, which sounds a lot like the English word), and it was not a big deal. No sooner had the word left my mouth, than the game came to an abrupt halt, with everyone turning and looking at me with eyes of disbelief.

"What did you just say?" One of the staff took me aside and very sternly informed me that this was not an approved word here on campus – oops, sorry!

The first meeting was conducted in a former swimming pool which had been turned into a chapel, simply blew me away. I had never been to a church meeting of such exuberance and expression of worship. There was loud music and even louder shouting, and at some point it seemed like everyone was "dancing in the Spirit," as it was called, and that was something I had never seen before. When things quieted there were numerous prophecies, and messages in tongues followed by an interpretation by another person. Those kinds of things happened occasionally in the churches in Sweden, but it was more like twice a year, and always by the same old ladies. But here there seemed to be one after the other, and even many of the students were involved.

This experience left me with two very diverse thoughts. The first one was a tremendous respect for the spiritual maturity of everyone around me, and the second was a great sense of inferiority, and feeling out of place. After all, I had not even learned to speak in tongues, let alone walk in any of the gifts of the Spirit.

Once classes began, I was faced with another challenge. My school English had in no way prepared me for all the Biblical terms and lingo to which I was suddenly exposed. I remember sitting in Pentateuch class, frantically flipping through my paperback German-English dictionary, looking for meanings of words like "atonement," or "Septuagint." The fact that we were to read only the old King James Version of the Bible did not help my limited understanding.

I worked hard and did my best, and when the first tests and quizzes came, I did much better than I had expected. I discovered very soon that the learning experience at FST went far beyond the academic accumulation of Biblical knowledge. As the name suggests, Faith School of Theology majors in learning and practicing faith. It surprised me to find out that none of the teachers and staff received any kind of salary. At every Sunday meeting there was a special offering for the "Levites," and that was evenly divided among the workers there. There was always talk of living by faith, and at testimony time there were countless stories of God providing for various needs.

The tuition was very low, and all students were required to work about four hours a week in what was called "duty." This could be anything from helping in the kitchen, to cleaning floors, to working in the gardens, or other types of maintenance. Whenever we got caught breaking any of the rules, we got what was called "extra duty," which simply meant that we had to work more hours. Often these extra hours had to be done at five or six in the morning, and involved such unpleasant things like picking out rotten potatoes in the cellar.

The Israelites had their manna, and we had our potatoes. Some of the potato farmers in the region tithed to the school in, well, potatoes. So after the potato harvest there would be huge trucks filling our cellars with literally tons of potatoes.

So we had hash browns for breakfast, potato soup for lunch, and mashed, or baked potatoes for dinner. Our gardens produced tomatoes, squash, and a variety of other vegetables. Whenever funds were low, the meat portions became rather small, and we were told that if we wanted more meat on the tables, we had better start praying. We guys really did that, and would be surprised to see a farmer in his old pickup truck pull up the next day, donating half a side of beef. We would have steak that night.

The winters in Maine are long and extreme. I was shocked to discover that it was even colder there than Stockholm, and with lots more snow, sometimes until April, or even May. All the buildings were heated by oil burners, and our heating bills were huge. Quite frequently throughout the long winters, we were asked to pray for the oil bill, or other pressing needs, and more than once there would be a real move of the Holy Spirit during these times of intercession. One particular Sunday, the Lord spoke very clearly through various sources that if we wanted Him to supply for our needs, then we would have to do our part as well. That triggered an avalanche of students, staff, and visitors literally running to the front of the hall, emptying their pockets and wallets into the offering baskets on stage. The only jewelry that was allowed on campus were engagement rings and wedding bands, and sometimes they were found in the baskets as well. We literally gave everything, and then watched in awe how God provided for our needs, both corporately, and individually! I am still drawing from that training today, many years later.

I valued the incredible respect and openness towards the Holy Spirit. Every morning, after breakfast the whole student body had a time of devotion together right there in the dining hall. There would be a song or two, some scripture reading, and often some announcements. More than once, God began to speak to us regarding things that He wanted to do in our lives, and the result was that we would spend all morning, and sometimes the afternoon as well in the dining hall, on our knees, weeping and laughing, being hit by wave after wave of His presence as He visited us. Classes were cancelled, and all leadership was relinquished and turned over to the Holy Spirit, until it was clear to all that He was finished.

One of the cultural differences had to do with the healing process in my life. Being raised in what used to be West Germany in the fifties left our generation without any national pride whatsoever. When it came to World History and the topic of the Second World War, I believe we learned less in school than anyone else in the world. All our teachers had been part of that particular history in one way or another, and there was this blanket of corporate guilt over the nation that did not allow for any expression of nationalism.

I was both intrigued and jealous when I saw all the blue and yellow Swedish flags displayed all over the country in the summer time. Now, here in the US I saw a similar expression of national pride. At FST we also had a flagpole, and at certain occasions we would gather around in a big circle to pray for America and pledge our allegiance. I felt I could not participate and there was a sense of longing to be able to be proud of my country. Initially, everyone thought that I was Swedish, since I had applied and arrived from Sweden, and I did not make any effort to correct them. But eventually word got out that I was German. There were occasional remarks and wisecracks, since everyone had seen the popular TV show "Hogan's Heroes," a comedy series that portrayed the anecdotes of U.S. and German troops during World War II. The Germans were featured as not especially shining with intelligence.

When it started getting really cold I had bought myself a long winter coat of fake suede leather. Some of the guys thought that made me look like Colonel Klinck from that comedy show, and when I walked into my dorm one afternoon, they had all lined up on the steps and saluted me with "Heil Hitler." Somehow they failed to see that I did not think this to be very funny at all. It would take many years for the Lord to heal that broken relationship with my own identity. I still can't say that I am proud to be German, but I realize now that this is part of what God has made me, and I am fully aware that God made all the nations of this world, and has a special role for each of them in His overall plan.

While I was getting used to the spiritual dynamics at FST, I was frustrated that I still could not speak in tongues. I thought it was proof that I had not yet been filled with God's Spirit, and that brought me to a point of desperation.

One morning I woke up and decided that I was going to do something about that. After breakfast, instead of going to classes, I locked myself into my room, knelt by my bed and announced to God, "Lord, I am not getting up until I can speak in tongues!"

Then I waited for Him to come and fill me with His Spirit. Nothing happened for the longest time, and I started getting more and more frustrated with God and myself. But then my mind wandered off, and I started thinking back to the night in Skellefteå, when I was so overcome by God's love and cried my heart out. And then it began to dawn on me that this was my baptism in His Spirit. It was not until much later that I learned that He wanted to baptize me again and again.

I was indeed spirit-filled, and I had not lied on my application to FST. That was a relief, but what about the tongues? Why was I not able to do that? Very gently, God began to instruct me. He simply said, "You do it, just start speaking in a new language."

I was appalled. There was no way I was going to fake this, by trying to do it myself! So I waited some more for God to take control of my tongue and cause me to speak in a language I had never learnt. Again, there was that whisper in my heart, "Open your mouth and start speaking."

Since I was alone in the room and none would be able to hear me, I decided to give it a try. It felt like I was making up sounds and syllables, and as I did, it began gushing forth like a stream. I could speak in tongues! I could start anytime I wanted to, and I could stop at any moment. There was no special sense of anointing, no thunder, no stars or angels – just that feeling that I was praying exactly what God wanted me to say. I felt almost disappointed. This was so easy, I could have done this a long time ago. I just wished someone had instructed me properly.

Now that I had my very own prayer language, I started feeling a bit better about my spirituality. It was not long afterwards that I gave my first message in tongues at a small prayer meeting, and someone else in the room promptly interpreted it – how cool was that?

* * *

During my time in Sweden I was at times overcome by a great sense of loneliness, and I began yearning for a girlfriend. Unlike before, I knew that it would not be right to pursue a relationship with any girl, without the assurance in my heart that we could actually spend the rest of our lives together. That limited my options greatly. Besides, it had to be someone who was totally committed to following Jesus, wherever He would lead us some day. I had my eyes on one of the girls in Sweden, but she made it quite plain to me that we could never be more than friends.

At FST, I had limited my choice on two girls in my class, but it became obvious before any relationship even developed, that they were not the right ones either. The rules regarding dating were quite strict, but friendships between boys and girls were quite common. You just could not get engaged until your senior year, and you could not get married while at school. The problem was, almost all the guys around me had girlfriends, except me.

Again, this led me to such frustration that I set aside one afternoon to complain to God about that. I took a long walk through the beautiful forests around the school, and poured out my heart to God. By then I had become more accustomed to hearing His voice, and it did not take all that long to hear Him whisper in my heart, "Who gave you the right to get married? Didn't you give up all your rights when you decided to follow Me?"

I was totally taken off guard by that revelation. Wasn't everyone supposed to get married at some point? But He had made His point – I had never even asked Him if He wanted me to get married. Having flash backs of my accident in Austria, I realized how important it was for me to obey Him in all things. I knelt down by an old tree stump, and rededicated myself to God. And then I told Him that I was giving up my right to get married, and if He wanted me to stay single, then that was quite all right.

Later on, I kept telling all my friends at school that I felt God asked me to stay single for the rest of my life. That was not exactly what He had said, but I was very serious about relinquishing that privilege. I actually felt a great sense of joy and freedom after that particular event.

This time I passed the test, and you'll never believe what happened just a few months later.

BOOT CAMP

I had made it through my freshman year at FST, and it had become clear that I was going to finish the school at any cost. Since I had come to the U.S. on a round-trip ticket, I started my summer break by flying back to Sweden. There was a great reunion with Willis and the rest of the gang in Norrtälje. I joined right back in their singing schedule, and was invited to help at a kids' camp on some island. Some of the others from the group were helping as well, and we had a wonderful time. I remember especially when the Holy Spirit fell on the children during the evening gathering, and then when we were all tucked away in our tents, we could hear them pray and prophesy over each other for hours into the night.

The two weeks in Sweden went by all too fast, and I was quite tense as I embarked on the next part of my journey. I had called my parents from Stockholm, and my father was concerned that I would be detained at the German border, because I had not yet served in the army there. So it was decided that I would meet them in Copenhagen, Denmark.

When I got off the train, they were already waiting for me – Mom, Dad, and my brother Winfried. There were some awkward moments as we greeted each other, but then we all piled into Dad's Volkswagen and started the long drive down to Nuremberg. There were many questions, especially from my father, and I tried to answer knowing they would never fully understand. They were worried that I had ended up in some religious cult, since in those days anything that was not part of the Catholic or Lutheran Church was highly suspect.

During the days that followed back in my old home, we had many, at times, rather heated discussions about spiritual matters. At one point my father shocked me by admitting that he had been part of the Salvation Army as a young man, preaching in the streets of his home town. When the war broke out, and he was sent to fight on the Russian front, he slowly retreated into a nominal kind of Christianity.

The next few weeks were frustrating and exciting at the same time. I met some of my old friends, and also Günther, but now we had even less in common than before I had left. Father introduced me to his Lutheran pastor, and I got to share a song at one of their meetings. I came in contact with a Pentecostal pastor of a small church in town, and started going there on Sundays. More than once my father joined me, mainly to find out more about that cult in which he thought I was captured. But more than once he was touched by the messages aimed at his heart, and God was at work in him.

The discussions with my sister and her husband were less fruitful, and everyone tried to talk me out of my missionary calling. I had lots of fun spending time with my little brother Winfried, who was not so little anymore, and I took him along to some of the meetings, and he was impressed and wide open. Later on he committed his life to Jesus, went to a Bible school, and has been in ministry ever since.

There were some good times with some of the young people at the church, and I was able to challenge and help them to new insights and understanding of God's will for their lives. But I began longing to get back to FST and the spiritual reality there. My parents helped me to get a ticket back to the US, and I was ready to leave again.

* * *

Since there were still a few days before school started, I spent some time with Tante Louise and her daughter's family in Pennsylvania. My friend John, who was going back to FST for his senior year, picked me up and we hung out at his parents' home in Trenton, New Jersey. We also did some last minute shopping for school supplies. The last Saturday of our break we had a hard time deciding what to do with our free time, so we scanned the newspaper. All we found was a notice that a certain church at the shore was having a picnic at the Shark River Park. Some of our fellow students came from that church, and so we decided to drive an hour or so to see who we could meet there.

It was a warm and sunny day, and soon I started getting bored, and did not feel like joining the softball game (I never did get used to some of the American games like football and baseball). In those days I had my guitar with me just about everywhere I went, so I found a shady spot under a tree, pulled out my songbook and guitar and started strumming away.

Quite some time later, two girls came over, sat down and started singing with me. As it turned out, they were sisters, Anna and Cathy. They too were not really part of that church, and had only come because they wanted to do something fun together. Cathy was the younger one with beautiful long and blonde hair, and a lovely voice that blended real well when she harmonized with me. After a few minutes Anna got up and walked away, and Cathy and I sang some more, and talked a bit. I thought it was so cool that her Dad was Norwegian, and her Mom mainly German. Later on, Anna came to pick up her sister. As they walked away, Cathy turned around and looked at me with her blue eyes, and it was like I was struck by lightning.

"Oh, Norbert, she is gorgeous," said John on our drive back to Trenton. He had obviously seen us together, but stayed out of the picture. I definitely thought so too. As a matter of fact I thought she was the most beautiful girl I had ever seen. But I did not want to get my hopes up again. Besides, what were the chances of me seeing her again?

The next day, John and I decided to go to that church for their Sunday night meeting. Glad Tidings Church had many young people, and a real charismatic pastor that could preach up a storm, as they say. To my utter amazement and delight, Cathy was there as well, and we spent a few minutes talking after church. She actually seemed to like me, which really surprised me, and I found myself thinking about her until I fell asleep late that night.

The following Wednesday, John's mother dropped us and our luggage off with a friend at the shore who was also a student and would drive us up to Maine the next morning. Since we were close to Glad Tidings and they had a Wednesday night meeting, we all decided to go there one last time. I thought it would be too much of a coincidence to see Cathy there again, but there she was, beautiful as ever, and my heart ached at the thought of having to leave her. This time we talked a bit more, and she suggested that we could write each other, and so we exchanged addresses. Before we parted ways Cathy totally surprised me when she invited me to spend the Thanksgiving holidays with her family! I was on Cloud Nine all the way up to Maine, and could not believe what was happening to me. This just seemed too good to be true, but the Lord reminded me that he was pleased with my willingness to give up my right for marriage, and now He was giving me something far better than I could have imagined.

In the weeks and months that followed, Cathy and I developed our relationship through almost daily letters, and an occasional phone call. It did not take us long to discover that this was getting serious.

Faith School of Theology had something called "outside ministry," and that could mean accompanying one of the teachers for a weekend visit to some church, or joining a team to visit a prison, or passing out tracts at the mall in Bangor. Once per semester, during extended ministry trips called "crusade," the students were assigned to a team to serve a local church, usually somewhere along the east coast, or Canada. There was always one team who joined "Brother Pier" on a speaking tour to numerous churches. Dr. Pier is the founder of the school and taught both Homiletics and Prophecy. Traveling with him was a very coveted thing, since it meant exciting meetings, and invitations to nice homes and restaurants.

In my junior year, I was chosen to be part of a singing group scheduled to travel with Brother Pier down to New Jersey. One of the meetings was at a church in Perth Amboy, NJ, and Cathy and her parents drove up from their home in Neptune to attend the meeting and to see me. After the meeting, Cathy's father surprised us all when he walked up to Brother Pier and asked permission for me to come and spend the night at their house. Brother Pier surprised us even more by saying yes!

That evening I got to meet Cathy's parents, and some of her siblings. She is "number 9" of ten children, and half of them had already left home by then. It was also the first time that Cathy and I got to be alone with each other, and we shared our first kiss under a big tree in the back yard.

* * *

Even though the junior year was considered the hardest at FST, it flew by quickly, and my biggest challenge was to keep my mind on my studies, and not constantly think about my future with Cathy.

We spent Thanksgiving and Christmas together, and the family had accepted me as part of them. By Christmas we already talked about engagement and wedding. I had shared my heart and calling with Cathy, for I wanted to be certain that she would be all right with living the life of a missionary (not that I knew what that meant…). I told her that we would not be living the American Dream, and that we might never live in a home of our own. Cathy had just recently rededicated her life to Jesus, and was willing to go wherever the Lord would lead us. She had recently turned 17, and I was 21. In so many ways we were both naive and immature, but God saw our heart and desire to serve Him.

In April, we had another ministry trip planned to New Jersey as part of a school choir tour, and we would sing at Glad Tidings church, where we had first met. I had written a letter to Cathy's father, asking for his blessing to marry his daughter, and he agreed. Cathy told me later that most of her siblings had opposed the idea of her getting married so young, but her Dad had stood up for her by saying, "Norbert is the one for her."

One of the seniors at school had to break off his engagement and gave me a good deal on a diamond ring, and so in April 1975, after our meeting at Glad Tidings, I took Cathy down to the basement of the church and asked her, "So, you want to get married?"

During my junior year at FST, I spent much time seeking God regarding my calling to serve Him in Asia. I had started to read many missionary books about Asia, but there was no particular country that stood out to me. I had hung a world map on the wall above my bed, and every morning I would look at the vast continent of Asia, and asked the same question: "Lord, where will it be?"

There never came an answer, and I understood that this was an area where I had to learn patience and wait for His revelation. God did speak in a way I never expected. We had just returned from another ministry trip to a rather large church in Baltimore, Maryland, where I had sung in the tenor section of the school choir. I had also been asked to give a short testimony about how I found Jesus.

After we had returned to Maine, there was a small parcel waiting for me. I did not recognize the name of the sender and was intrigued by this mysterious gift. The parcel contained a used book, and a short letter. In the letter, the lady simply stated that when she heard me tell my story at her church, she felt the Lord ask her to send me this particular book. The book was called "God's Smuggler", and the author was Brother Andrew.

It was the story of a man in Holland who was overwhelmed by the fact that most Christians in the Communist Countries in Eastern Europe were heavily persecuted, and could not even buy Bibles. These nations were behind what used to be referred to as the "Iron Curtain," and Brother Andrew risked both his life and freedom to smuggle Bibles in his Volkswagen Beetle to countries like Romania, Bulgaria, and the former Soviet Union. He described praying for God to close the eyes of the border guards while they searched his car at the borders. He told stories of pastors and believers being imprisoned and tortured for their faith, and of handwritten parts of the Bible, and believers learning large portions of the Bible by heart, because they had no access to the written Word of God.

I was deeply moved by this revelation, and even before I had even finished reading the last page of the book, I knew deep down in my heart that this was what God wanted me to do. This was the first of two incidences where God gave me clear guidance and direction by reading a book other than the Bible itself.

The next incident would not happen until five years later, but both times the message in the books profoundly changed my life. That may be the reason why I love to read books even today, and it is my hope that someone reading this book may receive direction from God.

* * *

The summer after my junior year would become one of many unforgettable experiences. Since my parents had paid for my ticket to come home, I flew back to Germany, and my time with my family was a lot easier than the previous year. I was way too restless to spend several months at home. To my great surprise, My father gave me his old Volkswagen, and for the first time I drove all the way from Germany to Sweden, to connect with my dear friends there.

But the new-found revelation regarding the persecuted church would not give me any rest, and I felt it was time to do something about that. I convinced my old friend Willis, and Donnie Archer (he was the American who had told me about FST), to accompany me to Finland, and the border of the Soviet Union. Since it was quite difficult to get a visa to actually enter Russia, we had decided to try to connect with Russians coming out into Finland.

We had loaded the trunk of my car with Russian Bibles, New Testaments, and tracts from the Bible Society in Stockholm. We took the car ferry to Naantali, and from there we checked the harbors of Turku and Helsinki for Russian cargo ships. We tried to strike up conversations with the sailors, and give them our literature, but we quickly discovered that they were very reluctant and fearful to talk to us. At one of the ships, we were invited to come on board and meet the captain. While Willis and Donnie engaged him in a conversation, I snuck off to find the sleeping quarters of the crew, and managed to slip a Russian New Testament under the pillows of their bunks.

In Helsinki, we went to the train station, and waited for the daily train from Moscow. The people on that train looked to us like businessmen and government officials, and we actually managed to give away some Bibles that we had gift wrapped for the occasion. With a smile and "Welcome to Finland," we blessed them with the Word of God in their language.

I wanted to get closer to "the enemy," and so we drove along the coast, passing Kotka and Hamina, until we actually saw the towers of the border crossing to Russia, and the main highway to Leningrad. We found a truck stop where many of the trucks coming out of Russia paused, and passed out our gifts to the drivers. As it turned out, our idea with the gift -wrapped books made it a lot easier to pass them on.

We wanted to continue meeting trucks the next day, and decided to spend the night in an abandoned barn, just one kilometer from the fence that divided Russia from the "Free Western World." But in the middle of the night we were rudely awakened by Finnish Border Patrol who told us to leave immediately, since we had entered a restricted security zone.

On the long way back to Sweden I could not help to feel quite satisfied about the success of our mission, and wondered if one day I would meet someone in eternity that would say, "I am here because of the Word of God you gave to me in Finland!"

After returning to my parent's house in Germany, I was surprised by another exciting prospect. During the Sunday meeting I met a man who headed up several ministries geared towards blessing Israel, and in an effort to facilitate reconciliation between the two nations, he organized for groups of German, Christian youth to go to Israel to volunteer in a kibbutz.

A kibbutz is a collective community that was traditionally based on agriculture. Today, farming has been partly supplanted by other economic branches, including industrial plants and high-tech enterprises. Kibbutzim began as utopian communities, a combination of socialism and Zionism. They still needed another member for the group that would depart in a few days, and I quickly signed up. Going to Israel was a dream come true, and the next four weeks would turn into an unforgettable experience.

After flying from Frankfurt to Tel Aviv, we were picked up by a representative of the kibbutz Urim in the Negev desert in southern Israel near the border of the Gaza Strip and about 30 kilometers west of Beersheba. Driving through the Negev desert, we began to wonder where on earth we were going until we saw the gate to Urim. Inside, the desert had been turned into a beautiful oasis through clever means of irrigation. There were lush green lawns and big palm trees, and there was a big swimming pool and a tennis court.

We were assigned to various bungalows, and all meals were taken at the communal dining hall. We had to get up at 6 every morning, and after breakfast were taken to our daily place of work. Most days we worked at the grapefruit orchards. Since it was not yet harvest season, we got a quick lesson in learning how to prune trees, and then were put to work, armed with clippers. It was hot and dusty, and the rows of trees seemed to stretch endlessly. The trees were quite big, and we had to climb in them to get to all the obsolete branches that needed to be cut. But occasionally we would cut the wrong branch, and you could hear the drop of an unripe fruit on the ground. Our overseers would get quite upset with us when they found out, and so we came up with this game, where we quickly rolled or threw the fruit to the next row of trees, so that they would get blamed instead of us. This soon turned into a full-blown war with the other volunteers, and you could see grapefruit flying back and forth between rows of trees, really driving our overseers crazy.

By three in the afternoon we were done with work, and enjoyed the rest of the day at the pool, eating chilled watermelons and other great fruit. Every evening we would sit on the lawn in a circle singing worship songs. Being drawn by the music, we often had some of the Jewish residents join us with their instruments.

As part of the program, the kibbutz organized several trips for us, so that we could see more of the country. The first trip took us to the Dead Sea. We got to swim in the waterfalls of En Gedi, and saw the caves where David and his men hid from King Saul. That night we all slept on the beach of the Dead Sea, and were awakened at 3:30 the next morning to embark on the long ascent on the "Snake Path" to the ancient fortress of Masada, where we watched the sun rise.

Masada had been built by King Herod as a refuge for himself. Later on, it was occupied by Jewish rebels who had fled Jerusalem in an attempt to defy the Roman occupational forces. In 72 AD, the Romans laid siege to the mountain fortress by building a huge ramp. When they finally breeched the walls, they found that all 960 inhabitants had committed mass suicide.

On our second trip, we finally got to see Jerusalem, an absolute highlight for me. Even though we were all a bit put off by the fact that there was a church, cathedral or monastery at every place of historical and biblical importance, we were overwhelmed by the spiritual significance of that ancient city. Walking through the narrow streets almost made you feel like you were living in biblical times and you could expect to bump into Peter or John at the next corner. We walked for long distances, and on our way to the Mount of Olives we connected with some sisters from a German order that invited us for a simple lunch with them.

We went on to see Nazareth, the Sea of Galilee and the slopes where Jesus preached His famous sermon, then up to Jaffa, and back to Beersheba. During one part of the trip, we travelled on a public bus and had a bit of a shock when someone in the back started to shout something in Hebrew. The bus immediately stopped by the side of the road, and the driver told everyone to get off at once. He then went back into the bus to retrieve a plastic bag from under one of the seats in the back. Some passenger had obviously forgotten it when getting off earlier, but since this was a common way for Palestinian separatists to leave a bomb behind, no one was taking any chances. It was not so much fear as a national alertness that made people very careful.

Some days later I got to experience personally how easy it is to get yourself in a dangerous situation in this nation that has never experienced real peace. One late afternoon, I had decided to take an excursion into the surrounding desert all by myself. I was fascinated by the barren, rugged and yet beautiful landscape that was so different from anything I had ever seen or experienced. To my surprise and delight, I was able to find pieces of ancient pottery that were so numerous that they had lost their attraction to the archeological community. I then sat on top of a small hill, reading my Bible and feeling close to God. On my way back to the kibbutz I heard gunshots and turned to see some older boys with rifles in the distance. At first I thought they were maybe hunting snakes or other desert creatures. But then I felt and heard a bullet buzz right over my head, which sent me sprinting for the gate in record time. When I told some of the kibbutz leaders about this they just shrugged their shoulders, and told me I was stupid for going out there by myself in the first place.

Too soon our four weeks were over, and I don't think that I ever took another trip that left me with such a sense of awe and wonder as this adventure in the Holy Land. I have not been there since, but I do have an appointment with Jesus there one day.

$$* * *$$

The rest of the summer flew by quickly, and I could not wait to get back to the US, and be with Cathy. I was able to spend a few days with her and her family before going back to Maine for my senior year. Since FST also had a Christian high school, Cathy planned to come up to Maine with me, finish her senior year, while at the same time taking the first year of Bible School. Since the requirements for graduating were lower in Maine than in New Jersey, she only had to take another class of English to accumulate enough credits for her high school diploma.

We were already engaged at this point, so we were a "recognized couple" at FST, which had its privileges. All the rules of interacting with the opposite sex still applied, but we were allowed to spend half an hour each night after supper sitting across a table in the dining room, with all the other official couples, being watched by one of the teachers or staff. On one of these occasions, we were caught holding hands under the table. Brother Godly (that really was his name) was a godly man, and let us off the hook with a warning.

Once a month we were allowed to go on a weekend date, but we had to ask one of the teachers to act as a chaperone. That meant if we wanted to go out for a meal we had to pay for their meal as well while they sat there with us, spoiling our romantic dinner. One of the most requested chaperones was the school's matron, Sister Doyle, and we soon found out why. Sister Doyle was blind in one eye, and we would ask her to drive the car on our way to town. On the way home in the dark she would be seriously concentrating on her driving, so that we would be able to sneak in a few hugs and kisses on the back seat without her noticing. Or maybe she was just a lot more tolerant than we gave her credit for.

* * *

Being a senior meant that we were given more leadership challenges, and I had been given the ungrateful job of the "dorm monitor." That simply meant that I had to make sure everyone on my floor obeyed the rules when it came to lights-out at ten, keeping their rooms in order, and making sure everyone was studying at the designated times. That also included turning those in for punishment who broke the rules and did not heed your warnings. That, of course did not earn you points with the trouble makers.

The workload was actually lighter than during the second year, and we had more time to spend on ministry related programs and projects. Already at the end of my freshman year, I was able to buy a secondhand electric bass and amplifier, and enjoyed playing for the various musical groups. During my last year at school, I joined a gospel group called "The Tones of Glory" as the only "white" member playing the bass and having lots of fun going on trips to various churches.

Since this was my last year, I was especially eager to hear from God regarding the future. God had answered my prayer for a wife and partner, and we were both ready to go wherever He would send us. And there was this prophetic promise to become one of "God's Smugglers," but I really had no idea how to go about this. Well, I need not have worried, for God had that covered as well. One day we had a guest speaker at our daily chapel service by the name of Mart Vahi. He was originally from Estonia, but now lived in Canada, and was about to move with his family to Germany in order to set up a base for a ministry smuggling Bibles into Iron Curtain countries. As I listened to his stories it became clear that God had brought him to the school as answer to my prayers. We connected and realized the obvious: God wanted us to work together, and Mart was to become my mentor and teacher for this very specific type of ministry.

The rest of my senior year went by in a flash, and in May 1976, both Cathy and I, respectively, graduated from Faith School of Theology and Higgins Classical Institute.

Tante Louise and Cathy's parents were able to come for the occasion, and I remember leaving Maine with both a joyful and a sad heart. Of course I was happy to have completed my course at FST, but there was also a sense of pain of leaving behind the place and the people that God had used to reveal himself to me in such a real and powerful way. Both Cathy and I had become close friends with some of the students, and we did not know if we would ever see them again.

No Longer Alone

Less than three weeks after our graduation, our big day had arrived. On June 5, 1976, Cathy and I were married at Glad Tidings Church in Tinton Falls, New Jersey, the very church that had the Sunday School picnic where we met for the first time.

My parents and my brother Winfried had come over for the occasion, as well as some of my distant relatives from Pennsylvania. The reception was held outside in the backyard of Cathy's parents, and it was a gorgeous spring day. Many flowers were in bloom, and the dear folks from the church had helped with food and the wedding cake, so it turned out to be a great outdoor banquet. We had asked for monetary gifts, rather than the traditional household gifts, since we knew that we would leave for Europe very soon.

Later in the afternoon, Cathy and I left for a three-day honeymoon to the Poconos in Pennsylvania. Cathy's brother Dan had let us use his souped up Datsun 240Z sports car, and with a great roar and racket from the tin cans that had been attached to the rear bumper, we left for our first trip as married couple, not knowing that in the years to come we would spend countless hours on the road together.

The next few weeks were filled with reducing all our earthly belongings to one suitcase each and making the rounds saying good-bye to friends, family and churches. When we finally left in July, we only had the promise of a few hundred dollars support from some friends, and the rest of our wedding gifts. My Dad had paid for our tickets to Germany, and his old Volkswagen was waiting for us in storage behind the house.

For me it was a trip home, but for Cathy it was a journey into the un-known, and from that day on she never again was to live in her home country.

For the first few weeks in Germany we stayed with my parents, and it seemed quite strange to live with my wife in my old room, surrounded by the painful memories of a different life. With my parents not speaking any English, and Cathy not knowing any German, communication was quite difficult, and I found myself constantly interpreting for both sides.

I was able to show Cathy the places of my childhood, and we even visited my old friend Günther who was living with one of his girlfriends at the time. It was quite obvious that we had grown apart even more, and though he respected the choices I had made in life, he showed no interest or desire to know more about them. Our paths had gone in different directions and would never cross again after that day.

We had decided earlier to meet Mart Vahi and his family in the city of Wiesbaden, and the day had come for us to leave Nürnberg to start our ministry as God's smugglers.

Wiesbaden is not far from the city of Frankfurt, and we were surprised to discover that the address we had been given was that of an old castle called "Schloss Freudenberg." The castle was rented by several Christian ministries. The basement halls were used by an American missionary family as a church and outreach to the numerous U.S. soldiers stationed in the area and on the upstairs floor, Mart and his family had their apart-ment, and office. We were assigned a corner in the huge attic of the castle, and we tried to create some privacy by connecting some of the wooden pillars with crude boards, constructing makeshift walls. The result was our first, one-room apartment that was quite cozy.

Soon the time had come for our first smuggling trip. We were given an ancient Volkswagen camper van to use. We followed Mart and his family who drove a huge Ford camper into Hungary. That was one of the easier countries to get into, and just perfect for our initiation as "God's smugglers". The only hiding place on that van was the spare tire mounted on the front, and we had stuffed it with New Testaments and other smaller books and prayed that we would not get a flat tire. We got to experience the thrill of our first border crossing behind the Iron Curtain, and all went well as we delivered the literature to our contact in the capital Budapest.

As we continued to work with Mart and his mission, we ran into an unforeseen problem. The German army had exempted me from military service while I was still studying. Those working as clergy and Christian workers were exempt all together, but since the mission we worked for was not recognized by the German authorities, I was mustered and evaluated, and declared fit for service. Something had to be done quickly, or I would find myself in the military for the next 18 months.

As we were searching for answers to our dilemma, we heard about a German mission that was involved in the same type of ministry, operating not far from the area where we lived. The ministry was simply called AVC which is an acronym for "Aktionskommitee für Verfolgte Christen" which translates to "Action-Committee for Persecuted Christians". Since they were recognized through the national Pentecostal movement in Germany, working with them would exempt me from the military. We met with their leaders, Waldemar and Hans, and they were eager to employ us as full-time Bible couriers. Though we were sad to have to leave Mart and his family, we knew that God was working on our behalf in providing a perfect framework for what God had called us to do. We were given all the tools needed, such as vehicles and literature, and even a small salary and health insurance. As it turned out, we would still partner with Mart on several trips, but we left the old castle and moved into a small apartment in a former farm building north of Frankfurt which became our base of operations.

For the next two and a half years, we took a trip almost every month into a Communist nation in Eastern Europe: Hungary, the former Yugoslavia and Czechoslovakia, Eastern Germany, Romania, Bulgaria, Poland, and several nations within the former Soviet Union, such as the Ukraine, Belarus, Russia, Estonia, Georgia, and Armenia. The only country we were not able to visit was Albania, which was totally closed towards tourism in those days.

The mission kept coming up with newer and better vans, and all of them had been converted into campers at the base. By doing the conversions ourselves, we could integrate various designs for hiding places. I can remember sitting at the breakfast table with Hans and his family, and Hans sharing the idea for a new hiding place that he had received from the Lord in his dreams. Even though the need for smuggling Bibles into Soviet Bloc nations has passed, I am not sure how much I should reveal about our methods back then, since there still are nations in this world where persecution of Christians is a grim reality, and even now there are ministries involved with smuggling Bibles and Christian literature into certain nations of this world. If you picture a van or closed truck, you can imagine that any hiding place would have to be in places like double walls, ceilings, or floors.

After several successful trips to Hungary, Poland, Romania and Yugoslavia, came the most feared of all: The Soviet Union! In those days you could not simply arrive at the border, and expect to be let in. Besides a visa from the Soviet embassy, you needed to submit an itinerary for every single day, six months in advance. Only certain roads were opened to foreign tourists, and there was a checkpoint in and out of every city, and if one did not show up at the given destination for that day, the authorities would come looking for you. Of course, we were never allowed to just park and sleep in our van anywhere but at the authorized camp sites, and if the city did not have one, then we were forced to book a hotel.

For our first trip there, we drove to Poland and the border town of Brest, and even though we had a long wait and thorough search by the Russian border guards, we were treated kindly and our hiding places withstood all their scrutiny. Greatly relieved, we drove on to the city of Smolensk, and then on to Moscow, where we had our first contact. The most crucial part of each trip was to connect with our contacts there without endangering them in any way. We knew that if something went wrong, then the local believers would be in much greater danger than us. We had memorized our instructions to connect with our contacts using public transportation, since we could not simply drive up to their address in our big camper. So Cathy and I tried to dress as inconspicuously as possible, and used buses, and the famous Moscow subway, called the Metro.

Delivery of our "gifts" was usually a late-night affair, where we met our friends in some remote place like a park, or forest, quickly transferring the books in potato sacks from our vehicle to theirs, and then go our separate ways, quite often never seeing each other again. For this particular transaction, our friends came to a secluded spot outside the camp site, and we shoved the sacks through a hole in the fence.

While we were in Moscow, we also took in some of the sights, and had to join some tourist tours organized by the state-run agency called "Intourist." Since it was our first wedding anniversary, I had decided to take Cathy to a huge restaurant right by the Red Square for a memorable meal. The waiter came with a thick menu that was just filled with the largest variety of dishes we had ever seen. When we had finally made our selections and told the waiter, he informed us that these particular meals were not available today. The same thing was repeated with each alternative we suggested, until I finally asked him, "Then what do you have tonight?"

"Beef Stroganoff," was his brisk answer, and that is what we had. As it turned out, that was the only available meal in most of the other restaurants we visited later on as well.

Driving through the Russian countryside on endless straight roads filled with potholes, we were amazed at the large wheat fields everywhere. We could see numerous work crews that mainly consisted of women, and many of them were just lying idly under some trees, or sitting in groups to chat. Whenever we met any road repair crews, they also were mainly made up of mainly women. They were armed with shovels, spades and pick axes, and did all the hard work, while the men drove the trucks and other road making equipment.

Everywhere were statues and billboards depicting Lenin, praising the accomplishments of communism. Often, when we paused for gas or a meal, people would come up to us and begin to ask us questions in either broken German or English. They wanted to know what we did for a living, how much money we made, how much we paid for a pound of butter, and so on. When we told them, they would always become upset, and often even angry, for they had been told that people in the West are quite poor, and many are starving. At one particular spot, we had gathered quite a crowd, and it looked like they were ready to start another revolution, so we quickly excused ourselves and drove on.

After Moscow we drove all the way north past Kalinin and Novgorod to Leningrad. There we headed west towards the capital of Estonia, Tallinn. The three Baltic states of Estonia, Latvia, and Lithuania share closely related languages and a common cultural ancestry with Finland. Under Soviet rule they had become states of the Soviet Union and were forced to adopt Russian as their national language, which they detested. We had proof of that when we rode in a taxi in Tallinn, and automatically thanked the driver in Russian. He turned to us and gave us that "when looks could kill" stare that reminded us of the pent-up hate of a subdued people.

Because of the proximity to Finland and Western Europe the churches in Estonia enjoyed more freedom, and we had some great house church meetings with several groups. Earlier on our trip through Russia we had been invited to an underground meeting with the Russian believers, and that had been a very interesting experience to say the least. We were stuffed in a room of a typical wooden house, with all the windows closed tightly. The singing was quiet and a capella, and it was there we saw our first handwritten hymn books and Bibles. Their traditions included the brotherly kiss and foot-washing, which were both new to us. After the service the leaders gathered around us and asked questions. One of the most common question was, "What is wrong with the churches in the

West that they don't get persecuted? After all, didn't Jesus say that we would be persecuted as He was persecuted?"

After Tallinn we made our way back to Leningrad and then turned north towards the border to Finland. It is hard to describe the sense of freedom and lightness that hits you once you cross over into the "free" world. I am convinced that communism is much more than a political ideology. No doubt, there are spiritual forces behind each system that shuts out God and persecutes His people, and, as a believer, you can sense them. Many years later I had the chance to do some work in Vietnam, and I recognized that feeling the moment I stepped off the plane in Saigon.

On our way back to Germany, we drove through beautiful Sweden and connected with our friends there, and showed off our very special camper.

Hans' ideas kept getting better and better, and there was one particular Peugeot van that was able to carry and conceal one metric ton of literature. Depending on size and shape that meant between 3,000 and 5,000 books! Our first trip with that van was into Romania, and all had gone well. But now came the real test: our second trip into the Soviet Union! This would turn out to be one trip we would never forget.

Coming through Hungary, we entered at the town of Chop in today's Ukraine. Right from the start we realized that this would not be as easy as our previous trip. After handing over our passports and other documents, we were separated from our vehicle, while at least ten border guards with grim faces and armed with tools and mirrors went to check out our camper. In the meantime, we were led to the main building and engaged in a lengthy conversation with a man in civilian clothing – obviously KGB (the feared Soviet secret police). After countless questions regarding the nature of our planned trip came some references to the severity of punishment for anyone smuggling anti-communist propaganda into the Soviet Union. We knew that officially, there was no law against bringing Bibles into the country, but no one had ever been granted permission to bring them in legally. If you were caught hiding

Bibles, then they would be classified as pornography, or anti-Communist propaganda, and then you were treated as a spy or political enemy.

Our "escort" shocked us by suddenly pulling a one-ruble coin from his pocket, and asking us, "Do you know whose face that is?"

"Yes," I answered, "This is the face of Lenin!"

He then leaned towards us in a conspiratorial manner and almost whispered: "You know – I pray to him!"

Either he was a really bad communist, or he just wanted to solicit some kind of reaction from us, admitting that we were Christians. We did not fall for it, and at that point one of the border guards came in and motioned for me to follow him out to the van. When I got to the vehicle I could see the tense faces of the other guards, they were obviously not happy with their discoveries. They had rightfully noticed that the measurements of the outside wall did not correspond with those taken from the inside, and they suspected that there was a double floor, which happened to be true, but they could not find any way to verify that. So one of them asked me in broken English while pointing at the floor, "What inside there?"

I played dumb, shrugged my shoulders and answered, "Insulation maybe?" Now, everyone knows that paper makes for really good insulation, so I did not feel too guilty about my fib.

They were not satisfied and ordered me to drive the van over a service pit. Some of the guards started poking around with screw drivers underneath the car, while others inside the camper were stamping their feet and jumped up and down on the floor, yelling to the ones underneath. Though I could not understand Ukrainian, the meaning was clear: "Can you hear this?" The guys below kept shaking their heads, and by this time I almost lost my cool and began sweating. This was getting way too close, but it got even worse. They produced a large x-ray machine on wheels, and maneuvered it inside the van, while the guys in the pit attached large plates all along the floor of the van.

By now I really began to worry, and wondered what the pictures would reveal. I was not sure if the plastic covers on the Bibles would show up on an x-ray, but we also had hidden some cassette recorders and teaching tapes, whose metal parts would certainly become visible.

When they were done we were led back to the building to wait, while they took the plates to be developed at the laboratory. This must have been the longest hour of my life, and in my mind I imagined all kinds of unpleasant thoughts of interrogations, prison and torture. But then the main guard came with a smile and handed us our passports. "Everything OK – you go now!"

I could barely keep from hugging him, and Cathy and I hurried to the car with a big boulder having rolled off our hearts. As we drove to our next stop, the city of Lvov (now called Lviv), I had some nagging doubts regarding what had happened there at the border. There were only two possibilities: either they had really seen nothing on the pictures, which would make it a miracle, or they had seen the Bibles, but let us go so that we could lead them to our contacts.

This was a six-week trip, and we did not find out until we got back home what had really happened. When we told Hans about the x-rays, he immediately got on the phone with the supplier of our building materials. After a few minutes he returned with a big grin on his face: "Guess what – the pressed particle boards that we used for the floor are coated with a white finish which happens to contain lots of lead!"

Lead – the very metal used to shield and absorb x-rays! The guards did not see anything at all, but we did not know that until it was all over, and now we embarked on the most exciting journey of our lives.

The roads to our next stop, Kiev, were worse than any we had ever been on before, and led through some pretty mountainous terrain that really tested the underpowered engine of the Peugeot, as well as my driving skills, but finally we reached the campground.

When we tried to make contact with a certain pastor there, we ran into another obstacle: the address was outdated and the family had moved. We could not draw any attention to ourselves as well as to them, so knocking on doors and asking the neighbors was out of the question. We sent up some desperate prayers for help, and after some minutes a young girl casually walked up to us and asked in passable English if we had come to see Pastor Ivan (not his real name). She then guided us to another huge apartment block nearby, and brought us to the right door.

Grateful and relieved, we met with Pastor Ivan, his wife and oldest son. Communication was not easy, and we had to be careful what we shared, since there was a good chance that his place was bugged. Ivan had just recently been released from a 25-year prison sentence, and I don't think I have ever been so humbled than to be in the presence of such a hero of our faith.

We made them understand that we had many gifts for them, and they understood with tear-filled eyes, what kind of gifts we were talking about. I had to find out how many Bibles he was willing to take, since I had to prepare for the transaction, and was surprised to hear him say, "We take all!"

He obviously had no idea about the capacity of our vehicle, but assured us he was ready to handle whatever we could give him. We could not talk openly about details, so he simply told us to be prepared for some kind of contact on the main highway leaving Kiev the following morning. I was not sure what to make of that, but had no choice but to trust him, so that night we opened up our secret compartment and filled several big sacks with literature, tape recorders and teaching tapes. We hid them in the wash cabin and under the benches in the camper, and prayed there would be no check point and control before we were able to transfer the cargo.

Tired and tense, we left Kiev the following morning on the six-lane highway heading towards Kharkov. Both Cathy and I kept looking for something that would indicate a contact with our friends, but for many kilometers there was nothing, and I began to think that I must have missed whatever sign they had prepared for us. Then the unthinkable happened: I heard sirens behind me, and one look in my review mirror confirmed my fear. We were being pulled over by the highway police in a Lada jeep. With my heart pounding wildly I moved over to the emergency lane and stopped. I started getting our documents out of the glove compartment, when a uniformed officer knocked on my window. He looked at me with a big smile, and gave me an exaggerated wink. I recognized him immediately. It was Ivan's son, disguised as a police officer! He then "officially" confiscated our cargo, and loaded it into his jeep. With a salute he roared off, while we were still recovering from the shock of what just had happened. We found out later that he had already been in prison for three years for refusing to join the Soviet army. His mother had sewn the uniform, and we never found out where that police jeep had come from. One thing was clear, if he was caught impersonating a police officer, chances were that he would be shot on the spot. To take such risks for a few hundred Bibles was beyond us, and demonstrated a courage and love for God's word that none of us in the West could match.

I will never forget what happened in the next city: Rostov-Na-Donu.

As the name points out, the mighty river Don flows through Rostov, and when you cross the bridge you are passing from Europe to Asia. We had an address to visit there and very little information. After we met the pastor in his home, he seemed very tense and let us know that he had something very important to tell us, but that it was not safe to talk at his place. So he invited us for a ride in his Jiguli (a very common Soviet copy of a Fiat), and as soon as we had left his house, he looked into his mirror and said: "We are being followed by KGB!"

Sure enough, we were obviously being trailed by a grey Volga car. The Volga was a bigger car and had been the choice of Soviet authorities for many years, and as our friend pointed out, the KGB cars were always grey. What happened next could have been a scene in a James Bond thriller. Our friend actually tried to shake the Volga by racing and zipping through narrow roads and lanes of Rostov. The secret police were right on our tail, and things did not look good at all. We shot up a dirt road leading to a restaurant with many cars in the parking lot. Our driver found a gap between two parked cars and squeezed through it, but the bigger Volga tried to follow and got stuck. If it had not been so scary it would have been kind of funny, but we realized that this poor man had no chance of escaping the authorities forever. He dropped us off at the edge of a forest and told us to run, while he sped away.

Cathy and I rushed through the dense forest and emerged right by the entrance to our camping ground. We nonchalantly walked in as if we had just returned from a stroll in the woods. We never heard of the pastor again, nor did we find out what he so desperately wanted to tell us, but there had been rumors that several church leaders in the city had been tortured and killed, and we hoped and prayed that he would not become one of them.

* * *

The next leg of our journey south turned out to be a grueling trip to another city with the intriguing name of Ordzhonikidze. We were now in today's Republic of Georgia. Again, it was like a totally different country with another language and different looking people. The roads seemed to get increasingly worse, and quite often the main highway was nothing but a wide dirt road with potholes and rocks strewn about. We were now faced with a new problem. Not only was it harder and harder to find a running gas station, but unlike in the Ukraine, they were not selling any diesel here, which is what our Peugeot required. I remember stopping at a gas station with an empty tank just to find out that they did not have any diesel either. We were effectively stuck, and I desperately asked some of the people there if they had any idea where we could find diesel. After a big and emotional discussion among them, one man motioned us to follow him, as he got into his car. He led us on a small dirt road up into the mountains, which I knew was off-limits to us, but we really had no other choice but to trust him. After what seemed like forever driving on nothing but fumes, we came to a huge stone quarry with all kinds of heavy machinery and a big fuel tank with an attached hand pump. We had to use a funnel to pump the diesel into our tank, and it looked more like black crude oil than refined diesel fuel. But our engine purred happily, and after slipping the man some rubles we were on our way again, all set for another 500 to 600 kilometers.

In Tbilisi, the capital of Georgia, we had another drop-off that was quite easy and almost routine after our previous adventures. The roads kept getting worse as we threaded our way through the mountains into yet another Soviet state, Armenia. Quite often we would literally inch by oncoming trucks and buses, either being squeezed against a rock cliff, or at the edge of a ravine hundreds of meters deep with no guard rails and any room to spare.

As we came close to the capital of Yerevan we were rewarded with an extraordinary sight. It was a hot and hazy late summer day, and we had been wondering about this huge white cloud in the sky that never seemed to move. As we came nearer we realized with a gasp that this cloud was in fact the snow covered tip of a gigantic mountain that had pierced the cloud layer. We were looking at Mt. Ararat, the very place the Bible mentions as the resting place of Noah's Ark!

When we contacted the believers there, and told them that we had brought around 1,500 New Testaments in the Armenian language, their tears flowed freely, and they entered an impromptu time of worship. This was the first shipment of New Testaments in their language, and their joy was a sight to behold. The transfer became a tricky affair on a deserted mountain track in broad daylight, but this was the rest of our load and we were greatly relieved.

The Armenian Christians had no Old Testaments in their language, but had one old copy of the whole Bible that they asked us to take out for reprint, and we put that in our hiding place for safe keeping.

The rest of our trip was meant to be more relaxing and a vacation of sorts. Before leaving Yerevan, we joined a tourist tour to an ancient monastery at the foot of Mt. Ararat that had been converted into a museum. Among many old artifacts and relics was a block of wood said to have been brought from the mountain by some St. Gregory 1700 years ago. Our Intourist guide was quick to add that this, of course, was a legend only.

We did end up playing tourists, and got to visit some of the famous Black Sea resorts on our long way back to Kiev, and then down again to Odessa. From there it was a relatively short trip to the border town of Kishinev in Moldova which would take us to Romania.

We were quite relaxed and tired from almost six weeks of daily driving, and were happy and thankful that everything had gone so well after all. When we got close to the border crossing we saw that something had gone terribly wrong. On the parking lot behind the main building were three campers that had obviously been confiscated. We recognized all three of them, as a matter of fact, we had used one of them on our previous trip to the Soviet Union. When the border guards saw us coming they were ready for us. They immediately demanded that I open the hiding place, and when I played dumb they came with axes and crow bars and started tearing apart the furniture in the back. The game was over and I realized it would be better for us if I cooperated to some extent, so I opened the double floor for them. When they saw the size and capacity of it they became really mad, for they realized the amount of material that had slipped through. Of course they found the old Armenian Bible which was proof for them that we were Bible couriers and Christians.

They then separated Cathy and me, and interrogated us individually. They used the old "good cop, bad cop" routine right out of a textbook. One guy in uniform acted real mad and threw threats and insults at us, and then there was our plainclothes interpreter who just wanted to be our friend. He looked at Cathy's passport, and sadly shook his head, saying, "Oh dear, I see that your wife is having her birthday soon. Surely you don't want her to spend it in prison, do you?"

The main problem was that we were not really prepared for this situation. Usually, we had rehearsed a story we would tell if we were to be caught going in, but none had briefed us on what to do and say when you were caught going out!

Under no circumstances could we reveal the names and addresses of our contacts, so I made some vague references to men with beards whose names we did not know.

After a few hours of this we were both given some paper and pen, and were told to write down our confessions: Cathy on one end of the hall, and me on the other. By now it was evening, the border was closed, and almost all the guards were in the next room watching an important soccer game on TV. I can't remember if it was the World Cup, or the European Championship, but they were obviously into it, with the Soviet Union playing against some other nation.

They had left one young guard to watch us, but the poor guy really wanted to watch the game instead, so he would disappear for a few minutes now and then when the game got hot, and we could hear loud cheering and shouting in the other room. While that was going on I seized the opportunity and yelled all the way across to Cathy, telling her what to write and what not to write. It was crucial that our stories matched, if we wanted to get out of this mess anytime soon.

When the game was over, they allowed us to get some food from our camper, and then we were locked into a cell with one bed for the night. We were certain the place was bugged and that they intended to get more vital information out of us, but we just talked casually and soon fell asleep, after an exhausting day.

The next morning they made us wait for a long time, but eventually the "good cop" came with our passports and told us they had decided to let us go. We could not believe our ears, but were not about to argue with him. He gave us a short sermon, praising the achievements of Communism, and told us what we had done was a great insult to the Soviet Union.

We had not expected to get off the hook so easily, especially since we had seen all the other confiscated vehicles, but all they really had on us was one hidden Bible that we had wanted to bring out, and for some strange reason they had decided to keep it. But we knew from now on our names were on the black list, and we knew that our trips to the Soviet Union were over.

When we crossed over into Romania, the guards there took pity on us when they saw the damage the "Ruskies" had done to the camper, and processed our paperwork with great speed and efficiency.

* * *

After that particular trip, we took several more to less dangerous places, but both Hans and I knew that our career as couriers was coming to an end. Our passports were filled with visa stamps from all over Eastern Europe, and even though we tried to use different border crossings every time, there were only so many, and some of the border guards recognized us. "Ah, Mister and Mrs. Bauer..., you on vacation again?"

On one of our last trips to Hungary, we brought in several boxes of books written by a certain Todd Burke, but since they had been translated into Hungarian we could not read them. Little did we know that some years later this same book would significantly influence our lives.

Together we made around 27 trips, and must have smuggled roughly 60,000 Bibles and other books in a period of two and one-half years. One day we will find out how many lives were touched and changed through them. It had been a season of sowing.

During our last summer with the Mission, we took a few weeks' vacation to reconnect with our friends in Sweden, and as always we had a wonderful time. As usual, we joined "Ungdomsgruppen" on their various outreaches. By now, the group had some new and younger members, and some of the old core had moved away from Norrtälje, but there were still quite a few from the old stock, and we always had much fun together.

One particular evening, we attended a tent meeting somewhere on the outskirts of Stockholm. That particular day I had thought much about our future in missions, and had asked the Lord to give us guidance. Still nothing had opened up in regard to Asia, and I did not understand why.

During that meeting, they had asked a man from Denmark to give a testimony, and he told us how he and his family had worked among the Eskimos of Greenland for the past ten years. He told us about the terrible darkness during the winter months, and how it made people there depressed and given to alcohol and promiscuity. As he described the situation there, tears flowed down his cheeks, and it was obvious how much he loved the people there in Greenland. He and his family had to go back to Denmark for educational reasons, and he had been praying for a replacement and made an appeal right then and there.

As I listened to him, my heart began to pound wildly within me, and I felt stirred deep down. Here we were, available for anything, and asking God for guidance, and then we end up at this meeting. This seemed to have God's fingerprints all over. After the meeting I asked the man for more information, and what it would involve to go to Greenland and work there. He assured us that his mission in Denmark would love to take us on, and even support us financially.

For the weeks that followed I could only think about Greenland and Eskimos. I bought some books and devoured them. We even contacted the mission in Denmark, and they seemed eager to meet us and train us for ministry among the Eskimos.

As far as I was concerned it was a done deal, and Cathy was willing to follow wherever, but then something strange happened. I woke up one morning, and all the excitement and desire for Greenland was totally gone! I could not understand how I could be so excited about a thing one day, just to lose it overnight. Did I totally miss God on that one? Did he not clearly lead us to go to that tent meeting right when we had asked for guidance and direction?

In the midst of my confusion God began to speak to me. He let me know that this had been a test to see if we were still willing to go wherever he would ask us to go. I could sense his pleasure for wanting to be obedient, and at the same time he removed the burden for the Eskimos people from my heart.

"But what then, Lord?" I asked desperately. He answered a few days later, while Hans and I worked in the barn on a new design for a hiding place. I shared with him my desire for missions in Asia, and how God had tested my willingness to go wherever he chooses to send us.

Hans paused from what he was doing, looked at me and said: "Do you even know what it means to be a missionary?" And then he said something that hit me like an arrow to my heart. "Missions is simply church work under more difficult circumstances. How much experience in church planting and church growth do you have?"

Well, we both knew the answer to that – zero! Oh I had ministered in many churches in Sweden and during my Bible school days in the US, but never from a position of leadership and responsibility.

I did not like what I heard, but I knew deep down in my heart that Hans was right. The problem was that I thought church work was boring, and lacked all the glamour and excitement that I envisioned in a life in missions. That very afternoon I received a phone call from Peter, the pastor of the small Pentecostal church in Nürnberg where we attended whenever we were in town. He had asked me before if I would consider helping him as a youth pastor, but I had never given it any serious thought. Now he made me an offer. He said that they could start us on a part-time salary with the prospect of a full-time job within one year.

I told him that we would pray about this and get back to him later. Then one of the biggest battles of my life began to unfold right in my soul. There were a couple of issues I had to deal with, and the biggest one was with going back to my home town! When I had run away 6 years earlier, I had sworn myself to never live there again. It was all part of my old life that I wanted to forget. And then, the prospect of helping out in a small church just seemed so far removed from what I perceived God had called us to, that I had a really hard time getting excited about this offer.

But Hans' words kept haunting me, and I knew deep down that I was not ready for any form of cross-cultural ministry. I had just passed an obedience test, and I was not going to fail this one! After talking it over with Cathy I got on the phone with Peter and gave him the news: "OK, we are coming!"

FULL CIRCLE

In the fall of 1978, we moved to Nürnberg where we had found a small apartment in the south of the city, about a 10-minute drive from my parents' house. Of course they were more than happy to have us that close, and we ended up there almost every Sunday for dinner after church.

Church was in a small, run-down hall in a workers' district of town. The congregation was around 40 people. It was a good mix of both young and old, and there were some immigrants from Eastern Europe, and a man from Indonesia who was married to a German woman.

Peter and Rosi, the pastors, lived just around the corner from us, and we spent much time with them there, getting to know them and learning about church life. We had to deal with some cultural differences between American and European Christianity. One was the whole area of drinking alcohol. In Sweden, it had never been talked about, but it was obvious that the Pentecostals there did not indulge. In the US, and especially at FST it was labeled sinful, and according to some, Jesus did not make wine, but grape juice.

On the first Sunday that we had communion at the church in Nürnberg, they served real wine. That was especially troublesome for Cathy who was brought up believing that drinking any kind of alcohol was sin. Now she tasted it for the first time in church of all places, during such a sacred act as communion! I wish I had had a camera to capture the expression on her face. Every place we were invited, our hosts served beer or wine with the meals, and even a little schnapps to help with digestion after meals was quite in order. We stuck to our convictions, and only drank soft drinks and juice. That would have been all right, if it had not been for the temptation to feel just a little bit superior, and to pass judgment on these "worldly" Christians. The Lord had a funny way of dealing with this problem in my heart.

Cathy had begun to cook some German meals, and many of the recipes called for red wine in the gravy. We felt that was justifiable, since all alcohol would be gone after cooking, so I had bought a bottle of cheap red Italian wine for that purpose. One night I woke up with the most excruciating stomach pain. I had never experienced anything like it before or since, and I thought I was going to die. In my agony I cried out to God for help, and he answered immediately. That famous verse popped into my mind, where Paul tells Timothy, "and drink a little wine for the sake of your stomach".[1]

At that point I was beyond any theological or spiritual consideration, and was desperate enough to try anything that would bring relief. So I dragged myself into our tiny kitchen, took the wine bottle from the fridge, and was then troubled by this profound question, "What did Paul mean by a little?" Pushing that question aside for the time being, I put the bottle to my mouth and gave it several good pulls. The wine had been in the fridge for weeks and had almost turned into vinegar, so needless to say, it tasted horrible. By the time I made it back to our bedroom, the pain was completely gone, and has never come back to this day!

Now that I had become a "worldly" Christian myself I could stop judging others, and even enjoy an occasional sip of wine – thanking God for liberty!

The other cultural difference was the whole viewpoint of Christians serving in the military. In the U.S. I had learned that serving and defending one's country was a Christian obligation, even if it meant killing people in the line of duty. In most of the European countries, however, the "thou shall not kill" commandment is viewed superior to any nationalistic obligation, and Christian young men generally do not serve in the

---

[1] 1 Timothy 5:23 (NLTse)

112

military. Instead, they became "conscientious objectors." In Germany in particular that meant defending your viewpoint in a court case, and once approved, you ended up driving an ambulance, or serving in a nursing home or other social institution for the duration of your usual military service.

This whole scenario did not affect us personally, and I had already been exempt from the military because I was now considered clergy in the eyes of the government. But since we were working with the youth, it became part of my job to prep our young men for this legal process.

As Peter had told us earlier, the church was not able to carry two full-time workers at this stage, and they could only afford to employ us part-time. To survive, I was forced to find another half-day job. After some searching, I found a job as a driver for a bakery. That meant getting up at 4 in the morning, because all the deliveries had to be made before 8AM. The bakery catered mainly to hospitals, nursing homes, and department stores.

The job was much more physically demanding than I had expected. The yellow Mercedes van that I drove had to be loaded with big metal baskets holding 10 five pound loaves of dark sourdough bread, and heavy pallets with hundreds of pastries on it. Everything was freshly baked and smelled delicious, but soon it became the smell of hard labor. I had to make several rounds and was on a tight schedule to deliver everything before breakfast. Occasionally, a load of goods had come out of the oven too late, and I had to race through the mostly empty roads of a sleeping city. Since it was winter, the roads were often slippery, and not yet cleared from the nightly snowfalls.

One morning the inevitable happened. I was late delivering several hundred pastries to a large nursing home, and the roads were icy. To make matters worse, I was driving on a cobblestone road, and the van had no snow tires. Going around a curve too fast I lost control and the van first fishtailed and then spun around a full 360°. Thankfully I did not hit anything, but as the centrifugal forces took hold of the vehicle, I heard a sound from the back that I knew spelled disaster. I quick inspection confirmed my greatest fears: Several trays with hundreds of apricot cheese cake squares had jumped off the shelf and landed upside-down on the dirty floor of the van!

I raced back to the bakery and thought for sure I would be fired. My boss took one look at the mess, and to my surprise was not even angry. He told me to get some buckets and a hand shovel and fill them with the gooey mess. He winked as he advised me: "Try not to get too much dirt in it!"

The next day I delivered hundreds of chocolate covered cones called "Granatsplitter", which literally translates to "shell splinters." They used to be my favorite when I was a young boy. Now I knew they were a clever disguise for unwanted leftovers.

After several months of this, I became more and more exhausted. Since most church meetings were in the evenings, I had no chance to go to bed early, and even though I tried to take naps during the day I was often awakened by phone calls or other disturbances. Most folks in church could see that this was not a long-term solution and were willing to make extra sacrifices so that I could be employed full-time.

With my three years of Bible college and the years working for the mission, I was now qualified to be ordained by the German Pentecostal movement. Looking back it seemed so right at the time, but today I could no longer justify giving anyone a title just because they had fulfilled some academic requirements, and "done the time." By now I had only preached a few times in church, and gained a bit of experience in running a youth group, but now I was "Pastor Bauer."

With the ordination came a new set of obligations and expectations. There were the quarterly regional meetings and the biannual national leaders' conferences. For reasons I could not understand at that time, I was not totally convinced that I wanted this. But I knew I was young and inexperienced, and needed to learn many things, so I suppressed my doubts and tried my best not to be critical and judgmental. Plus, I found it hard to put my finger on specific issues and call them wrong. Looking back, I realize that what I really missed in that setting was a sense of transparency and honesty. One particular conversation seemed to repeat itself every time we met, like a broken record:

"Oh hi brother, how are things with you and your church?"

"Thanks for asking. Things are just great, and the Lord keeps adding new members – hallelujah!"

The unofficial news was that the dear brother had great problems at home, his wife was suffering from depression, and his church was on the verge of a major split. One of the pastor's wives in Northern Germany had actually jumped from a bridge and killed herself. Why was none there to help them in their crisis? We called ourselves brotherhood, but what I saw were shallow relationships, and what I was really yearning for was community and family. At that point I could not have explained my frustrations to anyone, since I did not even know that what I was longing for actually existed.

So I "sucked it up" and tried to be a good pastor. Actually, things were going quite well at our church in Nürnberg. We started to grow and were considered one of the fastest growing churches in the region. Of course, much of that growth was transfer growth, but we did get to see a few unbelievers come to Jesus, and that made it worth it all.

During the summer months we would be out in the sidewalk corridor between two big department stores to sing songs, give testimonies, pass out tracts, and invite folks to our evangelistic meetings. We did this for several years, and one young lady actually came to our meetings and gave her heart to Jesus. She experienced a radical transformation in her life and is serving God today in Israel with her husband.

The church had moved to a larger building, and I was introduced to the whole realm of committees, task forces and church politics. I had no idea how much administration and practical work was involved in running a church. Since Peter was a real handyman, we would help many folks with construction type work. We would wallpaper the flat of an old woman, put in a wooden ceiling in the living room of an elder, or tile a young couple's bathroom.

By now our team had grown. We had employed Lennart from Sweden as choir director, and he and his wife Gabi became good friends. We had much fun making music together, and putting on programs for the youth.

* * *

Reflecting on those years I realize how hard they must have been for Cathy. During my years in Sweden and the U.S. I knew what it was like to be a foreigner. For her this was the first time away from her home country. I had bought her a German course with books and tapes, but it did not really help her to become fluent in the language. She became so frustrated with this dilemma of not fully understanding what was going on that she approached me one day and said: "From now on I want you to speak to me only in German!"

The following weeks and months were quite difficult, because our communication was so limited, but this experience helped her to learn quickly, and after some years she became totally fluent in the language.

While we were traveling for the mission, we had purposely waited to have children, but once we had settled down in Nürnberg, we felt it was time to start a family. No matter how hard we tried, Cathy did not become pregnant. We started to get worried that maybe one of us had some physical condition that had caused us to be infertile.

In April 1979 we had a surprise visitor. Sven-Erik was a Lutheran pastor in the city of Malmö in the south of Sweden. We had met in Maine, when he and his wife Helena had attended FST for one year, and we had become good friends and visited them on our trips every summer.

We were sitting on our small balcony, enjoying a cup of coffee and the early spring sun. In the course of our conversation we confided in him regarding our possible infertility problem. Sven-Erik stood up immediately, put one hand on each of us, and prayed for God to touch us and grant us many children.

Within one month after that day Cathy became pregnant, and we would have no problem with fertility ever since. Because of that powerful prayer we have prayed with many couples over the years, and have seen several of them have children against all odds.

On February 22, 1980 our son Björn was born in a Methodist hospital in town. In those days it was quite uncommon for the father to be allowed in the delivery room, but I was there the whole time, and with all the following births. At one point I did feel a bit woozy at the sight of things, and when Cathy's doctor checked on her the following morning, her first question was: "Mrs. Bauer – how is your husband?"

I had always liked children, but when I held our son in my arms for the first time, I felt a strong emotional bond to that child, unlike anything I had ever experienced before, and for the first time I understood in part how much our Heavenly Father loves us.

My parents enjoyed having us nearby, and often helped us out financially when things got tight. Almost every Sunday my Father would attend the morning service, especially when I was scheduled to preach. I had a sense that he mainly came for my sake, and that was confirmed later on when we moved away from Nürnberg. My brother Winfried became a regular member of the church and met his future wife Lydia at the youth group. I would have the privilege of marrying them before our time there was over. For special occasions we would also get together with my sister Monika and her family, but they showed little interest in our church activities and way of life.

In the eyes of most people in the state church, being part of a Pentecostal church meant you were part of a sect, or even a cult. Even among the other evangelical churches we were viewed with some suspicion. I tried to attend most ecumenical meetings for the pastors in the city, but was mainly viewed as an outsider by the other leaders. It was already back then that God gave me a great love for his whole church, and a desire to experience true unity among his children.

* * *

As time went on, I began to wrestle with some fundamental questions regarding church and our calling as church leaders. I had made an observation that I found quite disturbing. It seemed like we were missing something along the way. The few times we were blessed to lead unbelievers to the Lord, I saw the same story repeat itself. Depending on their sincerity and hunger, it would take new believers between two to three years to reach the spiritual level of most of the other people in church. Then they would either plateau, or leave the church in search of something more challenging and exciting. Whenever that happened I felt like we had failed them on some level, but whenever I raised the issue at our leadership meetings I met with opposition. I was told I should be happy for all the great things God was doing in our midst, and not be so critical. Then it hit me: We had become content with making members for our church. If people came to the meetings, read their Bibles and paid their tithes, then we were happy. If they even came to the prayer meetings then they were saints, and who was I to fault that?

I was on a quest for more. At one point I read a book on discipleship by a South American pastor by the name of Juan Carlos Ortiz. I loved his witty and straightforward approach to what he considered to be the truth, and for the first time I began to understand the difference between making church members and making disciples of Jesus! In one of his teachings he tells the story of a large pastors' conference in South America. After listening to hours of reports and bragging regarding their success in church growth, Juan Carlos got up to the microphone and upset several thousand pastors with these words: "God is not impressed by your church growth – the cemetery is growing too!"

It was then that I realized that there was no future for me in our present church setting. Oh, I tried very hard to convince everyone of my newfound revelations, but none of the others on the team seemed to understand my zeal. Everyone seemed quite comfortable with the status quo, and I fell more and more into the role of an outsider and trouble-maker. I was never one to run away from challenging situations, but I knew better than to take things into my own hands and run ahead of the Lord.

In March 1982, our second son Nils was born at the same hospital in town, and we were full of joy and gratefulness. Nils came two weeks early, and it all happened so fast that we almost did not get Cathy to the hospital in time. The great thing about living in Germany in those days was that the healthcare system took care of all the medical expenses, and even paid you a monthly compensation for the first year, so that the mother could stay home from work.

That summer Cathy's parents came to visit us for a few weeks, and we surprised them by taking a trip up to Norway, to Stavanger, the very place where her dad's ancestors had come from. We were all overwhelmed by the natural beauty surrounding us, and Cathy's father repeated over and over, "why did my mother never tell me how beautiful this country is?"

***

During that time I kept my desire to go to Asia alive by reading any missionary book I could get my hands on. There was one particular book that was a hot item on many church book tables. It was called "Anointed for Burial" by Todd Burke. It is the story of a young couple feeling called to the nation of Cambodia, and working there for about 20 months before the outbreak of one of the most terrible wars in modern history. They were evacuated with all other foreigners. Reading their account of what could easily be described as a revival among the Khmer people is almost like reading the book of Acts, and I found myself totally fascinated and absorbed by each page of the book. As I found out later, this was the very book we had smuggled into Hungary by the case when we still worked for the Mission.

By the time I was finished reading, I was totally convinced of two things. The first one was a strong conviction that we would go and work in Cambodia some day, and the second one was a strong sense that we would meet this Todd Burke some day, and work with him. I remember telling Cathy about that, and her reply was, "Well, I guess we'll see…".

I was shocked to discover that the media had been so quiet regarding the terrible events going on in Cambodia. Between 1975 and 1979 at least 1.7 million Cambodians perished by the hands of their own people, the notorious Khmer Rouge under a madman by the name of Pol Pot. By the time details of the holocaust emerged in the Western media, Cambodia was totally cut off from the rest of the world. Many more were to die from sickness and starvation until the borders opened again in the beginning of the nineties.

The city of Nürnberg had taken in over 80 Cambodian refugees from the camps in Thailand, and we decided to sponsor one family with three small children. We would visit each other regularly and try to be their friends even though we could barely communicate with each other. Though they could not tell us their full story, the sadness and pain on their faces was evidence that they had seen and endured unspeakable horrors.

We invited their children to a weekly program at church, and they loved going there. A few weeks later the kids stopped coming, and I visited the family to make sure they were all right. When the father opened the door to their apartment, his eyes blazed with anger, and he communicated very clearly that he did not want us to teach his children about Christianity! They broke off all contact with us, and we heard that they had moved to another city – we would never see them again.

This incident taught me something about the human heart that seems to resonate in and through all cultures. Whenever people are rescued from a situation of pain and suffering, and are introduced to the temptations of materialism, they shut their hearts to the efforts of the Holy Spirit to lead them to the light of the Gospel. While our dear friends rejected the truth of salvation through Christ, many thousand Cambodians in the refugee camps of Thailand opened their hearts wide to the love of God and had their hearts and lives changed forever.

✳ ✳ ✳

We continued our work at church, but I was frustrated. I felt like I was stuck in a cul-de-sac, and there seemed no way out. God was already working on a solution. I was thrilled when the church decided to send me to a pastors' conference in Stockholm Sweden to foster the relationships between the churches in Sweden and Germany. I greatly enjoyed these few days of worshiping in Swedish and listening to great teaching. During a break one afternoon, I strolled through the city and found a new Christian bookstore. I eagerly went in to see if there were any new missionary books, and there it was: "Anointed for Burial" in English. I had read it in German, and I eagerly flipped through the pages to see if the original version was any different. I only saw one difference, but it made my heart beat faster. At the very end of the book was the address of a church called "New Covenant Community" in Oklahoma City, where Todd Burke was the pastor.

As soon as I got back home to Nürnberg, I wrote a short letter to them, asking for more information regarding the work in Cambodia. One week later our phone rang at some odd hour, and it turned out to be a long-distance call from the US. Someone from the church office at New Covenant Community told me that they had received my letter, and gave me the phone number of a man in Switzerland by the name of Martin Buehlmann. Todd Burke and a team were there right now, if I wanted to meet them. Of course I wanted to meet them. I called Martin in Berne, Switzerland, and he confirmed that Todd was indeed there right now and invited me to come and visit. The next day I sat on a train from Nürnberg to Berne, wondering what to expect from my meeting with Todd. I had a premonition that I would come to a turning point in my life, but I had no idea how profoundly these next few days would shape and influence our future.

Coming Home

When I arrived at the train station in Berne, I was picked up by a lady named Klara who took me to Martin's house in a ritzy suburb called Muri. As it turned out it was not only the residence of Martin and his family, but also home to several single women, as well as the meeting place of their church plant called "Basileia Bern."

Todd had gone skiing with men from the church for the day and was not around, but I got to meet Martin, and I was surprised by the fact that we had so much in common. Outwardly we were of the same size and build, we both had brown hair and full beards, and we were almost the same age, Martin a bit younger.

We both were committed to serve God, and we were both on a quest to find our place in the Body of Christ and discover church. It seemed like Martin had found his place, and I envied him for that. He met Todd at a church parking lot in Oklahoma City, as he and his wife Georgia were touring the U.S. in search of a church model that they could embrace. They had connected and Todd had helped him to plant the church in Berne. It all sounded very exciting and intriguing, and I could not wait to learn more about their methods and beliefs.

That evening I got to meet Todd for the first time, and I was instantly gripped by his charismatic personality. He looked trim and fit, well-groomed, and of average height, but he bore the mantle of leadership unlike anyone I had met before. He would look at you with piercing eyes, and the words he spoke demanded respect. Some described his speech and mannerism as arrogant, and maybe that was true, but to me it was the

self-confidence of a man who had met God and knew what he was doing. In my eyes Todd could do no wrong, and I would defend him fiercely
whenever others criticized him in any way. I had found a friend, a mentor and a hero, and I received everything he said and modeled without
hesitation.

That night I met two more men on Todd's team: Mike Hudgins and
Charles Bello. After many years I still consider them some of my best
friends, and Charles turned out to become the father-in-law of our son
Björn. Later that evening I also overheard an interesting conversation
between the two men who had gone skiing with Todd that day. Though
it was initially quite hard for me to understand the Swiss German dialect,
I understood enough of their conversation. They told the others in the
house how Todd, who had never skied before, had made it down the expert slope unharmed, almost running down a few fellow skiers in the
process. That story should have put up a red flag in my heart, but instead
I could fully identify with that kind of recklessness from my own life.

I had to get home the next day, but before I left, they all assured me
of their help and support, and we decided to stay in touch, and develop
our relationships with each other. They gave me some teaching material
and tapes, and brought me to the train station. During the whole four-
hour trip home I was filled with excitement and the sense that something
very significant had happened in my life. I had no language for what was
happening in my heart, but realization emerged from deep within my
spirit: For the first time in my life, I had truly come home!

From that time forth things became increasingly difficult for me at the
church in Nürnberg. I felt like I had just learned to drive, but was pushing
the car instead! The teaching material I had received in Bern answered
many of my questions, and resounded with some of the growing values
in my heart. It was heavily influenced by the "Shepherding Movement"
that had influenced many Charismatic circles in those days, mainly in the
United States. There was a strong emphasis on true community and relationships – organism versus organization. The movement got its name

from the fact that every believer was challenged to have his or her personal shepherd to whom they were accountable, but that was the very thing that broke its back several years later. Even though there was a good biblical foundation to most of the teaching, it did not work. It was abused by many of the "shepherds".

Eventually, the very teachers that had started the movement recalled it later on, and asked forgiveness from the Body of Christ. Many had been wounded and hurt by the high level of expectation, control, and commitment to man that was placed on them, and a large number turned against the Church in general.

The relationships that were forged were called "covenant relationships", and amazingly, many of them still exist today. Initially, I was placed right under Todd, and we began to communicate by mail and telephone. I'll never forget Todd calling me all the way from India, just to "touch base", and see how I was doing. He used to travel around the world three or four times per year, working on church plants, evangelistic crusades, as well as leadership training seminars. Whenever he passed through Europe he would visit us in Nürnberg, or we would drive to Switzerland to see him.

I had begun to share some of my new insights with Peter and Lennart at the church in Nürnberg, but of course they were quite skeptical. Peter was worried that I had fallen prey to false teaching. Little did I know that his concerns were justified, but I was hooked and not willing to listen to his reasoning. It became more and more obvious that our days at the church in Nürnberg were numbered. There was never any pressure from Todd or Martin to leave, but I wanted to be more involved with what they were doing.

By that time there were a number of believers from Germany that drove several hours each Sunday just to be part of the church in Bern. Todd had sent his main worship leader, Earl Stuart, to Switzerland to help Martin. It was decided that Earl and his family would move to the border town of Lörrach on the German side, to plant a daughter church.

When I told Todd and Martin that we were ready to leave Nürnberg to work with them, it was an obvious choice that we would move down south to Lörrach in order to help Earl and Peggy with their baby church.

* * *

Many in the church in Nürnberg hated to see us go, and so did my parents, but we were determined to move on. In the fall of 1983 we moved to the small village of Binzen, just a few kilometers away from Lörrach. We had found a large apartment on the second floor of a house on the slope of the rolling hills. Behind us were the vineyards of this quite famous wine region, and from our balcony we could see France to one side, and Switzerland straight ahead.

The whole transition was done by faith. I had lost my employment and salary from the church in Nürnberg, and there were no resources available from Martin or Todd. I filed for unemployment and was granted some help from the government. Since their help was based on previous income, and they only paid two-thirds of that, we could not live on that alone. But they covered our health insurance which was a blessing, because Cathy was pregnant again, and in February 1984 our daughter Carina was born at the hospital in Lörrach.

Church life was very intensive. Some of the experiences Todd had in Cambodia had filtered through to all the other church plants he was involved in. One expectation was early morning prayer meetings several times a week, and the other was a very rigorous Bible reading plan designed by Todd which was obligatory for all members. Initially we read nine chapters every day. Three chapters from the Old Testament in the morning, three chapters from the Psalms and Proverbs at noon, and three from the New Testament in the evening. Later on they offered lighter versions of six, and even three chapters per day for the less spiritual among us.

Several of the early members had moved to Lörrach from different cities, just to be part of this new and exciting endeavor. Later on, my brother Winfried who had been youth pastor at a church in northern

Germany moved with his family all across Germany to join us. They found an apartment at the ground floor of the same house we lived in.

Initially, the church met in various homes throughout the week, and commuted to Bern every Sunday for their afternoon meeting. Then we would meet in the classroom of a public school.

For several months it was just us meeting for worship, teaching, and fellowship, but then came the big change. One of our young ladies had picked up a hitchhiker and brought him to the meeting. He walked into the room, dressed all in black, sat on a chair and never said one word. Throughout the whole meeting he simply stared at the floor, and did not respond to anyone trying to strike up a conversation. As soon as we were done he walked out the room without a word, and we thought we would never see him again.

The following week he was back again, looking and acting just the same as before. Somehow we found out that his name was Ralph, and that he came from a state-run drug rehabilitation center in a town nearby. Someone asked him if he would like to come with us to Bern on Sunday, and he nodded "yes".

The worship on that particular Sunday at the Basileia was especially good, and there was a real presence of God's spirit in the room. Ralph had been his usual self, barely speaking a word to anyone. Since everyone had stood up for worship, he casually leaned against the wall, looking at his shoes. I just happened to cast a glance in his direction, when I witnessed a powerful transformation in his demeanor. It was like he had lost all his strength, and he slowly slid down the wall unto his knees, and then he began to weep uncontrollably for a very long time. By the time he was done, he had given his life to Jesus and was a totally changed man. There was a smile on his face, and it was obvious that something very dark had lifted from him.

This was the first time in all my years as a believer that I had seen any-one saved, healed, delivered, and transformed during a time of worship, without being prayed for – it was awesome.

A few months later, a whole group of young men and women had joined us from the rehabilitation center, and after about two years the majority of our congregation were people who either had a background in drug addiction, or had psychological problems of some kind. Cathy and I were totally overwhelmed by their many needs, and felt so helpless since we both came from a different background. Neither were we trained to deal with their many phases of recovery. Often when there was a major crisis, we would just have them stay with us for a while. That sometimes led to unexpected dangers for our family.

At one point we had a young woman live with us who had severe psychological problems and was on several kinds of medication. She stayed in our guest room, and we had asked her to always keep her door closed, so that our young children could not get into her things. She was not very good at listening, and had left her door open numerous times. Then, one day, it happened. Our inquisitive Nils went into her room and saw what he thought was candy on the desk there. It was not until later that we noticed that he acted like he was drunk, and had lost all control over his bladder. He had eaten one of her "downers" and was relaxed to such a degree that his heart could have stopped beating! But God was watching.

None of the singles in our church were allowed to live by themselves, and we had rented several houses and apartments for the men and women to live in separate communities. I remember being called over frequently to one of the houses late at night to placate angry and disgruntled inhabitants, and try to mediate in their disagreements. Nevertheless, this proved to be a very effective way to disciple new believers, since none could hide their problems from each other.

It was during this exciting, but also extremely taxing season that our fourth child and third son, Lars, was born in June of 1986.

* * *

Since the church could not support us in the first few years, I was once again in search of a job. I found something that worked quite well for a season, by opening a small travel agency focusing on cheap long-distance flights. Since I knew so many people that traveled frequently, I was able to build a clientele mainly among Christians. At that time the US dollar was quite strong, and it was cheaper for Americans to book their flights in Germany because of the favorable exchange rate. Even Todd and his team booked their flights though us, and we were able to survive. About one year later the dollar crashed so badly, that I lost all of my U.S. customers overnight. In order to make the business work I would have had to invest more resources and time, and I had neither. The church agreed to pay us a small salary, and we folded the travel agency before we went into debt with it.

Since Todd knew that we would eventually end up in Asia, he prepared us to become part of his missions agency called "New Covenant Commission." So I took several courses and read through numerous books on culture and anthropology. One of the required courses was "Perspectives on the World Christian Movement" from the US Center of World Mission. Still today I consider this the best course for anyone preparing for cross-cultural ministry. There is simply no way to study it and then to turn your back on the nations and God's heart for them.

In spite of the challenges the church grew well, and there was great momentum. While we were part of the Pentecostal movement, we were always warned against ministries that practiced any kind of deliverance on believers. Their theology was quite simple in that regard. When a person comes to Christ he or she is automatically set free from any demonic influence, or oppression. Working with former addicts we learned rather quickly that they all required some kind of deliverance even after they had committed their lives to Jesus.

Repeatedly we found ourselves in situations where the forces of darkness manifested themselves in the lives of our members, and we had to learn quickly how to deal with that. That resulted in many hours of deliverance sessions. Some were set free and others were not. Some were free from drugs permanently, others succumbed to temptation over and over, and eventually left the church.

The biggest setback came through a young girl by the name of Kerstin. She had come out of an abusive situation at home and had become addicted to alcohol and drugs at a very young age. She was a mess when she came to us, but through much prayer and love from the other women she improved gradually, and when she was doing well she was the sweetest girl. The inside of her arms were scarred from where she had cut herself repeatedly with a knife or razor blade. I had never seen anything like it, and on one of her good days she explained to me what made her mutilate herself in such a way. She confessed that there were times when her emotional pain would get so intense that she had to cause herself physical pain in order drown it out. Wow – I could never have imagined anyone suffering such intense pain on the inside. Some Sundays she would come to the meeting with her arms all wrapped in bandages, and we knew she had had another "pain attack". We saw some improvement and healing in her life, but one day things came to a climax.

My office was in a large apartment where some of our members lived, and also Kerstin. One morning I unlocked the door and was just about to enter my office, when Kerstin jumped at me from behind. I quickly whirled around and saw her dressed all in black, with some black face paint marks on her cheeks, wielding the biggest kitchen knife from the drawer. At first I thought this was some kind of sick joke, but when she screeched like an animal and attacked me with the knife, I knew she meant business. Kerstin, or whoever was possessing her, wanted to kill me!

Out of pure instinct I picked up a kitchen chair and held it in front of me like I had seen lion tamers do on TV. While keeping her at a distance I tried calming her with words, as well as praying in tongues. She would settle down for a bit and then attack again, screaming with a voice I knew was not hers. Thankfully, after some time Earl arrived, and together we prayed, commanded, bound, and tried to reason with her. She did not respond at all, and this went on for hours. We had been able to take the knife from her, but had to pin her to the floor, because she tried to scratch and bite any chance she got. Kerstin was not very tall and quite skinny, but she displayed a physical strength that was more than human. In the end it took three of us to bring her to my van and drive here 50 kilometers to a psychological ward in Freiburg. On the way back we were crushed and felt defeated. What had happened to our spiritual authority that had enabled us to break through with some of the others? In the end we came to the conclusion that Kerstin simply did not want to be helped, and there was nothing we could do to change that.

From time to time I went to visit her at the hospital, but she was always in a drug-induced haze, and hardly spoke to me. After several months she was released and we never saw her again.

* * *

One of the highlights of those years was a trip to Birmingham, England for a conference called Acts 86. Martin had gotten to know John Wimber, the father and founder of the Vineyard churches. John started coming to Europe, and Martin had become his interpreter for the German-speaking world. John was one of the speakers in Birmingham, and Martin had signed me up as one of the interpreters for the event. The conference was huge by European standards, and around seven thousand had come from all over Europe to hear some of the best known speakers from the charismatic circles.

Every session was interpreted live on stage into German, while numerous interpreters in small booths in the back of the hall translated the teachings into many other European languages for those listeners who had been issued headphones.

I already knew that Martin would translate for John Wimber, and I hoped that I would get to interpret for Michael Harper, or Larry Christensen. When I looked at the roster I saw that I had been assigned to translate for Father Tom Forrest. I was deeply disappointed. Not only had I never heard of him, but to make matters worse, he was a Catholic!

Growing up in a nation where you were either born a Lutheran or a Catholic, you accepted what you were, and rejected the rest. All through school we had mandatory religious education twice a week, where the class was divided right down the middle according to your family's church adherence. Sometimes there would be fights between Catholics and Protestants over whose faith was the better one.

Walking in Pentecostal circles did not change any of this. Catholics were referred to as "sipping saints" and idolaters, and were generally not regarded as true believers. On the other hand, many Catholics made it very clear that theirs was the only true church.

At that point in time I was not even sure how I felt about Catholic charismatics, but the fact that I was to interpret for one of the leaders of the Catholic charismatic movement revealed that I still had issues in that department.

As it turned out, interpreting in front of seven thousand people was one of the scariest things I had ever done, but working with Tom turned out to be a pleasant surprise. His messages were inspired and anointed, and there was nothing he said that I could not agree with. In the end this turned out to be a very healing experience, and I was convinced that God was still at work in all churches – even among the Catholics.

John Wimber was not yet well known in Europe, and he was not one of the main speakers at the conference. He had a workshop on healing in the afternoons, and I made sure that I could attend.

John's style of ministry was unlike any I had ever seen and experienced before. His teaching was very inspiring, and he had a good sense of humor which made everyone feel very relaxed. There was no hype or religious language. After he had taught for some time he called people forward that needed a physical healing. He also called out some specific needs and problems that the Holy Spirit had given him. When he prayed for the people he did not shout and there were no dramatics whatsoever. He then asked one lady how she was feeling, and she confirmed that she her pain was gone.

John simply said, "Great! Now why don't you pray for that man over there. You've just received a healing – now give it away."

The poor woman was so shocked that she began to stutter, "B-b-but I can't do that... I don't have the gift of healing, and besides, I have never done that before..."

"Why don't you let the Lord worry about that, and simply give Him a chance?"

John did the same with everyone else that was in any way touched by God. After awhile there was a group of people on the stage praying for each other, and John simply watched from the back with a big grin on his face. To everyone's amazement, several people experienced a significant touch or healing from the Lord, and at the end of the workshop many left with the conviction, "Hey, I can do this too!"

I was so impressed by what I had seen, and simply loved this style of ministry. Later I would see John and his team minister to several thousand people in Frankfurt, Germany, and the presence of God was more intense than anything I had ever witnessed before. The worship times were awesome, and it was the first time that I heard demons scream and leave during worship.

Martin was totally hooked on the values that were expressed and demonstrated by the Vineyard, and his relationship with John became very close. That was the beginning of our history with the Vineyard, and it has been our home ever since.

✳ ✳ ✳

Three years after the church plant began, Earl and Peggy and their children moved back to Oklahoma, and we all hated to see them go. The transition that followed was difficult for the church as well as our family. My leadership style was quite different from Earl's, and no matter how hard I tried, I could never fill his shoes. Together, we struggled for about another year, and even though there was growth and many good things happened, things began to erode from the inside. I was totally clueless and thought we were actually doing all right, until one fateful day. Our strategy had been that I would pour myself into our four small group leaders, and they in turn shepherded those within their respective groups. So I meet regularly with these four men for prayer and training.

One Saturday morning we were meeting again in my office. By the time I walked in they had already met for some time without me, and then their spokesman dropped the bomb. They had talked and agreed that my leadership was no longer acceptable to them. They did not think that I was appointed by God for the job of leading them, and they felt they could do a better job of running the church without me.

What could I say to that? I was so shocked that I did not even know how to react, other than feeling hurt and completely devastated! Words cannot describe the agony of the next few days. All I remember is that I had never felt so hurt and rejected in all my life. Looking back I realize that I overreacted and let myself be pulled down by the pain in my heart.

From my perspective I only had two choices. One would have been to slam my fist on the table and say: "I am the leader appointed by Martin and Todd, and I have their and God's authority behind me. If you don't agree with that, then it is best that you leave the church!" I knew that if I had called Martin at this point then this would have been his instructions.

But I did not call him until I had made up my mind, and this was my reasoning: If they did not believe my leadership came from God, then I did not want to be their leader! I allowed myself to believe that their lack of approval meant that God did not approve of me either. Two days later I called a special meeting and resigned from my position as leader and pastor of the church, and turned leadership over to the four men.

Only then did I call Martin and tell him what happened. There was really nothing he could do at this point, and I could sense his disappointment and hurt, adding to the load of guilt I already bore.

Martin did not endorse the leadership of the four "rebels," and we both watched in agony as the church continued to disintegrate and finally ceased to exist just a few months later. We heard stories and rumors of some of the members joining other churches, but others totally fell away from their faith in God. It would take me years to accept and receive God's forgiveness for my part in this drama, and I could not even imagine that God would ever entrust me with a shepherding role again.

* * *

The following months were filled with a sense of grief and failure, and endless questions. Again we had lost our income and employment, and my options for finding work were bleak. For a while I tried selling different kinds of insurance, and spent many weekends at training seminars, where we were taught all the tricks in the book to manipulate our clients into buying the kind of coverage that would ensure a fat commission for us. I was shocked by this introduction into the ruthless practices of insurance companies, and simply could not bring myself to lie shamelessly to my clients. I would advise them to get the kind of coverage that I felt was wise and adequate for their current status in life. That meant that I never landed the kind of contract that made my work worthwhile.

Then I switched to another opportunity in sales that I hoped would be more honest and lucrative. This particular company spent the summer months sending a helicopter and a photographer to take aerial pictures of people's homes in the beautiful area called the Black Forest. I thought this would be much fun, and began training with the man who had recruited me. All we had was the name of the village, and a stack of photographs of all the farms and villas without any address. So we had to identify the houses by sight only. This was no easy task, since houses tend to look quite differently from the ground than from the air.

Once we had charted our course through the village we would knock on doors, and showed the house owner a picture of their pride and joy. Once inside the house we would unpack some sample pictures to show them what we could do with the small photo once it was enlarged and processed. You could have the picture blown up to just about any size, and have it processed so it looked like an actual oil painting.

And then it happened again. I watched my boss talk an older couple into buying the most expensive product we offered, with the most gaudy and expensive picture frame, claiming it would look absolutely stunning on their living room wall. Anyone with even the faintest trace of taste could see that the result would look absolutely horrific on their plain wooden wall, but my skillfully cunning boss got them to sign the order for a $2,000 picture that would ensure him a fat bonus of fifteen percent.

The following week I was turned loose on my own with a stack of pictures of a village I had never heard of. It took me more than two hours to get there, and as I climbed the winding road into the beautiful highland, I discovered that winter had unleashed three feet of snow the night before! Most of the roads had been plowed, but now all the houses were hidden behind mountains of snow that I had to climb to identify them. It was an endless puzzle, and I was not dressed for the occasion. By the time I finally knocked on doors I was miserably frozen to my bones.

Selling pictures was not that hard, since most home owners were intrigued to see a picture of their home taken from the air. As before, I recommended them to order a picture that would match their style and the size of the room. Those were never the biggest pictures, and at the end of the day my commission barely covered my gas and other expenses. Once again I had to realize that being an honest salesman would not feed my family. After a few weeks I quit and filed for unemployment once again.

Through all the driving and lugging of portfolios I had developed a terrible back ache, and found myself seeking treatment from an orthopedic surgeon. After the initial x-rays he revealed to me that I had a double curvature of the spine that could not be corrected. The only way for me to make life bearable would be to buy a better car, a better mattress, do daily exercises, and take pain killers. Either way, he left me with his prediction that I would be in a wheel chair by the age of fifty!

* * *

Over the years I found myself rejecting and breaking the power of that prediction over and over. How could I ever be a missionary living in much more uncomfortable conditions with this kind of outlook? In the midst of all the gloom there were some rays of hope. One of them was my first trip to Asia.

Todd's left-hand man Charles and his wife Dianna had come to visit, and they were on their way to Sri Lanka to secure a suitable building for a training school Todd was working on. They invited me to tag along, and I was beside myself with excitement.

We flew to the capital, Colombo, and I'll never forget the sights, sounds and smells of Asia on the way from the airport to the guest house where we were staying. This was my first confrontation with true poverty, and no matter how many times you may have seen it on television, there is no substitute to seeing it with your own eyes. It is more than just taking in the shacks and rags of the poor, it is sensing the spirit of death and hope-lessness that surrounds them, being reflected in the eyes of the beggars that assault you continuously.

One of my first memories of Sri Lanka involved food. We had joined a local pastor at a traditional restaurant, and just about any item on the menu included the word "curry". I remember ordering a chicken curry, and the pastor looked a bit doubtful when he asked me, "Are you sure you can handle that?"

"Oh, don't worry, I love curry!"

As it turned out, my idea of curry was quite different from what I was about to experience. Growing up in Germany, we had been introduced to a new and exotic kind of sauce, called "Curry Ketchup," and that is exactly what it was – tomato ketchup with a slight addition of curry powder. We used to put it on our hot dogs and brag about how tough we were eating such spicy food.

The dish that was set before me looked nothing like what I had ex-pected, but it smelled delicious, and I dug in. Only seconds after my first bite I was assaulted by the sensation of fire in my mouth that took my breath away and caused my eyes to tear up instantly. Everyone at the ta-ble had been waiting for this kind of reaction and had a good laugh at my expense. I found out later that Sri Lankan food has the reputation of be-ing some of the hottest in the world, and my mouth never quite stopped burning for days. After about one week of this, my gums and the whole inside of my mouth felt so raw that I knew I needed a break from this culinary torture. I remember walking down one of the main streets of Colombo in search of some Western cuisine. And there it was, a real hamburger place. It was a local chain, but how bad can a hamburger be? My first bite answered that question in a very painful fashion. The meat patty was heavily laced with chili peppers of the meanest kind!

Charles and Dianna left a few days before me, and I continued to explore the city and the culture of this nation torn and wounded by years of civil war between two ethnic groups and their religions – the Tamils who are predominantly Hindu, and the Buddhist Sinhalese.

For most of the people, the lines between their religious beliefs had blurred into a mix of most of the main religions in this world. Every time I took a ride on what they call a "mini bus," this became quite evident. On top of the dashboard right in front of the driver lay a long wooden box with a glass front. Inside was a whole row of figurines, depicting gods from all religions. Besides Buddha, and a whole assortment of Hindu gods and goddesses, there were also figures of Mary and Jesus, and one that looked like Moses. On the very left and right were bright red light bulbs that lit up every time the driver stepped on the brake, which made for a really cool disco light effect. The drivers must be the worst in the world, and I remember hanging on for dear life, praying in tongues, when an older man beside me sweetly smiled and said, "Don't worry, man, nothing can happen, we are protected by all the gods!"

Upon my return to Germany, my enthusiasm towards living in Asia had definitely cooled off some, and I seriously asked myself if I could really justify dragging Cathy and the kids to live in a place like that? Just a few days later I had a meeting with Martin in Bern. He had been on the phone with Todd the day before, and they had talked about our future. Martin totally shocked me when he said that they were ready to send us out to Asia if we still wanted to go. Cambodia still had not opened up, but we could go and join a church planting team in the Philippines for a few years.

This was the closest I had ever come to the fulfillment of my dream, and now I was not sure anymore if I really wanted to go. There was nothing left for us to do in Germany, and a door had opened that we could not ignore. The next few months would become some of the most memorable for our family.

Asia at Last

One month before our departure date, I flew to Manila by myself to meet the team there, and secure housing and schooling for us.

A missionary by the name of Andrew picked me up at the airport, and I stayed with him and his family for some days. The Philippines had a completely different feel compared to Sri Lanka. Though the people looked similar, the culture did not feel as "Asian". Having been a Spanish colony for 400 years, there were many European influences, the main one being Catholicism. Instead of Buddhist and Hindu temples with their myriads of idols and gods, there where churches everywhere, and even more statues of Mary. Many signs and street names sounded Spanish, and I could read them since they were in Latin script.

The sheer size of Manila and the crowds of people wherever you went became quite overwhelming, and I spent many hours in buses and taxis crawling through the congested streets of this mega city.

We were to connect with another family who lived in the northern part of the city, near a place called Antipolo. That area was towards the hills, and quite a bit higher and greener.

Mike and his family lived in a big house in a subdivision called Beverly Hills! Since the American forces fought side by side with the Filipinos against the Japanese during the Second World War, anything sounding American was attractive and desirable.

After some extensive search I found a suitable bungalow for us in the same subdivision, and wondered what people back home would think when they found out that we were moving to Beverly Hills?

One of the main reasons why we sought housing in that area was the fact that it was close to a well-known Christian private school called "Faith Academy." I visited there and got all the information and paper work to enroll Björn and Nils there for the following fall.

It was Easter time, and a group of missionaries had decided to go to a famous Cathedral in the oldest part of Manila in order to witness a real crucifixion. I tagged along with my camera hoping to get some good shots, but I was not prepared for what we were about to witness even before we got close to the venue. The streets were filled with processions, and throngs of pilgrims that had come from far away to celebrate Good Friday in a very painful way. Many were crawling on their knees, while whipping their bare backs with crude whips, and bamboo sticks. I had never seen such an expression of pain and agony, and so much blood! It all felt so wrong. I felt like screaming at them, "You don't have to do this – don't you know that Jesus already suffered for you?"

Then we stood for hours in stifling heat outside the Cathedral, waiting for a chosen young man to let himself be nailed to a cross. They stretched it out like an endless drama, and in the end it was like a farce of the event that took place 2,000 years earlier in Jerusalem.

The poor guy was obviously on drugs, or completely drunk, and throughout the ordeal he did not seem to suffer all that much. They had tied his arms to the cross in a way where he was held there even without any nails. Then they made a big show of sterilizing the nails in alcohol, while a doctor marked the right spots on his hands where they would do the least amount of damage, and not hit any bone. The nails were about two inches long and very thin, and from where we were standing we could barely see them at all. Finally, under the screams and sobs of the crowd they drove the nails though his hand with one swift pound of a household hammer, and carefully lifted the cross to an upright position. His feet were not nailed, and stood on a pedestal that was attached to the cross. After a few minutes of corporate wailing and prayers, the cross was carefully laid down again, while a surgeon supervised the extraction of the nails that had barely gone into the wood.

We drove back in the car in silence and exhaustion, and agreed that this had been the worst waste of time and energy. But this day clearly highlighted the fact that the people of the Philippines needed to meet Jesus in a real way.

Before I went back to Germany I took a trip with Andrew to a remote area in the north of Luzon. First we flew in an ancient twin engine plane for an hour, and then rode for several hours on the roof of a crowded Jeepney to a village in the midst of the most beautiful coconut tree forest. Here, all seemed so peaceful and serene, and we passed many farmers working in their rice fields, waving to us as we drove by.

Andrew and I had several open-air meetings in the somewhat cooler evenings, and I witnessed many conversions and a number of miracles. Never before had I witnessed such a hunger, desire, and openness towards the things of God than among these precious people that had so little, and yet seemed so content.

It was on the way back to Manila that I knew I had fallen in love with Asia and her people, and I could not wait to come and live among them.

Something bothered me on the long flight home to Cathy and the kids. It seemed like the two families I had met really were not a team at all. They both did their own thing, and when I asked them about Todd, they both confirmed that he had never come out, and they had no contact with him at all anymore. I thought that was rather strange, but in all of my excitement regarding the future I suppressed my feelings and concerns for the time being.

* * *

We had less than four weeks to arrange for our move, and to burn our bridges. Cathy was 6 months pregnant, and not as mobile as she would have liked to be. All our belongings were divided into three groups. One part was not worth storing, and was donated to different people and ministries. The second pile was to be stored in a barn of our dear friends in

VOYAGE OF GRACE

a place called Achern, about an hour's drive away. The last and smallest portion was packed into a crate to be shipped to the Philippines by boat. It mainly contained personal things, books, and some kitchen ware.

We had put an ad in the paper for some items to be sold, among them were the kids' bicycles. It was then I realized how hard it must have been for our children who did not share my zeal and excitement to move to the other side of the world. A woman had come to look at the boys' bicycles, and when I opened the garage I noticed that Nils' bike was missing. When he had heard that I was about to sell his precious bike, he had taken off with it into the vineyards. It was then it truly sank in, that all of us were going to pay a price in following what we perceived to be our calling from God.

On our last Sunday in Bern, Martin and the church blessed us and commissioned us as their first missionaries. The arrangement was that we should go for two years, and then reevaluate the situation. We did not receive any payment from the church, but had found a number of individual supporters from the Basileia, as well as some friends in Germany and Sweden who promised to help.

Finally, the big day arrived. On May 1, 1988, we boarded a Singapore Airlines Jumbo headed for Singapore, and then onward to Manila. We had to spend one night in Singapore, and the immigration officer showed great concern when he saw Cathy's tummy. Apparently, many people try to have their children born in Singapore, because it makes them automatic citizens of this wealthy island state. He let us pass once we showed him our tickets and he saw that we were leaving again the following morning.

It was a gloomy and rainy day when we arrived in Manila. We were picked up by a friend of Mike, who lived just up the street from our new home. Dennis and Jerry Gunderson were to become some of our closest friends and mentors for the first season in this new and strange world we had entered into.

The long drive seemed to last forever, and our jet-lagged minds were

144

on sensory overload, as we slowly moved through the noisy traffic. The humidity was close to 100%, and everything was gray in gray. Looking back I cannot even imagine what it must have felt like for Cathy and the children who had never seen and experienced anything like that before.

The next few weeks became a blur of new experiences, impressions, and a sense of complete helplessness. Our new friends were wonderful in showing us where to shop for what, and teaching us to cope with our new environment and cultural challenges. We did not have money for a car and were forced to use the public transportation system for shopping and running errands. Where we lived there was only one option, and it was called "Jeepney," the most popular means of public transportation in the Philippines. They were originally made from US military jeeps left over from World War II and are known for their flamboyant decorations and crowded seating. They had become a true symbol of Philippine culture.

Equipped with noisy and smoke-belching diesel engines, you could always hear their typical "roar" when they approached. Though there were designated stops along their routes, the drivers usually always responded to anyone waving them down. After entering through the open back entrance you tried to find a seat on the two facing benches, with everyone scooting closer towards the front of the vehicle, until there was absolutely no more room. Then you would pass the fare to the person next to you, who would pass it on until it eventually reached the driver. If you did not pass on the exact change, then the excess would be passed back to you in the same way. I'll never forget my first Jeepney ride, when the old man next to me passed me some Peso coins. When he saw the puzzled look on my face, he realized that I was just another ignorant foreigner, so he emphasized his request by doing something else I had never seen before – he actually pointed at the driver with his lips!

Oh, and there was always loud music, and the benches one sat on doubled as speaker boxes. Between the rumbling diesel engine and the pounding beat of the music one was assured to get a good massage while riding in close fellowship with at least twenty other passengers.

Being taller than most people riding with me, I always had to tilt my head to look out the open side windows so I could get a fix on where we were. When you wanted to get off, you simply yelled "para," or knocked with a coin against the hand rail under the ceiling, and the driver would pull over at the next possible stop.

* * *

Just a few weeks after our arrival, I became sick with the mumps. This childhood disease can do quite a number on an adult man, and having a high fever in tropical temperatures does not help with the recovery process. Again, our newfound friends were there to help and assist Cathy, and a real sense of community began to develop among the missionaries in the neighborhood.

In the midst of this incredible journey of learning and trying to make a home for our family, we were confronted with the news that all was not well with our missions agency called New Covenant Commission. Though all of us had a sense that there was something not quite right, none of us could have imagined the magnitude of the crisis. Word reached us that Todd Burke had totally fallen away from the Lord, and that his ministry and all aspects of it had ceased to exist! It would take some time for more details to emerge, but at that moment I was completely devastated!

In the days that followed, we three families that formed the local team of NCC met to discuss the future. Without our common focus and leadership we really had nothing that could keep us together, and we pretty much went our separate ways from then on. We occasionally touched base, or had some fellowship, but everyone began to work within the circles that had emerged for them. Since we had only recently arrived, we did not yet have any local connections, except our new missionary neighbors.

To make matters worse, we found out that the person at the NCC office in Texas had disappeared with a large part of everyone's support funds.

Here we were, without real leadership and direction, and barely enough support to keep us above water. On top of it all, I fell into a spiritual abyss of despair unlike anything I had ever experienced. Every time I thought of Todd, I could hear the voices of fear in my heart whispering, "If Todd can fall, what makes you think you can stand?"

In my desperation I cried out to the Lord with renewed earnestness and desperation. My disappointment in leadership had given way to the resignation that there was simply no way that I could ever finish the course, if even men like Todd could fall away. To make matters worse, there was not really anyone I could talk to. Our new friends were very understanding of our dilemma, but they really did not know how they could help us either. This was before the days of Internet, email and even cell phones. Long-distance calls were costly and of terrible quality, and letters took several weeks back and forth. I had entered a season of isolation, and I knew I had to learn to press directly into God if I wanted any help and comfort. It was not until many years later that I learned that isolation is a very common way for God to train up leaders.

Amazingly, one day I heard God speak very clearly into my heart, and He let me know that the fear I felt in my heart was not from Him, and that it was not His will for any of His children to live in fear. That day, in my Bible reading I came across one verse that changed everything. I happened to read in the Second Epistle of Peter, and these words literally jumped at me, "Do these things, and you will never fall away".[2]

Wow – there it was, a solemn promise from God that we will not fall away! Of course there are conditions, and I have spent countless hours studying the previous verses ever since. But this was the hope that helped me to expel all fear from my heart, at least the fear of falling away from God. I knew I was still capable of walking away from Him, but now I understood that God had put safeguards in place that would keep me safe. It was at this point in time that I knew God was still with us, and that He would use us for His glory in whatever circumstances we might

---

[2] 2 Peter 1:10b (NLTse)

find ourselves.

* * *

During this season of deliverance, Cathy gave birth to our fifth child and fourth son, Leif Johan. This was our first home birth, and it turned out to be a wonderful experience for the whole family. Dianne, a missionary wife in the neighborhood, was a midwife and trained others in midwifery. She did a wonderful job encouraging us, and coaching Cathy through the process of a home delivery. Both Diane and her husband Dennis would become close friends of ours in the years to come.

Even though I had been delivered from the fear of falling, there were still so many questions about Todd's change of heart. None of us could understand how a man who was so anointed and used by God would want to turn his back on him. Over the years I was asked that same question over and over, especially by people who had read the book. I do not think that we ever discovered the whole truth, but the stories that emerged were terribly sad and heartbreaking.

Since his worldwide ministry required lots of funds to operate, Todd was constantly on the lookout for new business opportunities. Apparently, he got himself involved in some gray-market schemes, and his closest coworkers tried to warn him of the dangers, but he would not listen. In his own mind, Todd always knew what he was doing, and a root of pride became evident to those close to him.

Since Todd did not heed the warnings of his closest friends, they all left him, one by one. That in turn hurt him deeply, and in the end he stood all alone. Somewhere in this process tragedy hit, when one of Todd and DeAnn's sons was killed in a shotgun accident. The story is told that after the funeral Todd went to seek out a spirit medium in order to talk to the spirit of his son. The parallels to King Saul are all too evident to ignore.

The timing is unclear, but we heard that Todd and DeAnn's marriage did not survive these tragic events, and one of the last things we heard was that Todd became a New Age teacher in Arizona. We never had any more contact with him after that, but some of his closer friends tried to stay in touch with him. When it became clear that he was so blinded that he could no longer hear the truth, they met together to perform one last act of friendship for Todd: They turned him over to Satan for the destruction of the flesh, so that his spirit may be saved in the day of the Lord.[3]

The very last news regarding Todd was that he was killed in a car accident in 2006. Rumor has it that he was on his way to visit an old friend with the intention to get his life in order and return to God. The driver following him reported that he saw what he perceived to be some sort of struggle going on which led to the fatal accident. Oh, how I hope that Todd had enough time to come home in the final moments of his earthly life.

* * *

Among our new-found acquaintances was a Swedish missionary family, Sven and Seidy Johansson, and their four children. They only lived a few miles up the hills from us, and we quickly became good friends. Sven and I had a lot in common, and I enjoyed the very fact that they were Swedish. Sven was helping to train leaders for a group of churches under the umbrella of "New Testament Faith Mission." He would invite me to lead worship for some of their meetings, and, later on I traveled quite often with him to encourage the various churches.

During that time I had the opportunity to meet many of his Filipino coworkers, and was able to gain some insight into the whole arena of what we call missions. I'll never forget my conversations with some of the leaders. I had asked one youth leader what he thought of all the missionaries in his country, and his reply was both a surprise and a disappointment to me. He said, "Oh, it is wonderful! They have money and resources to help us build churches and buy equipment."

---

[3] 1 Corinthians 5:5 (NLTse)

He was very sincere and I wondered if this was really all we were good for. A short while later I talked to an older pastor from the island of Mindanao, and when he heard I was a missionary, he became almost angry and said, "You missionaries have taken away our ability to trust God!"

"How so?" I asked.

"Whenever we need anything we don't ask God, but we come to you, and then you write home to your missions organization, and they send the money."

Later on I would find out that this was quite true, and that the traditional missions approach really did not facilitate a healthy growth and maturity in the hearts of the local believers. This was still the remnant of the "mission station approach" of the first missionaries to Africa, where the poor heathen would come to receive food, clothing and education in return for becoming converts to Christianity. In Asia they are called Rice Christians, and this, sadly, is still a reality today in some circles.

One day, one of the pastors from the province came to Manila and told us the story that the roof of his church had been destroyed by a recent typhoon. He asked if we could help them raise some money for repair? My friend Sven asked his missions organization in Sweden for help, and they sent a good amount of money. We handed it to the pastor, and asked him for receipts for the repair materials, as well as a photo of the completed church building.

Several months later, we still had not heard back from him, so one of the workers in Manila went down to see what had happened. He found that the roof had not yet been repaired, and when he confronted the pastor about this, he confessed that he had used the funds to buy gold -digging equipment. When we spoke with him later he was still totally unrepentant, and argued that he could have built a much better church building if he had found gold!

Sadly, this would continue to be an issue many times over in the future. How does one help the poor without creating dependencies and fostering abuse?

***

Sven had a passion to teach and preach in the style of some of the old -time revivalists, and I quickly learned that Asia, and particularly the Philippines, was an easy and rewarding place for any kind of ministry. By nature, the people are much more spiritual than in the West, and they love to listen to spiritual teaching, and to be blessed and prayed for by spiritual leaders. No matter how good or bad the preaching, a Christian from the West had an instant recognition and platform. You simply could not visit a church without being called up to preach the moment the pastor spotted you. I used to try and hide somewhere in the back, but they always found me and I was announced as that day's guest speaker!

It was fun and rewarding to minister to people that were so open and eager to hear the Word, and act on it. Often, their faith and expectation would supersede my own, and more than once I asked myself, "Who is teaching whom here...?"

Within the first year, I was invited to share my testimony on a Christian television station in Manila. This was both exciting and scary, since I had never seen a television studio from the inside. I have no idea how many people actually watched that program, but afterward I had several phone calls and visits from both pastors and believers who wanted me to come and help them in some way.

The boss of a sewing factory asked me to come and speak to his employees, since he always tried to supply them with some spiritual devotion and challenge. When I came to the factory, I had no idea what to expect. As soon as he saw me, he announced a break for all the seamstresses, and immediately over a hundred of them abandoned their sewing machines and gathered around me in expectation. I felt completely lost and helpless, but I figured everyone likes a good story, and out of the blue I told them the story of the Day of Pentecost in my own words.

When I was done I asked the simple question, "Wouldn't it be great if we would experience something like that today?" For me it was more of a hypothetical question, but they took it quite literally, nodded their heads, and assumed a receiving position. So I said a simple prayer and asked the Holy Spirit to come, and to my absolute amazement, He did! Within a few minutes many, if not most of them began to weep, cry, and speak in tongues. I had no idea how many of them were actual believers, but it was the first time I witnessed God work in this way, and I loved it!

* * *

Shopping for a family of seven in Manila without a car turned out to be quite a problem. From our house to the next big supermarket could take between one and two hours with a Jeepney So a simple task like shopping, or going to the bank, or the post office could easily turn into a whole day's work. One of the first things I learned about life in Asia was that everything took much, much longer than back in Europe. I used to come home completely drained and frustrated, having only been able to carry out a fraction of what I had set out to do.

I was surprised to find out how expensive even old cars were, and especially vans, which is what we really needed. The U.S. forces had had a presence on the island of Luzon since the Second World War, and the soldiers and officers were able to import their cars by ship. Most of them tried to sell them locally before their term was over. My new friend Sven was a lover of antique cars, especially American cars. He convinced me that an old American sedan would be big enough for our whole family. These kind of cars were not popular among the Filipinos and were a lot cheaper than some Japanese imports.

I had seen an old Chevrolet Impala parked in the neighborhood, and one day I asked the owner if it was for sale. He said it needed a little bit of work, but I could have it for one thousand dollars. We ended up buying it, and thus began my adventure of becoming a would-be mechanic of ancient cars. This particular one was a 1963 hardtop model, and the owner was not kidding when he said it needed a little bit of work. Amazingly, there were still places in the city where you could get necessary spare parts. If not, then you just used some Japanese component and made it work. I learned a new expression from one of the local mechanics. It is called "making remedy," and it simply means that if there is no spare part available, then you make one, and if that is not possible, then you just figure out a way to do without it.

The Impala had no air conditioning, so we were forced to drive with all the windows down. Cruising down a main street called "Edsa," with the radio playing a sixties station really made you feel like you were sitting in a time machine. My left arm soon turned dark brown from hanging out the open window several hours a day.

As time went on, we were able to upgrade to a 1967 Dodge Coronet which had recently been restored by another missionary and sported mag wheels and air conditioning. Then there was a Dodge pickup truck, and finally a 1978 Chevy Suburban with a huge V8 engine and a leaky radiator.

In between we "car-sat" a white and baby-blue 1958 Plymouth Belvedere for another Swedish missionary on furlough. Apparently there were only four drivable units of this car left in the world, and he wanted to fully restore it and take it home to Sweden, where it would be worth a fortune. He asked us to drive it occasionally, which I did with great pleasure – when it ran.

It also had a giant V8 engine and a push-button automatic transmission. The original mufflers had rusted out decades ago, and had been replaced by fat metal water pipes that came out under each front door. The sound was absolutely amazing. When it idled it purred like a tomcat, but the moment you pressed the accelerator it growled like a cougar in heat! It had huge fins on the back fenders, and when I drove through our neighborhood the boys would come running after me and yell, "Batman, Batman!" That was the fun part of driving an ancient vehicle, and Sven was right – there was enough space for our whole family in any of these vehicles.

There were also agonizing moments when one of them quit working in the middle of a busy intersection, or overheated on the way to the airport, and we ended up hours late picking up guests. It was during those times that we got to experience the amazing helpfulness and hospitality of the Filipino people. There were always helping hands to push the car to the next mechanic. And if the incident happened late at night, then you were invited to spend the night at their simple abode, and were treated like a special guest.

* * *

Once we had our first car, we decided to get out of the city for a short break to the beach. A dear friend had offered us the use of his hut, and so we loaded up the old Impala for the two-hour drive. It was October which is typhoon season, but we had no idea what that meant. If we had listened to the radio we would have heard about the typhoon warning for that weekend, and we wondered why there was so little traffic on the way.

By the time we got to our hut right by the beach, it had begun to pour down heavily, and during the night the wind picked up and howled unlike anything we had ever experienced. Our hut began to vibrate, and we began to fear that it would be blown away. It never stopped for the next two days. The winds and rain were so strong that we could not go outside. I had tried to go out with our video camera to film this assault by nature, but I did not last more than just a few seconds. The rain came sideways with such force that it hurt like bee stings!

We could hear the pounding surf and prayed that the waves would not reach our hut. On the third day it was still cloudy and windy, but the rain had stopped, and we decided to explore the beach. There were broken trees everywhere, the sandy beach was littered with driftwood and seaweed, but the water was warm, and the kids had their first swim in the South China Sea.

Soon we realized that typhoons were a regular occurrence, especially in the "ber-months," meaning all the months ending with "ber". These storms caused massive destruction, and claimed many lives every year, especially among the poor.

Storms were not the only source of danger in the Philippines. In July of 1990, a killer earthquake unexpectedly hit and extensively devastated the city of Baguio killing about 1,000. Though the earthquake was 250 kilometers north of us, we could clearly feel the tremors at our house, adding another scary memory.

Politically, the Philippines were highly unstable, with both Muslim and Communist insurgencies in different regions causing havoc and constant confrontations with the military. Rumors of coups were common, and one December, a faction of the armed forces staged the biggest coup d'etat against the current government. As a result, large parts of Makati, Manila's business district, were under siege, and resembled a war zone.

Our friends from the New Testament Faith Mission held a weekly prayer meeting at their office in Cubao, and I joined them whenever I could. That particular Monday, I was the only one there, and the door to the office was locked. Before going home, I decided to go to the rooftop of the ten-story office building. From there I had a grand view of the developing war between the two factions just a few miles south from where I was. Dense smoke was rising from several bank buildings, and there was an aerial combat between a modern fighter jet, and some Second World War vintage fighters that the rebels had stolen from a nearby air force base. While watching with fascination, it dawned on me that this was a real war, and that I would be better off being at home with Cathy and the kids.

I decided to take a different route home, avoiding some of the main highways, but that turned out to be a big mistake. As I drove down a narrow street in a densely populated part of Quezon City, I came to a T-intersection, and was about to turn left, when I saw a tank approaching, his gun turret aimed in my direction.

Looking to the right, I could barely believe my eyes when I saw another tank coming towards me as well. It did not take me long to figure out that they were not on the same team, and that I was caught in the middle of a tank duel! There was no room to turn around, so I slammed the gearstick into reverse, praying there were no cars behind me. Thankfully, the streets were empty, since none had been as foolish as I, venturing out into an obvious war zone. With screeching and smoking tires, I reversed a whole city block, until I could turn around and race home, with my heart thundering in my chest the whole way.

* * *

The first few years in the Philippines flew by very quickly. The older kids settled in well at Faith Academy. For two years I volunteered to lead a Cub Scout group there, and enjoyed some special times with Björn and Nils and a group of boys their age. The annual Pine Wood Derby was always a huge affair where the boys and their dads built a race car out of a block of pinewood, four plastic wheels and four nails. At the derby they raced down a track, four in a row, and the winner advanced to the next round, until the final winner emerged. It was really more a contest between the dads than the boys, since all the dads got involved in tweaking the racers to squeeze the best possible time out of them. Of course, the cars had to be within a certain weight limit, and were thoroughly checked before the race. Little lead pieces were super-glued to get the exact weight, and a little graphite on the axles went a long way. We never made it to the finals, but we won some of the races and it was much fun – at least for me.

Some of the boys in my den were boarding students, and it was so sad to see them clamor for attention from me as a substitute father. One day I sat in a school bus and overheard some older boarding students vent to each other, "Why do I have to live in this stinking place! I hate my parents, and I hate God!"

Cathy and I decided that no matter what, we would never send our kids to a boarding school. Little did we know that this resolve would be tested sooner than we thought.

* * *

By then, we had a dog and several cats which started a tradition we would follow wherever we went. Driving down the main street every day, I would see a man by the side of the road, trying to sell a Filipino Sea Eagle. I was intrigued by the beauty of that poor creature, and one day I stopped to ask how much he wanted for the bird. My thoughts were that I would set it free. Since it only cost about five dollars, I came home with an eagle!

They had clipped the wings of the poor creature; it would never fly again. The man who had sold it to me found out where we lived, and from time to time he would come to the house with another bird in a sack. Soon I had a whole collection of exotic birds: Several sea eagles, an old albatross, an osprey, and a pair of young water birds that constantly fought with each other.

I ended up building a big walk-in cage in the backyard, and since they all liked fish, we had the freezer full of small fish from the market. The albatross died of old age; the osprey of a sickness; and the fighting couple ended up killing each other. Eventually I was left with several young eagles that I planned to set free at some point. I was the "bird man."

* * *

Increasingly I traveled with Sven to a province called Bicol, where the New Testament Faith Mission had several churches. We regularly taught at seminars for pastors and leaders, and sometimes traveled to remote places by bus, Jeepney, or "banka," which is a narrow fishing boat with an outrigger on one side. We often slept in simple bamboo huts and occasionally on a bare floor. The heat and humidity were exhausting, and during services we had to shout in order to drown out the noises of playing children, fighting chickens, or passing vehicles. Many of the places had no, or only sporadic electricity, so there was no help from any sound system.

In spite of the hardships, I remember those times with fondness, because I often encountered the faithful mercy and power of God there. Sometimes, after hours of teaching, I felt like I had nothing more to say, but then the Holy Spirit would rise within me and I would cut loose and speak to their hearts in ways that I knew had to be supernatural, Those ended up being the greatest ministry times I can remember.

We saw many healed, touched, and delivered during that season, but two particular stories stand out in my memory. One happened in one of those remote villages in Bicol. We had a meeting in a simple bamboo church, and when we invited the sick to come for prayer, a young man came complaining of stomach pain. He said that he always had extreme stomach cramps when he came to church or was near Christians. He recalled being sick as a child, and his mother taking him to a witch doctor, which is very common among the multitudes of people too poor to go to a real doctor or hospital. The witch doctor wrote some words on a piece of "magic" paper, and told the boy to eat it. His sickness got better, but from that day on he suffered from these stomach cramps. We began to pray, and broke the curse that had come on him through that ritual over 10 years earlier. All of a sudden he doubled over in extreme pain and began to groan. We continued to pray, but he turned around and ran outside, where we could hear him wretch violently. We followed him, and could not believe our eyes at the sight that met us. There he stood, erect and with a big smile on his face, pointing to a bloody and foamy mess at his feet. Among the remains of his supper was a wad of paper – the very paper he was forced to eat ten years earlier!

By now I had become acquainted with the supernatural power of God, but I think this was the first time I had seen proof of the supernatural powers of Satan, and the intense warfare that we are engaged in. Sometime later, in the city of Cagayan de Oro, on the southern island of Mindanao, I would have a similar encounter.

The pastor I was visiting had taken me to pray for a family in the slums. I was led into a tiny hut that was filled with a large family. The father sat on the bare ground and had both of his feet and hands wrapped in newspaper. When he unwrapped one hand for me I saw that the skin on his palm had been eaten away, and was covered with festering and smelly sores. They were so poor that they no longer could afford real bandages.

As I began to pray in my spirit, I clearly heard the word "curse," and so I paused and asked him if he was aware of any curse being placed on him. His eyes filled with tears as he told me one of the saddest stories I had ever heard.

Not too long ago he had been the proud owner of a very successful bakery in the city. Someone very close in his family was filled with such jealousy at his success, that they sought the help of a spirit medium to cast a curse on him. Within days, the insides of his hands and the bottom of his feet developed ugly boils and sores. He spent all his money on medical care, but no doctor could cure the disease, and he lost his house and business and ended up in the slums. There, he and his family became believers, and yet his condition did not improve.

The pastor and I broke the curse over the poor man, but nothing seemed to change. A few weeks later, I received a letter from the pastor with a photograph in it. In the picture was the man holding up his hands towards the camera. The sores were gone and were replaced by the pink and soft skin of a baby. He had begun to work for a local bakery and was on his way to recover from the grip of poverty.

* * *

During the first two years in Manila, I was invited twice to join a team to India with the Basileia Bern, which had now become the Vineyard Bern. These trips became unforgettable experiences in discovering more about the diversity of Asian cultures. Both trips began in the mega-city of Mumbai, formerly called Bombay, where I met Martin, Mike, and the rest of the team.

The biggest difference in India I noticed immediately was the immense poverty and the hoards of beggars who would continuously latch on to any foreigner they could spot. Pleading and begging children would pull on visitor's clothing until given a coin. The moment a "giver" was identified the onslaught became even more severe, and the only way to escape was to enter a store, or restaurant where beggars were not allowed.

The second thing I immediately noticed was the increased spiritual darkness all around us. With the Filipino people you always met a friendly smile and acceptance, but some of the faces of Hindu Indians radiated pure hatred, intensified by the spirits living inside them. By contrast, the Christians we met were some of the most loving, friendly, and hospitable people I had ever met.

The first leg of our trip took us to the city of Nagpur by train, and that in itself was a new adventure. Sitting in the hot and stuffy train compartment for endless hours became another lesson in patience, especially when the trip was interrupted by several hours because of a broken axle. The sanitary conditions were poor, and the water in the toilets ran out after the first hour of the trip.

At some point a vendor came through with mouthwatering chicken curry in aluminum dishes. We were hungry and most of us tried it. It was spicy and delicious, but we had to eat it Indian style – with our bare hands – and were left with sticky hands, and no water to wash them with. Then we looked for a trash can to discard our dishes, but there were none to be found, so we asked the conductor what to do.

"Just give to me," he said with a smile and collected our trays. Then he walked over to the open window and tossed them out! Why hadn't we thought of that?

In Nagpur we connected with a local pastor by the name of Satish, an old friend of Martin. They were holding a pastors' conference during the day, and some open-air meetings in the evenings. Those drew around 4,000 people, which is not a large crowd by Indian standards. Both Martin and Mike preached evangelistic messages, and then invited people to come forward for prayer. Hundreds streamed forward, and our team joined the local believers in praying for them. There were not enough interpreters, so we often had to guess what the people requested for prayer.

I prayed along with a young girl from Bern for a man who repeatedly pointed to his head. He obviously wanted us to pray for his headache, and so I encouraged the girl to start praying. The moment she touched his forehead he went down as if he had been hit by lightning. Laying on his back and began to expel one demon after another. He hissed and spit, and there was a foul smell that had nothing to do with poor dental hygiene.

At first the girl was in total shock, having never dealt with anything like this before, but she quickly recovered and together we prayed and lost count how many evil spirits left the poor man that night.

Throughout the first two evenings there were a number of significant healings, but then the enemy fought back. After the second night the police arrived at the hotel where we stayed and arrested both Martin and Mike. The charge was "practicing medicine without license," and the remaining meetings were canceled. The church bailed them out of jail and we continued our journey to Bangalore. From there we did some sightseeing and connected with believers in each place to teach and encourage them.

The following year I joined the team again in Mumbai, and this time I brought my friend Dominik from Manila with me. We traveled north by van to a city called Nasik, where we had another series of pastors' meetings and workshops where I had the opportunity to teach as well.

Later on, a woman pastor and a local missionary joined part of our team to visit a tribal village several hours outside the city in a very remote area. On the way they told us the amazing story of this particular village.

The people there were not Hindu, but rather animists, praying to and worshiping the spirits of their ancestors. There was a man in the village in the final stages of leprosy, who cried out to the spirits daily for help. One day he heard a clear voice say to him: "The god who created everything can also heal you!"

Dragging himself to the opening of his hut, he asked everyone that passed by, "Do you know the god that created everything?"

Nobody did, but one woman said that her son who had moved to the city would know, and so she sent for him. He was a Christian and attended a Bible school in the city. He told the dying man about Jesus, and when he prayed for him the man was totally healed from leprosy! It did not take long for the whole village to become Christian.

When we had arrived, we saw that all the huts were made of cow dung and red mud with thatched roofs. All the huts were built around a large hut in the center, the church where the whole village met every evening for worship.

As special guests, we were asked to attend and lead the meeting. I lead our team in some worship songs, and the villagers listened politely, but could not join in. After our last song I asked the people to continue worshiping God. As soon as the words had left the mouth of our interpreter, they began to engage in worship in a way none of us had seen and heard before. They began to wail loudly, and some played home made instruments – different types of hand drums and one-stringed instruments. Many began to dance, and everyone was engaged wholeheartedly. Soon their tears mixed with sweat, and some looked like they were going to collapse any moment.

We watched and listened in complete awe. Even though their music was nothing more than noise to our ears, we could all sense the presence of the Lord hovering over the place. After about thirty minutes of this, the lady pastor who had brought us poked me and shouted in my ear: "You have to tell them to stop, or they'll go on all night!"

We waited a bit longer, and when the first woman fainted I knew that she had been right. We played another song, and it was like someone had pushed an "off" button. They stopped instantly and sat down to listen to us.

This had been the first time I had seen a truly indigenous church and worship, a group of believers completely untouched by Western Christianity, and sadly it was the last time.

I will never forget India, the multitudes of broken and suffering people living in a broken and dark nation. With a grateful heart I returned to my family and thanked God that he had called us to the Philippines.

* * *

After returning to the family in Manila I received a letter from a woman from my hometown in Germany. She was planning to bring a team to the Philippines, and asked if we could help them visit one of the hill tribes. I had never done that myself, but I knew I could arrange something through my friends at the Faith Mission.

Our Dodge was not working at the time, so I picked them up from the airport in the "Bat-Mobil," which gave me instant credit with the guys on the team. There were around six, and they stayed at our house for a few days before we set out for the northern province of "Zambales." In Iba, we spent the night in a church, and parked our car there. From there on we needed something a bit more rugged, and the next morning we caught a ride with a dump truck going up into the mountains to a quarry. For hours we drove on a terrible dirt-road, and I was so glad I had not tried to take the old Plymouth. We were thrown around on the back of the truck and were glad when the driver finally stopped at the end of the road. We would then have to go by foot to our destination, a remote village of the Aeta Tribe.

The church in Iba had sent two girls with us who would guide us and help as interpreters. We walked through total wilderness, and often there was not even a visible path. We would have been totally lost without our two guides who chatted cheerfully while they led the way. Though the path was not steep, we were climbing constantly, and it was very tiring. Twice we had to cross a small river, which was refreshing. The water only reached to our waists, but we had to hold our backpacks high so they would not get wet. By late afternoon we reached a small village with about fifteen thatched bamboo huts.

This was the first time I had seen such a "primitive" tribe. The Aetas are the Aborigines of the Philippines, and had been there long before the Filipino people. The Spanish conquerors called them "negritos" which means "little Negroes", because they are very short, with curly hair, and a dark complexion. Some of the men still wore G-strings and were still hunting with bow and arrow.

We were welcomed by a horde of dirty children, and the team made instant friends when they passed out balloons and candy. The headman gave us the largest hut for accommodation, and we were constantly surrounded by nosy kids and some of the younger women. We were touched by their extreme poverty, and it was clear that many of them were sick. All the kids had runny noses, and some kind of eye infection. They had cooked some rice for us, and we ate it with some canned sardines that we had brought with us. Through our interpreters we asked them to invite the whole village to a meeting that evening, after dark.

When the time came, nobody showed up, not even the children. We were puzzled by their behavior, especially since they seemed to be so pleased by our visit. When I looked out of the open door of our hut, I saw a little old woman rushing about the huts wildly gesticulating and chattering with the other women. I asked one of our guides if she knew what was going on, and she explained to us that the old lady was the village witch doctor, and she was warning the people not to come to our meeting.

We understood that this was a very graphic example of spiritual warfare, and we formed a circle in our hut and began to pray and worship. After about half an hour we could see the lights of lanterns emerging from many huts, as they came towards us.

Soon the hut was packed with men, women and children, and we were relieved that the witch doctor was not among them. The team taught them some simple children's songs with motions, and they learned quickly and participated joyfully. A bit later I told them a very simple Bible story, and they listened politely. We then asked them to raise their hands if they wanted prayer, and quite a few of them responded, and that is when we all learned a very valuable lesson.

Each of us found someone to pray for, and one of the young ladies on the team had chosen one of the tribal women. But the moment she laid her hand on the young woman's shoulder, it was like she was hit by an invisible fist in her chest, and she literally flew several meters through the air, landing on her back with a thud. Her eyes began to bulge and it was obvious that she had trouble breathing. She looked like someone was sitting on her, trying to strangle her! Immediately we stopped what we were doing and gathered around her. We cried out in desperation, praying in tongues, while those among the team with any nursing experience tried to get her to sit up. For a moment it seemed like we were going to lose her, but then things turned in the spirit world. Color started coming back to her face, and she began to breathe normally again. We found out later that the young woman our team member had tried to pray for was the assistant of the witch doctor, and had been sent to disturb the meeting – well, it worked.

We were so shook up by this incident that we finished the meeting, and talked until late into the night about what had just happened. We all understood what the apostle Paul meant when he had told Timothy to not be hasty in the laying on of hands. Again, we were reminded of the severity of the spiritual war we all face.

We spent part of the next day in the village, and then some of the men invited us for target shooting with their bows and arrows. It was much fun, and in the end they presented me with a hunting bow and three arrows. Each arrow had a different metal tip. One was for birds, another for wild boar, and the last one was for "enemies."

We said our good byes and set out on our long trek back to civilization. I thought for sure that this would be my last time to ever see them again, but I was dead wrong, as I would discover some time later in the future.

The heat was overwhelming, and we spent an hour just sitting in the shallow waters of a creek to cool off. As the sunlight filtered through the trees above us and hit the water we saw sparkling particles in the sandy bed of the creek. At first we thought we had found gold, and took some of the glittery sand with us, but we soon discovered that this was just worthless "fools gold."

By the time we reached Iba and our car, I started feeling very sick to my stomach and bowels. We had run out of drinking water a long time ago, and we had refilled our canteens from the creek where the whole village drew their water. We purified the water with purification tablets that were supposed to make if safe. I found out later on that the particular brand that I used kills all kinds of bacteria except for one: Amoeba.

That is what I had for the next few weeks. With a high fever and extreme body aches and headaches I managed to drive us back to Manila, and spent the following week in bed. Thankfully, our friends with some medical training told me of the only type of antibiotic that effectively cures this sickness. If not treated properly, Amoeba can kill you!

Soon the team left to visit some of the other islands, but we were soon to be caught up in events that would change the course of our lives quite dramatically.

* * *

The date was June 12, 1991, and Cathy and I were shopping at a large supermarket during the afternoon. When we pushed our loaded cart out to the parking lot, I was shocked to see that it was already dark. It did not seem possible that we had been shopping for that long, and a glance at my watch confirmed this – it was only four in the afternoon! We could see that the people around us were just as confused and scared as we were, and there was an eerie atmosphere all around us, and, in fact, the air definitely smelled like sulfur.

We drove home as fast as we could, for we knew that whatever was going on, it would lead to even more chaotic circumstances than usual.

I barged into the house and turned on the television to find some news update. It did not take long for all channels to report that the Mount Pinatubo, a dormant volcano in Zambales, had erupted, and was spewing out such immense clouds of ashes, as to block out the sunlight.

By the next morning, the sun shone through the haze, and the ground around us was covered by a layer of gray ashes, several centimeters thick even though Manila is about 220 kilometers away from the volcano. The news that emerged in the days to come was bad. This had been the greatest volcanic eruption in living memory and was felt all around the world with eventual climate and temperature changes.

It turned out that I had only been several kilometers away from the crater when we had visited the Aeta tribe. On the news we could see streams of thousands of tribal people fleeing the destruction of their villages into the lower regions. The government quickly set up a huge refugee camp outside of Iba which swelled quickly to about 15,000 homeless tribal people. During one of these reports on television I even recognized the faces of several people whom we had met in the village with the witch doctor.

Being nomads, the Aeta usually live and travel in groups of thirty or forty people, and here they were all squeezed into tiny makeshift shelters that consisted of nothing more than some poles and a blue plastic canvas. Soon, the camp would be referred to as "Tent City."

As I watched one of the daily updates on the news, God began to speak to me so clearly, that I have never forgotten what He said: "This is the first time in history that these people are all in one place, and it will never happen again!"

That is all He said, but I understood the reality that this was a window in time, an open door for a season, and the challenge was clear: "What are you going to do about it?"

* * *

The weight of that challenge rested heavily on my heart, and would not go away. We knew there was only one thing for us to do – move to Zambales and bring the hope of the Gospel to the Aeta!

That decision had some very weighty implications. By now we had Björn, Nils, and Carina at Faith Academy, and they had adjusted well. In Zambales, there were no English speaking schools, and that left us with only one solution: home schooling. That was a huge challenge for Cathy and me, since we had no experience with that, and felt totally unqualified to be in charge of our children's education. Boarding school was not an option for us, and so we sought help from some of our missionary friends that had successfully schooled all their children at home.

Since it was summer break, we did not sign the kids up for the next school year at Faith, but ordered home schooling material instead. We took some scouting trips up to Iba, and eventually found a small house on a hill just outside the city, and only a few kilometers from the "Tent City."

It took us a few months to wrap everything up in Manila, but then the big day arrived. We were about to embark on an adventure unlike anything we had ever experienced. We hired a truck to carry our furniture and other belongings, packed up the old Suburban, and felt a bit like loading Noah's Ark. We were seven people as a family, but we also brought our helper, Bing, and her little son, and three dogs, several cats, plus three of my eagles. One of our tomcats refused to come out of his hiding place, and had to be left behind which caused some tears and sadness among the kids.

It was the height of the rain season, and it poured throughout the whole trip. We passed through the cities of Olongapo and Subic Bay where the American Forces still operated a naval base. There was some flooding along the way, but we managed to pass through until about fifty kilometers from our destination and new home.

The heavy rains had washed masses of volcanic ash down the slopes of the mountains, and into the rivers. The mixture of ashes and water turned into a powerful compound that the locals called "lahar." It filled the riverbeds and caused the mud to search for a new path, destroying everything in its way. Whole villages had been washed away, and bridges and roads were damaged by this powerful mudflow.

We had just left a small town, when the road disappeared into a lake of muddy water so large that we could not see the end of it. Only some trees hinted where the road went. We stopped to see if any other cars dared to go any further, but there was just us and the big truck behind us.

Some teenagers sat on top of a wall by the road, and so I rolled down my window and asked them if the road was passable.

Asia at Last

"Sure, man, no problem," was their casual reply. I was not so sure I could trust their judgment, but, on the other hand we had nowhere else to go, and it started getting dark.

I muttered, "In Jesus' name," put the Chevy into "drive," and eased into the water ahead of us. For a while all seemed fine, but then I noticed that the water got deeper, and there was a strong current from the side that threatened to push us off what was left of the road. Soon, the car's mufflers were submerged and started blubbering like an outboard engine. The water started slowly seeping through the doors, and the carpets became soaked.

Trying to stay on the road became harder and harder, especially when there was no point of reference like a fence or trees. And then it happened. Right in front of us the blacktop had been torn away by the mud current, and the front end of the car dipped into a crater, taking us all by surprise. The kids screamed, the dogs barked, and Cathy and I started praying in tongues! The water had reached the bottom of the windshield, and the engine quit with a big hiss. Steam rose from the submerged hood, and we were stuck at an angle of forty-five degrees.

Now what! I saw some men sitting in a tree nearby, and I rolled down my window again and shouted to them to help us. Their reply was not helpful at all, "Your car too big, man, cannot push!"

Then one of them said something so stupid that I almost laughed, except I had this sense that somehow his words were prophetic:

"Just start you engine and drive on!"

What was he talking about? The engine was totally submerged, and there was no way it could start up. But I was desperate and thought it could not hurt to try. I turned the key in the ignition, and the six-liter V8 started with a mighty roar! Somehow we made it up the other side of the crater, and after that the water level slowly receded. The truck behind us was able to negotiate around the crater and followed us all the way to our little house on the hill.

It was dark by the time we got there. We quickly unloaded the truck and were so exhausted that we all slept on mattresses on the floor.

169

The next morning I got up and opened the hood of our Chevy. I was shocked at what I saw. The whole engine was covered with a thick layer of mud, including the air filter. That engine should not have been able to run like that, but it had, and I understood that we had just witnessed a miracle of God.

* * *

Our little house on the hill was not much to look at, and only had two bedrooms. The covered front-porch became our dining room, and the older boys slept in a simple hut right next to the house. The walls and the wooden floor of the house were infested with termites, and the door frame to our bedroom felt like a sponge underneath several coats of paint.

But the view was priceless. Behind us were lush green hills, and in front we had a view of the South China Sea. There was no fence or gate anywhere, the entire hill was our backyard that we shared with some goats that came to graze there from time to time. There were large patches of volcanic ash everywhere that looked like white sand, and the dirt path up the hill became hard to negotiate when it rained.

I had set free the three eagles that we had brought from Manila, and they seemed to adjust well to life in the wild. In the beginning they kept close to the house, and when I threw up a small fish, one of them would swoop down and catch it before it hit the ground. After several weeks they hardly came close, but we could see them soar in the clear blue sky. I had asked some of our neighbors, and they told me that they had not seen any eagles in the region for several years. So whenever I saw one in the sky I knew it was one of "mine," and that became a great way to close my season as the "bird-man."

* * *

The older kids adjusted well to being home-schooled, and enjoyed the freedom of being outside most of the day, exploring their surroundings, and taking a swim down by the beach just a mile away. On the other hand, they had no friends, and there was nothing else to do. We must have been the only foreigners in the whole region, since all other missionaries had fled from the volcano when it became active.

Never before had we been so isolated. There was no telephone service whatsoever, and I had to drive two hours to Olongapo whenever I wanted to make an international call or send a fax! Sister Ofie from the New Testament Faith Mission came once a month by bus to bring our mail from the post box in Manila. Shopping was very limited in Iba, with only the market and one small grocery store. There was no international banking, and no automatic teller machines, and we were forced to drive down to Manila about once a month to get money and supplies.

We had sent out many fax messages and letters to anyone we could think of to come and help with us with the refugees. The government and other NGOs had started to work in the camp as well, but in these first few weeks the situation there was pitiful.

The Aeta were displaced in more ways than one. Not only had they lost their homes and fields, but also the land of their ancestors, as well as the favor of the spirits they had worshiped. We heard stories that some had offered water buffaloes into the crater of Mt. Pinatubo when it first started becoming active. Now their gods had forsaken them.

Having lived in small groups in the hills all their lives, they now felt like caged animals in a situation that was totally foreign to their culture and lifestyle. They sat all day under a blue plastic canvas stretched over a few bamboo poles with nothing to do but wait for the meager food rations provided by the government. Since it was still rain season, the whole camp soon turned into a field of mud, and the sanitary conditions were terrible. Soon diarrhea and other diseases spread like wildfire, and within one week over sixty babies had died of the measles. Volunteer medical teams arrived with vaccinations, and others taught basic hygiene, or dug wells.

Soon we had teams come from Malaysia, Germany, Switzerland, Sweden, as well as the U.S. Besides bringing food, medicines and clothing, some came to do Bible studies and programs for the children. Everyone was amazed to find the refugees wide open for the Gospel. They were in a spiritual vacuum, with no hope for the future, and they soaked up the message of God's kingdom like dry sponges.

One day I brought a group of American pastors who wanted to preach the gospel. We simply stood in the shade of a tree, and while we sang some songs a group of around sixty Negritos began to gather. We had brought a young girl from one of the churches in Manila to be our interpreter. We asked her to introduce the visiting pastors, and then let them speak, but everything turned out quite differently. When she began to talk to the group, the Holy Spirit came on her, and she began to preach the salvation story. After five minutes all hands went up, and when we asked her what was going on she said sheepishly, "They all want to become Christians now!"

She led them through a simple prayer, and then began to preach again, while the rest of us just looked at each other. This time she got real fiery in her exhortations, and ten minutes later, all hands went up again. "What is it now?" we asked.

"Oh, I told them about the Holy Spirit, and they all want to be filled now."

We really did not know what else to do, so we joined her in prayer by laying hands on them and asking the Holy Spirit to fill them. If I remember correctly, almost everyone began to speak in tongues immediately. The whole event had not lasted more than twenty minutes, and here we were confronted with a newly born church of about sixty believers ready to be baptized!

I will never forget one particular evening when I entered the camp after dark. As I walked down the main pathway, I could hear people praying in one sector, while there was singing in another corner, and further in someone was teaching the Bible to a group gathered around a fire. I looked up at the star-filled sky and would not have been surprised to see some smiling angels. It was the closest thing to revival I had ever witnessed, and I was totally overcome with thankfulness for an awesome God.

Within three months we were aware of at least six new churches among the Aeta, and we called in pastors from all different denominations in the area to come and pastor them.

* * *

Another story of visiting pastors stands out in my memory, and I am sure in theirs as well. Two dear brothers from the mission in Sweden that stood behind Sven and the NTFM came to visit, and Björn and I had driven to Manila in the old Suburban to pick them up. Because of the mudflows continuously destroying roads and bridges, we were forced to take a detour of several hours around the northern coast of Luzon. Our trip there went well, and we were able to connect with our Swedish visitors.

We drove right back, hoping to get to Zambales shortly after nightfall. Well, our Suburban had different plans and shortly after leaving Metro Manila the engine quit for the first time. We found a mechanic who took a look and he was able to get us on the road again, just to repeat the same maneuver an hour later. It was some mysterious problem with the carburetor, but nobody was able to tell us for sure, and after some adjustments the engine would fire up again.

By now we were already several hours behind schedule, and it was close to midnight when we pulled into another small town. Right in the center the engine backfired loudly and quit yet again. I let the truck coast as far as possible, looking for an auto repair shop. We rolled to a stop right in front of a building with many red neon signs, and to my absolute horror it turned out to be the town brothel! Several "working girls" came out to welcome the new customers, and I wish I could have captured the faces of our two pastors as this whole scenario unfolded.

It took us awhile to get through to the girls that we were looking for a place to sleep without their company, and they were very understanding.

That night, Björn and I shared a small room with a narrow bed and a red light bulb hanging from the ceiling, but I was too exhausted to even wonder what he might be thinking about this strange setup.

At seven in the morning, one of the girls knocked on our door, and let me know that she had found a mechanic who was waiting outside. While I watched the man take our carburetor apart for the fifth time on this trip, our dear guests had a leisurely breakfast with the whole staff of the establishment, sharing the gospel of Jesus, and praying with several of them. As we continued our trip, they told me some of the heartbreaking stories of several of the girls that had been lured away from their villages with the promise of a well-paid job as a chamber-maid in a hotel. We all realized that this had been a divine appointment, and it revealed the heart of the Father for the plight of the poor and the lost.

* * *

It was in the midst of this in-breaking of God's kingdom that we were immersed into an adventure that would shape our work in Asia for many years to come. Back in Switzerland, the Vineyard Bern was confronted with the reality that more and more young people wanted discipleship training and to become involved in cross-cultural ministry. To keep them from running off to the various para-church organizations, Martin asked us to partner with them in a discipleship training school right here in Zambales.

We called it the DMC which stood for "Discipleship, Missions, and Church-planting." The idea was to have classroom teaching for three weeks, followed by one week of practical involvement after each of the three blocks. At the very end the whole school would do a four week outreach in Cambodia.

Setting up the school with our limited avenues of communication turned out to be a logistical nightmare, but in the end it all worked out, and we launched our first school in November 1991. We had rented several houses at the Sand Valley Beach Resort as dorms. There was also a small hall with an adjacent Kitchen that doubled as a class room and dining room.

We had wanted the school to be multicultural, and this first one turned out to be quite a mix. There were eight students from Switzerland, one American, ten Filipinos, and six Cambodians from California.

I was in way over my head, and looking back, I realize it was just the grace of God that got us through that first school. For every week and topic we had another teacher, and often I had to drive down to Manila to pick them up from the airport. Among others, we had Martin come from Bern, and Mike from California. I got to teach some classes as well, and my days were full. We always started the morning at six with prayer and worship. After breakfast we had school until lunchtime. The afternoons were usually free, and there was a personal study time in the evenings.

It did not take long for some cultural differences to surface among the students, and I still consider that the strongest learning aspect of the whole program. We had made sure that the cultures and nationalities were well mixed in the various houses, and it was interesting to see the different cultures cope with their differences.

When the Westerners became upset they would shout at each other and slam doors, while the Filipinos would withdraw and pout, not speaking to anyone. Our two Cambodian young men would take their differences down to the beach for a quick fist fight! I remember spending many hours in the role of a mediator, trying to make peace. Everyone learned a lot about culture in those days, and in the end we all parted as friends, and quite a few are still in touch with each other today.

For their practical outreach times, the students served in the refugee camp, and some actually lived there for some time. The New Testament Faith Mission had built a simple bamboo church with the help of donations from Switzerland, and some of the students were involved in the actual construction.

We also had lots of fun together, with numerous beach parties for birthdays, Christmas and New Year, and some of the greatest fish barbecues I can remember. Those were the times when Cathy and the kids got to be involved and interact with the students. Every day I would bring one or two students home for lunch and family time.

When Martin came to teach, he told us about some exciting developments going on in Cambodia, and asked if I was still interested in going there. Was I interested? Even though I was extremely thankful for all our experiences in the Philippines, my longing to go to Cambodia had grown into a burning desire. The upcoming outreach to Cambodia would also serve as a scouting trip for me to see if the time was ripe for us to move there as a family.

Land of Broken Hearts

Around 1990 Cambodia started to open up its borders for certain government agencies and humanitarian organizations to come in and help rebuild the war-torn country.

In the years just previously, the Vietnamese occupation force had overpowered the Khmer Rouge, and brought some semblance of peace and stability to the country. Though traditionally the Khmer people hated the Vietnamese, they had recognized them to be the lesser evil after the holocaust they had endured under Khmer Rouge rule. Vietnam had installed a puppet president and withdrawn their troops, but now the United Nations stepped in and embarked on the greatest peacekeeping mission in their history – to facilitate the first democratic elections in Cambodia.

In his story about prewar Cambodia, Todd Burke had mentioned several men that were close to him, and some had become elders and leaders of the church that emerged. One of them was a man by the name of Sophal Ung.

Sophal's story is one of the most remarkable tales of a overcomer that I have ever heard. Through a series of supernatural events, Sophal and his family reunited after the war and managed to escape into Thailand, from where they were repatriated to the U.S. Sophal lived there for seven years and raised his children by himself after his wife died of cancer. He had a strong desire to return to his country and serve his people so he connected with some of Todd's old friends, Mike and Martin and they traveled to the capital, Phnom Penh. There, God opened up doors for them by connecting them with some government officials who promised to help them with a building and other assistance in order to establish a base. Sophal then began to plant a mother church in Phnom Penh.

* * *

The twenty-five DMC students and I arrived in Phnom Penh in February 1992. We had flown from Manila to Bangkok. The flight from there to Phnom Penh demonstrated how fragile the whole situation still was. Since part of the country was still in the grip of the Khmer Rouge rebels, the twin turboprop plane did not fly the direct route, but made a long detour along the coast of Thailand and Cambodia, and then angled back towards the Cardamom Mountains, and down into Potchentong airport.

In the arrival hall we were greeted by Sophal and some of his coworkers. We had never met before, but he walked right up to me and said, "You are Norbert – I saw you in a dream last night." Wow. What an introduction! I quickly learned that Sophal was a man deeply in touch with the supernatural, constantly hearing from God through dreams and visions.

They brought us on the back of a big truck to a five-story building in the heart of the city. The building used to be a Catholic school built in the fifties, and over the entrance hung a big sign that said "Global Network" in English and Khmer.

I could not believe how different Cambodia was from the Philippines in almost any aspect. It seemed so much more "Asian", with Buddhist temples and signs with a squiggly, very exotic looking script. Yet, here and there you could see the European influence in some of the buildings, a reminder of French colonialism.

The level of poverty was even below that of the rural Philippines, and we saw beggars and street children everywhere. The whole infrastructure of the city was far from rebuilt, with roads and buildings in dire need of repairs, and a very erratic supply of water and electricity. Very few people spoke English, or any other language besides Khmer. Communication became a real problem, with very few interpreters available, since the Khmer Rouge had killed almost everyone who had spoken a foreign language.

The Global Network building was home to a number of missionary families; some local families from the church that met on the fifth floor, as well as about thirty street children. The classrooms were used for teaching English, a small medical clinic, a sewing factory, a work shop, and as dorms for the orphans and teams like us.

As an introduction to the recent history of the country, we were given a tour of the two main attractions in the city. One was called "Toul Sleng," another former school building, which had been used as the main interrogation and torture center of the Khmer Rouge regime. Words cannot express the amount of grief and suffering that were represented in that place. Besides seeing all the torture equipment used for the killing of thousands upon thousands of innocent men, women, and children, there were halls filled with the photographs of the poor victims taken just before their execution. On a wall in the entrance was a large map of Cambodia made entirely of human skulls, and the rivers drawn with human blood. No one that ever visited that place could possibly be prepared for such a display of cruelty and agony.

The "killing fields" were the other main attraction, just outside the city. As you walked on paths between open mass graves, remnants of bone and rotten clothing were seen everywhere. Crude signs near each grave explained the number of skeletons found there, and the means by which they had been executed. The bones of over 17,000 people had since been buried elsewhere, but about 5,000 skulls were on display in a tall Buddhist stupa. A closer look revealed the crude way of execution used by the Khmer Rouge: death by a blow to the back of the head with a garden hoe.

Sophal told us how he himself had stood in a long line of Christians and other "enemies of the revolution" waiting for their execution by the hands of two teenage soldiers armed with hoes. The line of the condemned was so long that they had stood in the blistering sun all day. By sundown, Sophal was only a few individuals away from his execution, when an army commander came riding on a horse, asking the executioners how many they had already killed that day. Their answer was, "Around one thousand," and the commander told them to call it a day and to continue the next morning. That night, Sophal managed to escape from the prison camp.

In the following days, months, and years we heard so many similar heartbreaking stories that could fill many books. In 1984, a Hollywood movie with the title "The Killing Fields," was released telling the true story of the New York Times reporter Sidney Schanberg and his local photographer, Dith Pran, being caught in the midst of the Khmer Rouge takeover. The movie very graphically displays some of the atrocities and the suffering of the people at that time. Most of the Cambodian people we asked had seen that movie, and they all agreed: The reality was much worse than what the movie portrayed. For once it seems that even Hollywood could not exaggerate the true events.

The first few weeks in Cambodia were totally overwhelming and left me drained both emotionally, as well as spiritually. In the midst of that, I tried to hear from God if this was really the time to move here with Cathy and the kids. One late afternoon I set aside some time to seek the Lord about that on top of the roof of our building, where I had a great view over the city, and on the horizon I could see big, black storm clouds building up.

"Lord, I believe that you have called us to this place, but I need to know if this is the right time for us to move here!"

As I spoke those words, something very scary and unusual happened. For just an instant the large black clouds took on the shape of a huge and frightening looking evil spirit. I gasped at the sight of this, and immediately I heard the Lord speak to my heart, "This is what you are up against. These spirits have ruled and reigned here for thousands of years, and they are not intimidated by anyone not willing to lay down their lives!"

I was reminded of the verses in Revelation chapter twelve, where it says, "And they have defeated him by the blood of the Lamb and by their testimony. And they did not love their lives so much that they were afraid to die."[4]

The message could not have been any clearer, "If you are not willing to lay down your life, then don't bother coming at all!"

It took me awhile to digest the truth in that challenge, but in the end I was able to say "yes", and that settled it: We were moving to Cambodia!

＊＊＊

Those few weeks in Cambodia went like a whirlwind and left me in a flurry of new challenges and impressions. The time had come to say goodbye to my students, for we would all go home from there. Some we would see again, and with others we lost touch over the years.

I could not wait to get home to Cathy and the children, and tell them the news of our upcoming move. Little did I know that they had lived through their own personal drama while I was gone.

When Cathy told me the story of what had happened I felt so bad for leaving them stranded in such a remote place, but thankfully God had been merciful to us.

Around our bungalow in Zambales were several tall trees, and one of them was a cashew nut tree. Cathy had watched the gardener take the nuts in their shell and roast them in the fire he made when he burned the leaves. Since we all love nuts, Cathy decided to speed up that process, by roasting the nuts in her oven. What she did not know was that the fumes released during that process are poisonous, and that she was highly allergic to them. Soon her body reacted in several different ways. The glands in her neck swelled up, and so did her ears. She had itchy skin in several places, but worst of all were the severe heart palpitations.

Our son Björn understood more than the other kids how serious this was, and laid hands on his Mom and prayed for her. She did get better, and at some point she found a way to the little clinic in Iba where she received some antihistamine pills. It took quite some time for all the symptoms to subside, but we found out later on that she could easily have died during this ordeal.

[4]Revelation 12:11 (NLTse)

* * *

Before our move to Cambodia we had our first three-month furlough after four years in Asia. The church in Bern had set aside a certain amount from our monthly support for that purpose, and so we drove to Manila to catch the very long flight to Zürich.

It is hard to express what one feels when coming back after a long time to what once was your home. On one hand there is that familiarity to things from the past, but then there is this strange detachment to your own culture that keeps you from truly feeling at home. All of a sudden you see the people of your own race and culture with different eyes, and even though you look and sound just like them, you no longer feel a part of them.

This particular phenomenon would become more complex with each following subsequent trip "home," until you come to a place where you really don't know where home is anymore. This disorientation can become a huge problem to one's personality and identity, or it can turn into this liberating revelation:

This earth is really not our home anyway, and in the meantime, home is where God is leading us, and where we can be together with our loved ones.

But it took many years for this truth to sink in, and these first trips back to Europe were quite disconcerting for me. How much more so to the mind of a child? I often wonder how this has shaped the minds and personalities of our children, and there were times when I felt overcome with guilt. Then I remembered that it was God Himself who had given me this calling, and I had to learn once again to trust Him with my loved -ones.

Despite that we had some wonderful times enjoying the beauty of Switzerland, Germany, and all the way up to Sweden. It was wonderful to connect with family and friends everywhere, to enjoy familiar food, and the wonderful long evenings of the European summer. We visited and spoke in many different churches, sharing our stories, and trying to get others interested in this great adventure we call "missions."

The responses we received from different parts of the Body of Christ were quite interesting, and sometimes quite alarming. Some would treat us like "war heroes" coming home. There was a true sense of respect and admiration, but it raised a wall between us.

"It is so great that you have this calling, but I have not been called," is what we heard often, and I tried with limited success to drive home the point that as believers and followers of Jesus we have all been called to serve Him – wherever that might be!

It also became clear that for many churches, inviting a missionary to come and speak, and give him a good offering, took care of their responsibility to be involved in the evangelization of the world, for at least another year. Occasionally, we would meet someone who became agitated and almost angry at us, since they felt the need for cross-cultural ministry was just a waste of time since, after all, there was now a church in every nation of the world. As we know, even many years later, nothing could be further from the truth!

* * *

Our furlough was overshadowed by some bad news that reached us while spending time with friends in Sweden: Our house in Zambales had been broken into, and we were robbed of many valuables, such as computer, sewing machine, guitar, tools, and other things. Not being there for three months was just too great a temptation for some of the local thieves to ignore, and the police were not really interested in finding the perpetrators.

Again it was time to say good-bye and begin the long journey back. We had visited our friends in the Black Forest where we had stored many of our belongings, and retrieved a number of things that we wanted to bring back to Asia, such as photo albums, Legos, and other toys. The airline allowed us to check in our luggage in Bern, and though I knew we must have been over our weight limit, no one mentioned it, and I thought they simply had been generous to us. But when we reached the counter at the Zurich airport, the representative presented us with a bill over 1,500 Swiss Francs for excess luggage!

I explained to her that we did not have that kind of money, and that they should have warned us about the cost when we checked in our luggage earlier. After explaining that we were missionaries returning to the field, she looked up from her computer screen and said, "Well, I suppose we could make an exception," and tore up the bill.

* * *

We returned home to Zambales in the midst of the typhoon season, and now we experienced reverse culture shock again. After the clean and efficient environment in Switzerland, coming back to the Philippines was a shock to the system, though not as bad as the first time. Now we had four months to wind things down, and prepare for our move to Cambodia.

Just like four years earlier, we were now faced with a number of decisions in regard to finding homes for our pets, deciding what to sell, give away, or bring. Since we knew how hard it would be to buy new things in Cambodia, we decided to ship most of our belongings in a twenty-foot container.

By November 1992 we were ready to go. The kids did not have many friends to say good-bye to, but it was heartbreaking for them to have to part with their beloved dogs and cats. Cathy was pregnant with our 6th child, and we prayed this move would not trigger another miscarriage.

The work in the refugee camp continued to be carried on by various international groups, and a good number of local churches, including our friends at the New Testament Faith Mission. By now, some of the Aeta families had already been relocated to different areas, and some had left on their own to return to their home region to find a possible place to start a new village.

* * *

Our move to Phnom Penh truly marked the beginning of a chapter that was totally new to all of us. We had moved from a little house on a hill, surrounded by mountains and sea, to a five-story former school building right in the heart of one of the poorest cities in the world! We moved into a three room apartment on the third floor that had been occupied by another missionary family who had returned to the U.S. just a few days before our arrival.

The biggest difference was that while we had been quite alone and isolated in Zambales, we were now part of a large, international team, all living under the same roof. We ate most of our meals in a common dining area, together with some Khmer staff and a growing number of street children. We now had regular team meetings and prayer times.

On Sunday mornings, the building turned into a beehive of activity, with several hundred people showing up for church on the fifth floor. Several times throughout the morning, the big truck was sent to a large slum area near the Tonle Basac River to pick up folks who wanted to come to the meeting. They were packed like cattle, and each trip could haul sixty people, or more.

These were the poorest of the poor, and many of them were illiterate, but they had a hunger for spiritual things. Many had become believers through the ongoing work there by a team from the church. Of course, it helped that many of them were there when one among them was raised from the dead. When that sort of thing happens you don't need much advertisement.

It had happened several months before our arrival, and I can only recall the story from the many witnesses who could not stop talking about it. "Uncle Cheu," as we called him, must have been in his late fifties, or early sixties and lived in the slum with his wife. He had been sick for some time. Almost everyone in that age group seemed to be suffering from the after effects of the years of war during Pol Pot's regime and the ordeal in the labor camps which followed.

One evening Cheu simply passed away. All the neighbors heard the wails of his wife and came to comfort her, and even a Buddhist priest came by to pronounce him dead, saying he would arrange for the body to be picked up for cremation the following day.

It just so happened that both Cheu and his wife had begun to believe in Christ just a few weeks previously. The wife was mostly illiterate and had never read the Bible herself, but she must have heard the stories of Jesus and Paul raising people from the dead, because she decided she was going to pray for that to happen!

All night long she sat by the body of her husband and prayed. After eight or nine hours it happened. Cheu opened his eyes, sat up, and proclaimed to his astonished spouse, "I am feeling great, and I am hungry for some breakfast!" I would have imagined that his wife came running to the church, shouting from the top of her lungs, "Hallelujah – he is risen from the dead!"

But that is not at all what happened. It seems like the church did not hear about this until days, or even weeks later. She was not nearly as surprised as we would have been in the light of such a miracle. After all, Jesus had said that we would see even greater things than he had done, if we would believe.

This is what struck me repeatedly about the Cambodian believers: They may have lacked in education and knowledge, but they had a child-like faith that would put all of us Western believers to shame. In the years to come they would prove this to me again and again.

∗ ∗ ∗

The church meetings upstairs were quite an adjustment from what we were used to, especially for Cathy and the kids. It was very loud, and the hall was very hot and had no air-conditioning. People were walking around throughout the meeting, and children and babies played unattended. Obviously, the poor parents could not afford disposable diapers, so the babies would relieve themselves on the tile floor. The fact that everything was in a language totally unknown to us made matters even worse.

The meetings were very, very long, with a minimum of three hours. Needless to say, our children soon hated going there, and we would allow them to stay at home more and more. From time to time one of us missionaries would speak, or we had a visiting pastor preach, and that made all the difference in the world to us.

There was one international fellowship in town, but we were committed to serve Sophal and the churches he oversaw. As we met as a team to discuss needs and problems, we realized that we would be most productive if each one would be allowed to work in the area of their expertise, gifting, and calling. That sounded really good, and is certainly a healthy approach, but the problem is that there will always be things that nobody really wants to do.

My biggest wish was to help train leaders, but there was no infrastructure in place for this, and I would have to create my own. In the meantime, I was put in charge of teams coming through. So I took care of the planning, the logistics, and the actual program of quite a number of short -term teams passing though. Some came with groups like YWAM[5], and others were sent out by a local church. Some came to serve the poor, or the children, and others came to "preach the gospel." Those were usually the most problematic. They asked us to call people together, and then they would preach to them for many hours on end. I would stand on the sidelines and watch our Khmer believers politely listening to message after message that went right over their heads.

Then there were the medical teams. Many Christian doctors like to donate time, energy and medication for charity in the so-called Third World nations, and there are a good number of organizations facilitating these kind of outreach programs.

At one point we were visited by a dentist from the U.S. who had come with a small team to serve the poor. We went to some of the poorest villages, and set up a canvas chair that served as dentist chair either under a tree, or inside a cottage.

---

[5]Youth With A Mission

Since they could not possibly do elaborate fillings and root canals, they were restricted to cleaning teeth and extractions. It was often my job to hold the flashlight on the offending tooth, while the dear doctor did his job. My knees turned soft more than once, but I got to carry home the trophy of the day, a bucket full of bloody teeth and tooth fragments. I kept thanking God that I had not been called into the medical mission field!

There was one team that touched my heart in a way that I did not understand until many years later. They had come for two weeks, for one purpose only: to pray for the nation and to lift up the Lord through worship. They hardly ever left the meeting room assigned to them, and for hours we could hear the sound of their worship echo through every part of the building.

They left without having brought one single soul to believe in Christ. They had not given food to the poor, or spent much time playing with the orphans and street children. In terms of visible fruit, they had nothing to show, and yet I believe with all my heart that they were more effective in changing the world around them than any of the other teams. Back then, I just thought they were "cool", but many years later the importance of their ministry hit me and would become the focal point of our involvement here in Asia.

* * *

On a family level, the first 18 months in Cambodia were tough, to say the least. Of course we resumed home schooling as it was our only option, and the kids were confined to our cramped apartment for most of the day. The only other alternative for them was to play in the courtyard with some of the other kids, and that was it. There was no mall where they could hang out, nor was there a place where they could do sports and get some fresh air.

Whenever we went out as a family, we found ourselves surrounded by beggars, or fascinated mothers who got a thrill out of pinching the cheeks of blond toddlers. No matter where we went, we attracted attention, and soon the children resented going outside at all.

One day I decided to take our older kids to a public park to fly a kite. Soon we were surrounded by numerous kids who wanted to touch and help, until it was utterly impossible to do anything, and we returned home frustrated and with a broken kite.

When we were offered a small parcel of land in a very rural area outside the city, we bought it, and had it fenced in with bamboo for some privacy. We planted some trees and often went there on weekends just to enjoy nature. There were also some trails we could walk on, something which was not possible in many places because of the abundant land mines left from the war. We even heard of landowners protecting their land with mines, because it was cheaper than building a fence.

Years later we found out that we really did not own that parcel of land, since the title-deed was bogus. The fact that we had bought it from a local pastor illustrates the level of corruption even among believers.

Early on in her pregnancy Cathy showed similar signs to her two previous pregnancies. The local hospitals had such a bad reputation that we found it hard to trust their services. We urgently needed help. At that time, the UN forces were still in the country, and the German delegation had set up and staffed a field hospital at the outskirts of Phnom Penh. Without hesitation or asking for payment they offered us their help and treatment. Since there were a number of female UN soldiers they even had a German gynecologist at hand.

When it looked like Cathy might lose this child as well, they came with a UN ambulance and took her to the field hospital for observation. After a few days she stabilized and was allowed to come home.

Since Leif's home birth in the Philippines was such a great experience for her, Cathy really wanted to have another baby at home, but where could we find a good midwife?

About one month before her due date, we received a surprising fax message from our friend Dennis in Manila, the husband of Diane, the very midwife who had delivered Leif five years before. He wrote that he planned a trip to Vietnam, and could pay us a visit on the way. He also asked if there was anything he could bring for us.

I sent a message back to him and wrote half-jokingly:

"We are having another child, why don't you bring Diane?"

His reply came only hours later and got us all excited:

"OK, we can both come, but are only able to stay for three days!"

That was exactly what Cathy had asked for in her heart, and when we found out we just knew everything was going to be great with this birth.

And so it was. Dennis and Diane arrived in Phnom Penh one week before Cathy's due date. We spent the day sight-seeing (which meant going to the killing fields...), and that night Cathy went into labor and gave birth to our daughter Eja Christine right in our bedroom. We ended up having another midwife there as well, plus the UN doctor on standby in case of an emergency.

That story signifies and demonstrates the reality of those years in Cambodia: We were covered by the grace of God.

It was a time of great contradictions in my heart. On one hand, I struggled with the difficult circumstances of living in a war-torn country, seeing my family suffering in the confinement of a very simple and highly restricted lifestyle, and yet my heart was bursting with the joy of fulfillment that only comes when you know that you are where God wants you to be. That joy would be tested repeatedly in the years to come, but I know that we would not have lasted there for long without it.

When I went to the German embassy to apply for a passport for Eja, I stirred up the righteous indignation of the clerk processing the papers. When he saw that this was our sixth child he looked up from the application form, and with color darkening his face he all but screamed at me:

"Living in Cambodia, with six children..., are you out of your mind?"

I was so shocked by his outburst that I did not know what to say, and as I drove my motorcycle back to our building I thought that just maybe he was right. But then an incredible joy rose from deep within me as I realized that this was the safest place in the world for us to live, sheltered under the wings of the God who had called us there.

These wings proved to be real, time and time again. They were real when Björn contracted some mysterious rheumatic fever, and when Nils got sick with hepatitis.

After about one year and a half, the UN pulled out of Cambodia, and as a result the prices for housing dropped significantly. We finally could afford to move out of the city and the big building, and were able to move into a bungalow with a yard in a suburb called Toul Kok.

The back of our house connected with a police station, which made us feel kind of safe, but as it turned out it was quite hazardous to live there.

Often the police officers were drunk and started firing their weapons for no apparent reason.

One evening our oldest daughter Carina set the table in the dining area of our house. That particular part of the house was only covered by a corrugated iron roof, and as she was about to leave the room, a bullet tore through the sheet metal and hit the wall less than a foot from her head. She has kept that bullet as a reminder of God's grace.

There seemed to be gunfire of some kind almost every night, and sometimes in the daytime as well. At first we would wake up at the sound of it, wondering if we were in any kind of danger, but after some months we barely took notice anymore.

Sometimes we could see one of our neighbors standing on the flat roof of his house firing long bursts with his Russian made AK-47 at approaching storm clouds, convinced he could keep them at bay.

Another stray bullet barely missed Lars' leg as he was playing in our driveway one day, just to remind us that we were still covered.

* * *

Crime was an ever-present reality in those days, and the level of corruption was unimaginable. The sufferings of many years of war and the constant fight for survival had created a culture of dishonesty and deception. Not only were the authorities totally overwhelmed by this, but more often than not they were part of it.

When the UN pulled out they sold hundreds of vehicles they had brought into the country, mainly vans, trucks, and four-wheel drives, all painted white. The Cambodian government had expected that the UN would simply turn these vehicles over to them, but instead they were sold to non-government organizations for rock bottom prices. Even Global Network was able to purchase a van and an Isuzu jeep for Sophal.

The government was so angry they were left out of the deal, that they hired local thugs to steal back many of the vehicles. They were then re-painted and showed up around government institutions. This would happen in bright daylight, with a thief walking up to a missionary or NGO worker as they unlocked their parked vehicle, pointing a gun at them, and holding out the other hand for the keys. Every mission or aid organization lost vehicles in that way, and nothing could be done.

Sophal, who was well known by some of the current leaders in government, was often called in as an advisor, which was quite amazing, considering that they all knew he was a Christian who opposed any form of corruption. One day, as he met with some of the ministers he jokingly asked them if they were going to steal his vehicle as well. The answer revealed what everyone already knew: "You have Isuzu – we only take Toyota Land Cruiser!"

We had bought an old Toyota Carina from a man at church who had used it as a taxi for many years. We figured that no one would want to steal such an old car, which was true. One morning, as I backed out of our driveway, Björn pointed at the front of our car and yelled, "Dad, your lights are gone!"

"What do you mean, my lights are gone?" I got out of the car just to discover that both sets of headlights, plus the indicator lights had been removed! This was just unbelievable. Our yard was surrounded by a high fence in the front, and a wall spiked with broken glass on the sides. We had hired a night guard, and I had bought a German shepherd to help guard, and yet someone had waltzed in at night, and had taken the time to quietly remove my lights? I just would have to get new ones, since

I already knew that there was no help to be had from the police, even though their station was right behind our house.

I went to every shop I could imagine looking for another set of lights, but they were not available anywhere, until I was directed to a place which sold stolen articles. There they were, and I was able to buy my own lights back for the bargain prize of only 150 dollars!

Electricity turned out to be another sore spot in our existence. Twice a month, a man would come and collect the electric bill, which was a handwritten piece of paper. We already knew that foreigners had to pay about triple of the regular rate, but our bill would just sky-rocket and one month we ended up paying over 500 dollars for only five to six hours of power every day. I knew something fishy was going on, and decided to get to the bottom of it.

Rather than having a meter at the house, there was a wooden shack at the end of the street where everyone's meter was mounted on a wall. So one evening, we shut off all our lights and appliances, and I stomped over to the shack and asked the guard there to let me see my meter. He consulted a chart, and then pointed to a meter that was churning away so fast the numbers were blurred.

"Aha – got you!" Then I explained in broken Khmer that we were not using any electricity right now, and that obviously, we were being ripped off! To which he just shrugged his shoulders and fired back:

"You no pay, I shut off your line!"

The next day I went to see our land lord to tell him about our problem. He too just shrugged his shoulders, and said with a pained expression on his face: "This is Cambodia, there is no justice here."

As it turned out there was no one to complain to, and none of the authorities would help a foreigner. But, he suggested, I could hire a guard to patrol the street at night and remove any unauthorized hookup to our line. That little remark confirmed what I had feared: We were paying the bill for our whole street!

A few days later, I talked to a Swiss friend about this situation. He was an electrician and had a grand idea. Since the power was so sporadic anyway, everyone that could afford it had a generator for lights and re-frigerators when the power from the city was off. That meant that our generator was feeding the whole street as well. His idea was to adjust our generator to put out 360 Volts, instead of 220, and that would fry all the appliances connected to our line illegally.

In my mind I had visions of exploding light bulbs, smoking refriger-ators and sizzling television sets, and I was sorely tempted to have him come and make the necessary adjustments. Then I was reminded that we had not come here to wage war with the people, and I knew that this would end any chance of them ever opening their hearts to the gospel. Instead I did what I should have done all along. For the first time in my life I earnestly prayed, "Lord, you give me justice!"

Our next electric bill turned out to be considerably lower, and it seemed like the thieves had found another victim from whom to steal power. Another lesson learned.

* * *

In the midst of all these exciting developments, I finally got a chance to do what I really had on my heart. It started with teaching one-month courses to some of the aspiring leaders in the church, and I was overwhelmed by their hunger and ability to receive and believe everything they were taught. I found myself praying hard before every session that the Lord would keep me from saying things that were not right or true, for I knew my students would trust my words without question.

Then, one day, Sophal came to me with a clear assignment. He wanted me to open a one-year training school preparing potential leaders for ministry in the many new churches he was planting all over the country. He wanted me to take them through the Bible as well as prepare them for the practical aspects of pastoring churches of new believers.

I was excited and eager to get started – this was what I had come for! Sophal hand-picked the students himself, eleven women and twelve men. Among them were Uncle Cheu and his wife, and I was thrilled to be able to teach them, but at the same time I was wondering what that would be like. After all, it is not every day that you get to teach someone raised from the dead!

After the first day of classes, I found myself facing a real dilemma. I realized that their level of education was so low that I was not able to use any of my material from our discipleship schools, not to mention that some of them were almost totally illiterate.

This became one of the busiest seasons of my life. From 7 to 8 in the morning I studied Khmer with my private tutor at the university. Then I rushed over to Global Network where I taught my students from 8:30 to 12:30 PM. In the afternoons and evenings, I wrote the next lessons for the following day. This went on Monday through Friday for one year.

In most Asian schools of any kind, students learn by repetition and learning by heart. You can walk by a primary school and hear the kids chanting the alphabet or timetables in unison at almost any given time. No one questions what is being taught, and there is no challenge to form your own opinions whatsoever.

Whenever I asked my students anything, they dutifully repeated what I had taught them, but when I challenged them on their own opinions there was no response. I had to do some kind of testing in order to establish that I was getting through to them at all. When I gave them a simple multiple-choice test they did not know what to do, but if I had asked them to quote a certain scripture, most of them were able to do that.

I was constantly hitting walls and borders. For instance when we talked about Moses in Egypt I discovered that most of them had never studied geography in their lives.

"You know, where they have the pyramids…." To which they replied: "What is a pyramid?"

I had to decide what really was important for them to know. After all the main goal was for them to gain a better understanding of the heart of God, and to be able to disciple others in their relationship with God. I did end up buying a large world map, and it was amazing to see their shocked faces when they discovered how small their beloved country was. Every morning for the next few weeks they gathered around that map before I came in the morning, and after some time there was a hole at the spot where Cambodia used to be from all their pointing.

The best parts of the training were the practical outreach times. After three weeks of studying, I would break them up into teams and send them to various villages for a few days of ministry. After they returned, we had one morning of debriefing, and those were my favorite times of the whole program. Listening to their stories was like reading the book of Acts. Because of their childlike faith and trust in God, they experienced pretty much every type of miracle mentioned in the New Testament. They had many stories of physical healings and deliverance from demonic possession, and in one case they even healed the sick pig of the headman of the village they had visited.

One of the stories I remember so well was from the team who went to one particular village where no one wanted to listen to them. Usually people were very open to hear what visitors would have to say, but not in this place. There was an atmosphere of fear and desperation among the people that caused them to deny our students any of the traditional hospitality.

It did not take them long to discover the reason for this strange behavior. For the Khmer people in rural areas, rice means everything. Before the rice can be planted in the fields it is grown in containers until the seedlings are big enough to be transferred. The timing and the weather are very crucial to this process. If the seedlings stay in the pots too long, they die. But they cannot be transferred to the fields until the first rains of the season have softened the ground and flooded the fields.

This particular year, the monsoon rains were late, and the ground was hard and dry after four months of the dry-season, when it usually does not rain at all. The seedlings were overdue to be planted, but the ground was not ready to receive them, and so their whole rice harvest was at risk.

Once our team understood the dilemma of the villagers, they gathered to pray and ask God what they should do. One of the young men felt he had received a word from the Lord, and boldly proclaimed it at the market square where most people could hear him:

"Our God in heaven has seen your plight and will demonstrate his love for you by sending the rains you have longed for. Bring your seedlings out to the fields tomorrow morning at nine, because then it will begin to rain!"

Talk about boldness. I don't know how this man could sleep that night, but the next morning most of the farmers had decided to take him seriously, and transported their seedlings to the fields and waited. Sure enough, around nine o' clock big fat raindrops began to fall, and within minutes the fields were flooded.

The students worked side by side with the villagers all day long, and in the evening had a willing audience to hear more about the God who cared so much for them. That night many decisions were made to follow Jesus.

One day, after about three months of training, Sophal walked into the classroom for a surprise visit. He barely acknowledged me, but quickly looked at each of the students, and then pointed at three of the younger men and ordered, "You, you, and you, come with me now! I need you to pastor some of the new churches in the province."

Turning to me, he added, "Sorry, Norbert, but I cannot wait another nine months, I need them now!"

Sophal had grown into a very apostolic leader, and spent more and more time in various provinces, evangelizing and starting new churches. For him, a church that did not take care of the poor was not a real church, and every church plant was immediately involved in some form of social project. Because of his incredible generosity, Sophal had not only God's favor, but also the favor of many donors in the Western churches.

He received funds and goods from many sources, and I have never seen him misuse anything for his own good. Because his generosity and love for the poor were so spontaneous, he often angered his donors by using gifts differently than intended by them. His philosophy of handling money was very unique, and often misunderstood. Any funds received ended up in the right pocket of his pants, and were referred to as "new money." But whatever was in that pocket for more than three days became "old money" and was moved to the left pocket. "Old money" had to be given to the poor, otherwise there would be no more "new money."

When initially living in the States as a refugee, he had many children and no car. A small church sacrificed greatly by raising money for a good used car for him, for which he was very grateful. But just a few days later, he was visited by a missionary on his way to Mexico who desperately needed a vehicle. Without hesitation, Sophal gave him his car, to the chagrin of the dear folks who had worked so hard to get it for him. The following weekend Sophal was invited to a large church to speak, and after the service the pastor handed him the keys to a brand-new van in the parking lot.

Years later, Sophal received the funds to build a million-dollar church in the heart of Phnom Penh, and many criticized him for that. For me it was just a normal response from God to a heart that would always put the poor before itself.

* * *

It was the summer of 1994, and I had planned a trip to Europe to visit my parents, as well as to visit many churches in Switzerland, Germany, and England. As it turned out, it became my longest trip away from home, six weeks in all, and afterwards I swore to myself to never do that again.

When I visited the Vineyard Bern, I was in for a big surprise. Martin and some of the others on the leadership team had recently been to Toronto to check out the renewal going on at what used to be the Toronto Airport Vineyard. When they had returned to Switzerland they saw the same kind of phenomena breaking out in their church.

When I arrived there, the effects were visible everywhere. At the parking lot of the church office I saw an old friend arrive on his bicycle.

"Hi Phillip," I shouted and walked up to him to give him a hug. As I reached out to put my arm around him, he said, "Don't...," but it was already too late. As soon as I touched him, he started bouncing off like "Tigger," moaning and praising God at the same time.

What on earth...? I had no idea what was going on, but this was just the beginning of a whole string of bizarre encounters. When I took a look at the newly renovated youth room, I witnessed some young guys praying, and one of them was so overcome with joy that he vaulted over the pool table, making sounds like one of our monkeys back home in Phnom Penh.

That evening at a meeting, I saw some young boys standing at the only entrance to the hall, waving at the people trying to get in as if they were pushing something invisible towards them. Many of them fell right there under the power of God, blocking the entrance for others, while the boys giggled at each other.

The worship time was long, and there was a new sense of celebration, with exuberant shouts of praise, not typical of Vineyard meetings. Then, when Martin got up to speak, some people were toying with him, by shouting a loud "Hallelujah," or "Praise God," and every time Martin would jerk and become increasingly more drunk in the Spirit. At some point he just had to sit down at the edge of the stage with a lopsided grin on his face, as the worship continued.

On Sunday afternoon, the church met at a large exhibition hall seating over one thousand people, and the celebration continued. Even before it started, folks would sit in their chairs trembling, jerking, laughing, or "manifesting" in some other way. I remember a Cambodian pastor living in Switzerland getting up on stage to give a testimony. But he was not able to utter a single word, and when people tried to encourage him he just went down as if he had been hit by lightning.

I tried to come to grips with my own emotions as I watched these happenings, not quite sure what to think. Even though things seemed so strange and a bit disconcerting, I did feel a deep sense of peace and God's presence, and I knew it was all right, even though I did not understand what it was all about.

Several friends came and prayed for me, and I was a bit disappointed that there seemed to be nothing happening – or so I thought. There was no uncontrollable urge to twitch or laugh, just a great sense of peace.

When the meeting was finally over, I could hear people shout and laugh all around the parking lot and down at the bus stop, as if we had just left an incredibly awesome party.

The next day I left for England for a series of meetings and the last leg of my journey. I remember having some good meetings there, but nothing came even close to what I had witnessed in Bern.

When I finally landed in Phnom Penh, I was picked up by one of the assistant pastors, since Sophal was in the U.S. at that time. On the way to our home he asked me if I wanted to preach that coming Sunday. Having spoken at over 30 meetings in Europe, I was totally exhausted, and asked if it would be all right if I could wait another week? When I saw the disappointment on his face, I felt a bit guilty and told him I would give a short testimony that coming Sunday.

And so I did, not in the least prepared for what would happen. It was a normal service, with a normal time of worship, but when I got up to tell them about my trip, and some of the things I had witnessed in Bern, I saw them become extremely attentive and intrigued by my account of the move of God there. I could see a growing hunger and desperation in their eyes.

Before I sat down I wanted to say a quick prayer, and so I closed my eyes, but all I could say was, "Holy Spirit, come!"

All I heard was this "whoosh" sound all over the auditorium, and when I opened my eyes, I could not believe what I was seeing. Almost all the three hundred or so listeners were scattered all over the floor, as if knocked down by a huge wave. Then it dawned on me – I had just brought the "Toronto Blessing" to this church!

Feeling a bit wobbly myself, I sat down on the edge of the stage and watched with amazement how God seemed to move through the ranks, touching people here and there. Some began to moan and cry, while others fell into fits of laughter. There was some shouting and praying, and then I saw one man trying to get up. He only managed to crawl on his hands and feet, and he made his way towards the stage. When he came close to me, he tried to grab the microphone I was still holding, and I was not sure what to do. He was not one of the leaders, in fact I had never heard him say anything. He had this desperate look on his face, and I had the feeling if I would not give him the mike, he would fight me for it.

The moment I handed it to him, he began to sob and wail, and then he confessed his sins in front of the whole church! Whenever that happens, you know it has to be God – even more so in an Asian context, where "losing face" is about the worst thing that can happen. When he was done, there was a whole avalanche of men and women coming to the front to confess as well. One visiting missionary came and sat next to me, pouring out his heart, and confessing that he had entertained plans to visit a local brothel that day. As shocked as I was, I felt compassion for him, and the tears flowed heavily, as we prayed together that morning.

From that Sunday on, everything was different at church, and I could hardly wait from one meeting to the next. I remember driving to church before, thinking about whose turn it was to speak, and who would lead worship, and basing my expectations on that. Now, it didn't matter any-more if the speaker was a good teacher, or if the guitars were in tune, because every time we met, God showed up, and it was different all the time.

Overall I would describe this move of God as a healing renewal. And why not? Everyone in church over the age of forty had their personal hor-ror story to tell. I was looking at some of the women laying on the floor one of the following Sundays, laughing uncontrollably for the longest time, and then I recognized one of them. I remembered her story how she had been made to watch as her baby was thrown into the air by a Khmer Rouge soldier, and then caught on the bayonet of his rifle. Just to see her face glow with the joy of the Lord made being there worthwhile. In just twenty minutes the Lord had brought more healing to her soul than years of professional counseling could have achieved.

Later on, we discovered other parts of the story, and why God had chosen that particular time to begin to move. Without a doubt, the years of early morning prayer had prepared the foundation for it, but there was another element as well. I am not totally sure, but it could have been the exact same Sunday that Sophal was visiting the Anaheim Vineyard, and had a special meeting with John Wimber and John Arnott, the pastor from the Toronto Airport Vineyard. At the end of their meeting, John Arnott asked Sophal, "Sophal, what do you want God to do for your nation?"

Without hesitation Sophal answered, "I want the fire of God to fall on Cambodia!"

I don't know how much of that was felt and experienced by any of the other churches, but we enjoyed a very special presence of the Lord for the next 18 months. But something else happened, and it turned into a story that went around the world.

One day two Buddhist monks appeared on the news on national television, visibly shaken and beside themselves over what had happened at their monastery. As they were in prayer that morning, they heard the sound of what could have been a dozen freight trains, and when they rushed outside to check, they saw something fiery fall out of the sky, and hit the main building. It demolished part of the building and crushed the large Buddha statue in what they considered the most holy part of the temple. Their abbot, who lived in a separate small building, injured his back as his whole house began to spin around and was moved around 50 meters away from its former location.

What a bizarre story, and it shook the faith of the whole nation. Sophal sent a team from the church with a video camera to go and document the events, and they confirmed what the two monks had stated on television.

This period in Cambodia has shaped me in many ways, and I was forever spoiled for what I consider "ordinary church".

* * *

On the family front, things became tougher and tougher, and at the time I was quite ignorant of the warfare going on all around us. Looking back, I realize that God in His mercy had answered my prayers, when I had told him as a young believer back in Sweden that I wanted to see the same type of miracles that I had read about in the Book of Acts. The level of anointing that was released during this very special visitation of the Holy Spirit had become almost addicting. Every time anyone was prayed for in church it turned into a demonstration of God's power and authority that had the effect of one feeling blessed and gifted in ministry. But there was a danger lurking that I almost didn't see. It was so easy to simply neglect my devotional life. Working on my relationship with God was no longer a priority since, after all, He was using me in ways I never thought possible. I had grown in knowledge, experience and anointing, but I was further away from the heart of God than I had been in a long time, and it was only His grace that kept me from falling into the snares of the enemy.

Since life was not very exciting for our kids, especially the older ones, Cathy and I had been quite reluctant in denying them some wishes that we would not have considered under different circumstances. Most of our shopping was done at a big market in town, and the children were always attracted to one area where you could buy all kinds of exotic animals. There you could find leopard cubs as well as a young sun bear next to all kinds of dogs, rabbits and animals we had never laid eyes on before. So it did not take us very long to acquire a small private zoo.

There was a small civet cat, which is not a cat at all, but looks more like a miniature raccoon. The cutest of all was a slow loris that the girls dressed up in doll clothes. But none of us will ever forget Toby the monkey. We bought him as a baby for a few dollars, and initially he lived with us in the house. He would sit next to Eja in her high chair, and sleep in bed with Lars, curled up by his neck. We figured he would be tame since we had him since he was quite young, but that was not to be. As he became older he became quite wild, and would sometimes bite the kids.

One night Toby came into our bedroom, sat on Cathy's head while we were sleeping, and peed on her! The next day Toby moved out of the house. I built him a nice walk-in cage with a tree and a tire swing, but he was never happy there. We were his clan, and he wanted to be with us in the house. So he would sit on his branch and bend the strands of the chicken wire back and forth with his little hands for hours, until one of them would break. Then he would start on the next one, until he had made an opening big enough for him to squeeze through. Then he would come barging through the screen door of the house and attack whoever crossed his path by jumping on them and biting their cheeks.

Soon the smaller kids were quite scared of him, and whenever he had managed to escape there would be this warning scream, "Toby is loose!"

Not only did he terrorize our kids, but he would visit the neighbors as well, stealing bananas from their kitchen and chasing their children. One time he ripped the clothes from the line and dragged Cathy's bra down the street to the neighbor's yard. The only one that could really master him was Nils, who would let him out each afternoon, and quite often they could be seen sitting on the roof together, sharing some fruit. Since he seemed so lonely, we even ended up buying a young female companion for him, but he kept hurting her, and she ended up dying not long after we got her. We have a family video with Toby playing with one of our puppies and a cat, and we used to call them "the three amigos".

One day we found a medium-sized snake on our front porch, and since none of us knew if it was poisonous or not, I tried to chase it away with a broom. When this did not prove successful, I opted for some more drastic measures. Our only weapon was Nils' BB-gun that we had brought from the Philippines, and so I attacked the snake by shooting it in the head with pellets. It took about seven or eight direct hits before the poor creature finally turned on its back and opened its mouth wide before it died – there was not a single tooth in its mouth, and it had obviously not been poisonous. I felt rather stupid and threw it in a dumpster out by our gate.

Toby must have watched the whole thing, and when he was let out later that day, he dashed straight for the dumpster to have a look. The moment he saw the snake he let out a shriek and fainted. After about 10 seconds he got up and climbed up to take another look, only to faint again! How I wish I would have had a functioning video camera to capture this comic encounter. We were laughing about it for a long time.

* * *

By the beginning of 1995 Cathy was pregnant again, and we were happy that Eja would have a sibling closer to her age. By then the UN had completed their assignment in Cambodia and had completely pulled out of the country. That meant no more field hospital and no more German doctors. The local hospitals had a bad reputation, and when Cathy and I went to have a look we decided that we would not have the baby there. Plus, there was another possible complication: We were told that almost all Asians have positive blood types, and that there were no blood reserves for Cathy's negative blood type anywhere in the country. In case of some kind of hemorrhage, there simply was no blood supply, and my type was not compatible either. On top of it all we had a strong sense from the Lord that this child should not be born in Cambodia.

One of the visiting teams had told us about this church in Malaysia that had a great interest in missions and an open door for teams and visitors. We contacted the pastor, Dr. Joy, by fax and explained our situation. Shortly after we received a warm invitation to come and stay as long as we needed. They lived on the island of Penang, and there was a well-known hospital run by the Seventh-Day-Adventists.

We made arrangements and flew to Penang about one month before Cathy's due date. The church there gave us a royal welcome, and provided everything we could ever need. We even got to use Dr. Joy's private Toyota van. It was perfect for our whole family to take us around this beautiful island. Coming from Cambodia, Malaysia seemed like a modern paradise with all the conveniences of life in the West in a culture that is very Asian and international, with English spoken throughout.

We enjoyed some downtime while having good fellowship with dear folks from the church who invited us to dinners and brought food to the house where we got to stay for free.

Cathy had her checkups at the hospital, and everything seemed all right. When the time came for the delivery, we got there in good time, and on September 22, 1995, on Cathy's birthday, our third daughter Helena Catherine was born. After a few days, both mom and daughter were released with a clean bill of health.

Since there was no German Embassy in Penang, I had to take the train down to the capital, Kuala Lumpur, to get a certified birth certificate, and to apply for Helena's passport. When I came to Penang the next day, I was shocked to find out that Cathy and Lena, as we ended up calling her, were back in the hospital. After rushing there I was informed that Lena had contracted a severe case of spinal meningitis which is highly unusual for a child less than two weeks old. The right side of her body had begun to convulse, and after a spinal tap the doctors put her immediately on an antibiotic drip.

For the next few days things were touch and go, and we were so thankful for teams from the church coming daily to pray over Lena and worship Jesus right there in the hospital room. It was then we understood that we had heard from God when we decided to not have the birth in Cambodia. Without the quick and proper treatment she would surely have died, or ended up handicapped for the rest of her life. Lena's pediatrician told us clearly that she would need special supervision for quite some time to come, and that there was no way we could return to Cambodia with her. We were shocked to the core!

Our home and work was there, and now it looked like we would be stuck in Malaysia. We know that it was because of all the prayers that things started turning around very quickly. Not only did Lena recover fully, but by the time Cathy and she left the hospital, she had gained one whole kilogram. When we saw the doctor at a follow-up appointment, he changed his prognosis and assured us that she was totally fine and that there was no reason for us not to return to Cambodia.

When Lena's passport finally arrived, we said good-by to our dear church family and returned to our home in Phnom Penh.

∗ ∗ ∗

It is always harder to return to a place less nice than where you just were, but after a few days it seemed like we had never left, except for the fact that we now had a new family member who brought great joy to our lives.

After this three-month break, I continued teaching at the Bible school, and by the beginning of 1996 we had a sense that things were winding down for us here. I think I wrestled more with the idea of leaving than the rest of the family. The call to Cambodia had been so strong and special that I had felt I would spend the rest of my life there. But when I looked at my family, I realized that they were my first calling, and right now they were suffering. Having tasted how much easier life could be in Malaysia, it was even harder for them to return to Cambodia than the first time. Especially Björn and Nils became more and more depressed with their restricted lifestyle, and all the pets and other perks could not change that. So we took a hard look and made some difficult decisions.

∗ ∗ ∗

We were getting ready for our second furlough in eight years, and we knew that God would help us find the next stretch of road on his journey he had planned for us. Coming for a visit to Europe with 7 children was even harder than the previous time with "only" four. Many folks simply were not comfortable to invite a family of nine over for dinner, which we understood, but it did make it harder to connect with our roots and former culture.

We had rented a large van, and so we drove long distances within Switzerland and Germany, all the way up to Sweden, where we connected with my dear friends from Norrtälje and other places.

In Bern we had a long talk with Martin and some other leaders, and we all agreed that our days in Cambodia were numbered. There was really no room for us at the church in Bern, and I was not yet ready to leave Asia. It was then we realized that the Lord had already opened a door for us during our time in Penang, and we all felt that this would be a good place for our family to return to a somewhat more normal life. Yet we all had mixed feelings about being uprooted once again, and Carina burst into tears when she found out she was going to lose all her friends and pets.

On the way back to Cambodia, we had a stopover in Penang and left Björn there to attend Dalat International School while the rest of us went back to wrap things up in Phnom Penh.

The last few months there were quite hard as we began packing and letting go of responsibilities at the church. Some of the leaders there were so disappointed that they would no longer speak to us. On top of it all we hit a financial crisis when the daughter of our domestic helper stole a whole month's support money from us. Initially, her mother tried to cover for her and quit working for us, but much later, after we had already left she tried to pay some of the money back.

Finding a home for all the critters turned out to be quite a challenge as well. Almost until the very end we still had Toby the monkey, Civvy the civet, and Akela, a sickly and inbred female German Shepherd. We thought we could just set Toby free in the countryside, but that proved to be impossible. He would cling to us in great fear, and there was just no way to get rid of him.

In the end I had a brilliant idea: I posted a flyer at a very popular store and restaurant for foreigners, and it simply said in big letters, "Free German Shepherd", and then in small print on the bottom, "Comes with two friends…."

After a few days I got a phone call from a Swedish missionary, and his first question was, "Who are the two friends?"

He ended up taking all three of them, and he even kept in touch and told us how things turned out later on. Akela had one puppy, the civet was fine, but Toby had gotten caught with a rope around his neck and had died.

In October 1996, almost exactly four years after we had first arrived, we drove to Potchentong airport for the last time to leave this "land of broken hearts." In the decades to come I would realize how those years had shaped me in so many ways, and I will never forget the sweet presence of the Father among His children there. Still today, as I am writing these lines, I miss that intense presence and favor of God that I experienced at the church in Cambodia.

NEW HORIZONS

Just like the first time, we felt like we had arrived in paradise, when we finally landed in Penang, Malaysia.

Dr. Joy helped us find a great house near the beach and within walking distance to the international school where initially three of the kids would continue their studies. The house was quite narrow, but had three stories with plenty of rooms for us all. We found out later that it had once been a YWAM base.

Only a few weeks after our move we heard stories of another rebel uprising in Phnom Penh, which resulted in heavy fighting and numerous casualties. Some of the worst confrontations happened right in our old neighborhood, and on the news I saw the gas station just a few hundred meters from our home in flames. Later on, I was told that there were dead bodies all along our old street for days. We were so grateful that God spared us the agony of having to live through that, but at the same time our hearts ached for the people of Cambodia who never seemed to be able to enjoy any lasting peace.

Though life was so much easier in many ways, it was quite an adjustment to move from a Buddhist country to a Muslim nation. Though we lived quite far from the next mosque, we could clearly hear the call to prayer five times a day. The loudspeakers installed at each minaret made sure that no one could miss it. Since there was no air conditioning in our house, we slept with the windows wide open, and heard the first call before sunrise, After a while it became as normal as the gunshots in Cambodia, and we barely noticed it anymore.

Malaysia is a very unique country with a very diverse ethnic population. Only half of the population are Malays, and Muslim, while one quarter is Chinese, and the rest Indian and tribal. There are plenty of churches, but only the non-Malay population is allowed to worship there. The Islamic religious police enforce this by sending plain-clothes officers into the churches to make sure no members of the Muslim faith are attending.

There are many missionaries, and as long as they stay away from the Malays they are tolerated. We heard several stories of Westerners being deported because they were caught trying to evangelize the Malays.

In general, the different ethnic groups coexist well with each other, but there are tensions under the surface that erupt from time to time. Since the Malays are a majority, they make sure that the country is run according to Muslim ideologies and Islamic laws. Most government agencies and the banking system are run by them, with members of the other ethnic groups only allowed in lower positions. We got to meet an Indian architect working for the city who could never be promoted, being forced to work under leadership less qualified than himself.

That is true for the educational system as well. Students of Chinese and Indian origin have to achieve higher grade averages to attend university than their Malay counterparts. Those who can afford it will send their children to Singapore or the UK for higher learning.

All of that left me wondering if there were any Malay Christians at all, since we never met them in any of the churches we visited. We were assured that they existed and that their number is growing, but because of the strict laws and controls they either have to leave the country, or worship underground by continuing to visit the mosques and praying to Jesus there. Repeatedly, we heard stories of Muslims having visions of Jesus, or having Him appear to them in dreams.

The island of Penang is quite different from the rest of the country. The fact that there is a much higher population of Chinese and Indians there, plus its attractiveness for Western expatriates and tourists, has created a culture much less influenced and controlled by Islam.

The island is in the Strait of Malacca, has the shape of a turtle, and is connected to the mainland by a 14 kilometer long bridge. Apart from the city part called George Town, the island is hilly and covered with rainforest. With its close proximity to the equator, it is always hot and humid with plenty of rain all year round, though there is a relative "dry season" during the winter months.

* * *

For the family, life was so much easier now. There were plenty of shopping malls and other attractions, like the botanical garden, or an all-new water park. The kids quickly found new friends and could engage in activities they had missed for so long, such as playing sports, taking piano lessons, going to see a movie, or simply hanging out with friends. The advantage of living in a Muslim country was that things were relatively safe, and we could let the older kids go out by themselves. With an enforced death-sentence for drug dealers, and public caning for drug users, there was no great danger and temptation in that regard, and the overall crime rate was probably lower than in most Western countries.

For the first year, we attended Living Waters Church, pastored by Dr. Joy and his wonderful family. We helped with worship and occasional preaching, and enjoyed great fellowship with amazing Asian food. Penang is known for its diverse cuisine, and people come from far and wide to sample the most exquisite dishes from China, Indonesia, India, Thailand and other places.

Another big breakthrough for us was the amazing advantages of the Internet. I will never forget the first email from Martin appearing magically on the screen of my laptop computer. All of a sudden communication had turned into something that was easy, quick, and cheap.

One day there was an email from the pastor of a small Chinese Brethren Church on the other side of the island. He had read about John Wimber and the Vineyard movement on the Internet, and somehow found us in that context. He was very hungry for spiritual renewal for his flock, and asked if we could help them with that. Soon, we became good friends with Teng Huat and his wife Oi Ching. It took us almost 45 minutes to reach their church building every Sunday, but for the next few years we poured ourselves into that little church, helping them to get better acquainted with the Holy Spirit through teaching and leading worship.

For me this became another lesson in cross-cultural ministry, both on an ethnic level, as well as in trying to function in a church culture we had never experienced before. Seeing how hungry and open most of them were for a genuine move of God made the experience very rewarding, at least for me. But since the children had their friends mainly among the expat community, they found it quite hard to connect with the few young people at the church, and more and more sought to stay home on Sunday morning. Of course it did not help that all we had was an old and small Subaru, which made going anywhere together a real challenge.

It did not take us very long to acquire another house full of pets. The day we moved into the house, an old Chinese dog came into the yard and wanted some attention and food. We thought he was homeless, and when we asked our neighbors about him they just shook their heads. So we adopted him and called him Cheng. It was not until years later that the daughter of our neighbors came home for a visit and told us that Cheng was actually their dog, but Asian hospitality forbade them to refuse us looking after him - okay... plus we were the ones feeding him.

Then there was Dingo, a Dalmatian/Boxer mutt that kept climbing over the wall into our yard. One day he was just lying in front of our gate when the official dog catcher came and quickly put a rope around his neck. Then he rang our door bell and asked Cathy if he was our dog. When Cathy denied that he was, the guy just nodded, pulled out a hand gun and was getting ready to shoot him right then and there. Cathy stood there with Eja and Lena in utter shock, but managed to quickly blurt out, "We'll take him!"

Then there was a miniature-pincher puppy that melted our hearts.

About a year later, she died a few days after giving birth to four tiny puppies that had to be bottle-fed for the next few weeks every few hours. Then of course there were cats and kittens galore; we seemed to attract them like a magnet, and the kids and Cathy had their hands full looking after them.

During all these years in Penang, Cathy was busy home-schooling our youngest two, while the rest went to Dalat International School which provided them with excellent education from dedicated, Christian teachers. But the cost for tuition was way beyond our means, and we soon found ourselves in financial trouble by falling behind in our payments.

* * *

Nineteen ninety-seven became a very special year for me. In November of that year I received an invitation to the first Vineyard Asia Summit to be held in Manila. John Wimber was to be one of the main speakers, and I was excited to finally have a chance to meet him up close. Until then I had only seen him from a distance at conferences in England and Germany, and I was looking forward to finally shake his hand. When I arrived in the Philippines and found the venue for the conference, which was just down the street from where we used to live, we were told that John Wimber had passed away the day before. Not only was he not coming, but some of the other key speakers had to leave right away to make it back to the US for the funeral.

In spite of my disappointment, it turned out to be a very powerful conference, and I was encouraged to hear about the growth of the Vineyard in many countries of Southeast Asia and the Far East. The worship times made me realize how much I had missed that authentic, intimate style of worship that differs so much from the more flashy and showy version favored by many Asian churches. Meeting other Vineyard missionaries and seeing some of our core values expressed in the various local cultures once again gave me a sense of coming home — this time in Asia.

After one very sweet time of worship, one of the leaders from South Korea came to the stage crying and sobbing. He then explained to us how he and his family had suffered much at the hands of the Japanese soldiers during the final years of the Second World War. That had resulted in a deep-seated hatred towards all Japanese. After he became a Christian, he thought he had overcome these emotions, but when he sat across from one of the Japanese pastors at lunch, all these old feelings had resurfaced. He was so broken over his inability to love his former enemy that he had to come forward to confess this sin to us all. Partially understanding Asian cultures, I realized what it must have cost him to come forward and share this.

But that was just the beginning. While he and the Japanese brother hugged, wept, and prayed for each other, there was an avalanche of people coming forward to confess more sin. A man from Hong Kong asked forgiveness of all the Filipino women who are being abused as domestic helpers in his country. Other local leaders confessed their hurts over bad treatment by missionaries in the past, and we spent the next few hours weeping together, praying for each other, giving and receiving forgiveness. No one could have possibly planned or orchestrated such a meeting, and we were at awe at the sovereign move of God's Spirit among us.

But it got even better. The evening sessions had been moved to a larger hall in a part of Manila called Cubao. On the way there by public transport, we passed many beggars who were lining the main streets. That night our special speaker was Jackie Pullinger, an English woman who had lived and worked among drug addicts in HongKong for many years, and who has a special anointing to minister to and together with the poorest of the poor. When she taught about God's love for the poor, it cut very deeply into all of our hearts, and I realized that after the four years in Cambodia I had hardened my heart towards the poor. I had hidden behind the fact that so many of the beggars there were not genuine, but were the slaves of a corrupt network of Mafia-style thugs that took all the money for the drug trade. Furthermore, it had become so annoying to always be assaulted by those who were too lazy to work and expected constant handouts from the rich foreigners.

Jackie said something I will never forget, "As a Christian, you can never walk by a beggar and not do anything! You may not have money to give, and you may not feel like laying your hands on them in prayer, but the very least thing you can do is to bless them as you pass by. After all, there is a chance that the Lord Jesus himself is sitting there, and we can't afford to take that chance of ignoring Him."

Then and there I made a pact with God that from that day forth I would never pass by a beggar and not do anything. To my knowledge I have kept my part in this. It has not been any loss, but quite often I feel a profound sense of God's pleasure and favor, as I stop to bless a beggar by the road side. After the meeting, we all walked by the slew of beggars again, and they didn't know what hit them, when all these pastors and missionaries blessed them with money and prayers.

From then on, we have had Asian summits every two years, and they have always been extremely uplifting and encouraging.

* * *

That same year I took a trip with one of the doctors attending Living Waters to Chiang Mai, in Northern Thailand. There we visited a tribal leader by the name of Timothy Laklem, who had a compound outside the city which served as a training facility for Christian workers and leaders of the Karen tribe.

I was introduced to a reality in that part of the world that most people in the West know little about. Around 50% of the population of Myanmar, better known as Burma, consists of large tribal groups that have for centuries been under the iron rule of the Burmese people. When the British ruled the land for over 120 years, they had tried to stabilize the tension among these many ethnic groups, and even preferred Karen soldiers over the Burmese. Before pulling out in 1948, they installed a Burmese prime minister who had a heart for these tribal groups within their boundaries. But even before the pullout was completed, Aung San was assassinated, and the nation has been ruled by a brutal dictatorships of the military ever since. That means that the tribal nations within

Myanmar have been suffering with extreme oppression and persecution that has caused a permanent civil war that is continuing to this day. This conflict is so old that the news media stopped reporting about it a long time ago, while the suffering of literally millions of people continues.

Some of these large tribes, such as the Karen, the Shan, or the Kachin live in their ancestral territories along the border with Thailand. The Burmese military regularly launches attacks on their villages in the dense jungles, killing, raping, and taking the young men as slaves and porters. Though they try to secure the border to Thailand with land mines and patrols, it is impossible to secure a border that is over 2,200 kilometers long, and so there has been a constant stream of refugees into Thailand. Many disappear as illegal immigrants in the cities, or the countryside, often being exploited for cheap labor with no rights or justice whatsoever. Around 160,000 of them are held in refugee camps along the border which puts a huge burden on the Thai government who really does not care about these refugees, but they have the international community watching over them, and they are concerned about keeping a good image and public opinion. However, they can only supply the refugees with a staple of rice and dried fish, and if the NGOs would not step in to supply clothing, food, medical treatment and schooling, the situation would be far worse than it is.

Together with Timothy and some of his coworkers, we drove to the border town of Mae Sot, to visit one of these camps. On the way there, we passed several roadblocks, and Timothy had to pay off the soldiers with special treats to let us pass. When we arrived at the camp, we encountered the aftermath of an attack by some Burmese soldiers a few nights earlier. There were between ten to fifteen thousand refugees, divided into Buddhist and Christian Karen. The huts and shelters on the Buddhist side were still standing, while the Christian part was completely burned to the ground. High on drugs the Burmese soldiers had crossed the narrow river which serves as the border between the two nations, told the people to get out while torching their huts with flamethrowers. Apparently this had been the second attack like this in one year, and the handful of Thai soldiers guarding the camp pretended not to notice. There was nothing but smoldering ashes everywhere, as children searched the rubble for anything useful while the adults erected simple shelters made of four posts and a canvas to protect them from the powerful sun.

Apart from the slum in Phnom Penh, I had never seen such poverty and suffering. As we were walking through the large camp, we heard singing from further on and followed the sound of worship to a large makeshift tent filled with maybe 100 men, women and children, singing on the top at their lungs what I recognized to be John Wimber's "Spirit Song" in the Karen language. What a testimony of faith to see these dear people who had just lost everything once again, worship Jesus with all their heart in the heat of the day. Their worship leader had a guitar with three strings left on it, but the singing was beautiful and often in several part harmony, something I had never heard in all the years living in Asia. Two hundred years ago the Karen were evangelized by British Baptist missionaries who must have taught them how to sing.

We had a sweet time of ministry and fellowship with this group, and heard many more sad stories about mistreatment and discrimination. Basically, none of the refugees are allowed to leave the camp, and we met some that had been there for eight years. Those who managed to find jobs in town had to give half of their salary to the guards in order to be let out each morning. And yet, there was a sense contentment and joy among them that was so humbling to us from a better world. They had a network of evangelists who moved back and forth across the border and reached out to those from their tribe who did not know the Lord. Timothy provided training and support for many of them.

I returned to Penang with a better understanding of the underlying struggles in the region, and would be confronted with them many times in the years ahead. Whenever I tell these stories, I realize that most people in the world have no idea of this piece of current history and the plight of this forgotten part of God's family.

* * *

In 1999, Martin helped us revive the DMC, the international discipleship school we had started in the Philippines. Using his many relationships, we were able to put together an absolute dream team of well-known pastors and worship leaders to come and teach for one week each. Besides coming himself, he recruited our old friends Mike Hudgins and Charles Bello, as well as David Ruis, Scott Underwood, Derek Morphew, and others. We ended up with over twenty students from Switzerland, Germany, England, Australia, and Hong Kong. Though it became an extremely intense and busy time for me, I realized again how much I enjoyed guiding these young believers through a time of transition and growth in their lives and seeing them get in touch with their calling, purpose and destiny in God.

The practical aspect of the program was a bit more complicated in a Muslim country such as Malaysia. Since our school was underground, we had to keep a low profile in order not to draw too much attention to ourselves, and for the final outreach after eight weeks of training, we broke them up into teams and sent them to the Philippines, Thailand, and the island of Borneo for three weeks. There, they connected with local churches and served them in any way they could.

After they returned, we had a time of debriefing, and they swapped stories of their experiences and adventures. One of these stories still sticks with me after all these years. The team to Borneo had to take a trip to a very remote area which involved a massive hike through the jungle. When they finally reached the village where they would serve for a few days, they were utterly exhausted, dirty and sweaty, and obviously longed for a cool shower. One of the girls on the team spotted a deep hole in the ground filled with what seemed like clean and cool water. In her desperation she asked the other girl on the team to hold up a towel while she undressed and jumped into the water hole. There she could wash up and even shampoo her hair. Later that day they found out that this water hole was the drink-water supply for the whole village! Rather than being angry, their hosts shared a good laugh with the team, retelling and acting out the story over and over.

The following year we had another school like that with even more students. We have obviously lost touch with many of them, but others became close friends and even supporters. Many of them ended up in leadership positions in various churches, and some returned as full-time missionaries. This turned me into a firm believer in this type of training school, and I am convinced that the true value is not so much the teaching, as the cross-cultural experience and communal life. It was noteworthy that some of the ones who came with a long list of recommendations from their home church often struggled more than those that were still very new in their faith. At that last school in Penang we had a girl from Switzerland who brought her Muslim friend. By the end of the program, she had become a true disciple of Jesus. I offered to baptize her in the sea, but she said she wanted to do it back home in front of her family, which she ended up doing.

* * *

At one point during the years in Penang, I was invited to join our friend Peter Davids to a family camp of the Methodist churches of Malaysia. When Peter was asked to be the main speaker for the event, he asked it would be possible to bring a ministry team from the Vineyard. Our ministry team consisted of over 20 persons, with leaders from Hong Kong, Thailand, and Canada, which included Gary Best, the leader of the Canadian Vineyards.

The teaching seminars went very well, but after the first day it became obvious that some of the 400 attendees were becoming a bit uncomfortable with our style of ministry and the move of the Holy Spirit. The next day, the former bishop of the Methodist church in Malaysia got up to speak in the morning, addressing some of the concerns he was sensing. He explained to them the origin of the Methodist movement and read stories and quotations by their founder, John Wesley. This made it obvious that in the very beginning Methodists were part of a great Holy Spirit revival with genuine manifestations among them. That eased the fears of most, and we enjoyed wonderful times of fellowship and ministry with them.

Most of the participants were of Chinese origin and quite traditional in their style of behavior. They watched the way we Vineyard folks interacted with each other, how we joked around and had a lot of fun.

At the very end of the conference, they had the usual farewell and thank you speeches, and then one of the local leaders surprised us all, when he announced, "And now there is just one thing we still have to do…." At these words, four young men came to the front and without warning picked up the main leader's chair, carried him outside the hall, and unceremoniously dumped him into the hotel swimming pool, chair and all! Once everyone had overcome their shock and horror at what had just happened, the event closed in waves of roaring laughter. We felt we had left our mark in more ways than one.

After this camp, the ministry team split into two groups to go and visit the Methodist churches in two different places, one of them being Penang. I was privileged to accompany Gary Best for another set of powerful meetings, especially among the youth. We were encouraged by the renewal that was sweeping across these churches, which was obviously due to the hunger and openness of their bishop, and we were saddened to hear that he had been killed in a roadside accident less than one year later.

＊＊＊

The years in Penang were a turning point in our family life with Björn our oldest taking the lead to leave the nest. When our friend Charles Bello came to teach at our school, he extended an invitation for Björn to join their family in Oklahoma City. We gratefully accepted. They offered to help him get started with his studies, as well as to get a foothold in the American culture quite foreign to Björn. All along, Björn had shown a natural gift for art, which was confirmed and developed during his short time at Dalat International School. So he left our home to study art and to become an art teacher.

The following year, I met Charles at an event in Germany, and I was glad and relieved to hear of things going well for Björn. He had begun to work at the bakery section of a supermarket. Soon his artistic skills in decorating cakes had people coming from near and far to place special orders. Eventually, he was "discovered" by another store and offered better pay. Charles and Dianna have six children of their own, and Charles and I were joking about getting Björn hooked up with their oldest daughter Laura. Little did we know that Laura had "discovered" Björn on her own, and they were soon dating, and building a serious relationship.

* * *

When we were finishing up our second training school in Penang, I was invited to speak at a Methodist Church one Sunday morning, and I took some of our students along for the event. At the end of the meeting, two African men approached me, and asked me to pray for them. With tears in their eyes, they told me one of the most moving stories I had ever heard. Their father back in Sierra Leone had been a prominent leader in the struggle against the corrupt dictatorship, and had recently been killed by government soldiers. Before he passed away, he commissioned his sons to escape the country with a large amount of money supplied by the CIA to support the resistance, which was now crushed.

They asked me for a Bible, and I promised to bring one to the hotel where they were staying temporarily. When I got there, they told me some more details of their gruesome saga, and then they showed me something that I would have never believed if I had not seen it with my own eyes. They had a small suitcase packed tightly with what looked like small pieces of black paper. One of them pulled out one of those pieces, while the other one brought a brown plastic bottle. He then poured a few drops of a yellow liquid on the paper and rubbed it into the paper with his fingers. I front of our eyes the paper changed color and turned into a fifty dollar bill! After rinsing it with water and drying it off, we then went to a money changer who examined it and changed it into Malaysian Ringgit without hesitation.

Back at the room they explained to me that this was a special way of the CIA to finance certain struggles in developing countries, and since the paper was useless without the chemical solution, they could make sure that it did not fall into the wrong hands. They showed me what looked like official documents from the CIA regarding the use of this "Black Money," and a certificate of ownership with their father's name on it. They told me that their father had insisted that the money would only be used for humanitarian purposes, and since they trusted me as a man of God they asked me to help them spend the money helping the poor - all two million of it! There was one catch: the chemical had all but dried up on their long journey by boat from Africa, and they needed to find a way to get more.

I went home with my head spinning and my mind working in over-drive thinking of projects in the slums of Phnom Penh and of building an orphanage for the street children. The possibilities seemed endless with that kind of money. There were not many people I could tell about this, but I told Cathy who had a hard time believing the authenticity of it all, but, of course, she had not seen the money.

A few days later, I got a call from one of my new African friends. He said they were at the American Embassy in Kuala Lumpur where they had explained their situation. Upon checking their documents, they were told that a new bottle of the chemical solution could be sent from the U.S., but the cost for it was close to $2,000. Could I forward them the money, since they did not have enough solution to "make" more? We were in such bad shape financially that I could not have given them even two hundred. He seemed crestfallen and asked if I could send them anything at all. That is when I finally got suspicious, but still wanted to give them the benefit of my growing doubts. They called several times every day, always requesting money, and getting more and more angry and agitated when I told them that I had nothing to give them. It was their change of attitude that finally helped me understand that I had been conned by real professionals who knew how to press my buttons.

A few days later, I opened the morning paper and there on the front page was the article of the police arresting a whole gang of Nigerians, who had conned many local businessmen into buying cases full of worthless black paper. In my case, they had tried to abuse my love for the poor and my willingness to help out. Then I realized how easily I could have gotten myself in trouble by even associating with them. What a sneaky attack of the enemy to use my naïvety and gullibility to take me out! Thankfully, the Lord had answered Cathy's prayers and prevented what could have turned into complete disaster.

When I visited Bern a few months later, I told Martin the whole story, and he suggested that I contact the CIA and tell them about it. All I had to prove my story was the newspaper article from Penang, and one sample of the black paper my "friends" had given me. So I called the American Embassy in Bern the next day and asked if I could speak with the CIA. There was a long pause on the phone, and then the clerk informed me that there was no CIA in Switzerland, but that I could make an appointment with their security personnel, which I did. The agent, I am sure he was CIA, politely listened to my story, and showed great interest in my sample which would be sent to Washington for analysis. He then told me that they are aware of these kind of cases that are springing up all over the world. A poor farmer in Denmark had paid 5,000 dollars the previous week for a case of one million dollars in "Black Money." If the scenario with the magic money was real, he was not willing to confirm it one way or another, but I did some research later on which seems to confirm its existence.

Before I left the embassy, the agent said something which totally surprised me, and it was like a greeting from the Lord himself. He said that due to his job he was trained to never trust people, and then he said, "But you do, don't ever stop!" He did not know, but those words were like ointment for my sore heart.

* * *

It was during that particular visit to Switzerland and my visit with Martin that we discussed the future of our family and the training schools. Our financial situation had deteriorated more and more, and we needed more schools than one per year to justify and support our existence in Malaysia. The biggest drawback to continuing the schools there was the lack of freedom. The fact that we had to send our students so far for their outreach made the schools more expensive than they should have been. Together we came to the conclusion that it would be much better to run the schools in Thailand, where there were many opportunities for ministry everywhere. At the same time life for us a family would be cheaper, giving us a chance to recover from our financial troubles.

I flew back to Penang with the news of yet another upcoming move to yet another country. By then it had almost become a routine for us to move every four to five years, so neither Cathy nor the kids were too surprised, and together we prepared for another epic transition.

* * *

In the midst of our planning, there was one event that took me by surprise and shook me to the very core. In the spring of 2001, my mother called one evening, informing me that my Dad had passed away. He had been in hospital for water in his lungs, but then released since his condition had improved. The following day he had a heart attack, and the doctor could not save his life. I remember him saying many times that he just wanted to become eighty — he died at the age of eighty-six.

That night I spent hours walking up and down the beach near our house, with one question reverberating in my mind over and over again: "Why must people die for us to know how much we loved them?" Over the years I had often felt guilty for not having as much love for my father as I thought was right. That night the guilt was drowned by waves of grief, a grief I never thought I was capable of, and then I knew that I had truly loved him.

I managed to make it back to the funeral just in time, and it became one of the few occasions where we met all together as a family. It would take months to get over the sense of pain and loss, but it helped that we were totally absorbed by our upcoming move.

Our family went through the procedures that we had become quite accustomed to, such as trying to find homes for our dogs and cats, and deciding what to sell, and what to take along. Though the distance from Penang to Chiang Mai is roughly 2,000 kilometers, there is a train track all the way up, and we could ship most of our belongings in a container that would take less than two days to get there. Together with Eja and Lena, Cathy and I had taken a short trip three months before, and had been able to find a big house in a beautiful suburb, close to the International school where most of the kids would study.

In June of 2001, after five years of living in Penang on tourist visas, we boarded a Thai Airways plane to Bangkok, and from there on to our next home, Chiang Mai.

LAND OF SMILES

Chiang Mai is the second largest city in Thailand. It used to be part of the Kingdom of Lanna, near what is also referred to as the Golden Triangle, where Thailand, Myanmar and Laos meet. It has always been a spiritual center for several religions, and is sometimes referred to as the "Missionary Capital of the World," because of the large number of missionaries living there. When we moved there in 2001, we were told that there were over 1,500 missionaries in town, and that number might be higher today.

Just as the ancient city of Antioch in the Book of Acts, Chiang Mai is also a gateway city to the surrounding nations, and beyond. We soon discovered that around 90% of all missions activity there was not targeting the Thai people, but extended into Myanmar, China, Laos, Cambodia and Vietnam, as well as the many hill-tribes in the region. Many missionary and aid organizations have their regional headquarters in the city, and some have even moved their world headquarters there. The reasons are manifold: Being situated a bit further north, the climate is more pleasant than most cities in Southeast Asia, except for the month of April, which is extremely hot. There is also less traffic, and the overall cost of living is one of the lowest in the world. The many international schools and churches, new malls and medical centers all add to the attraction.

Though also a Buddhist nation, Thailand comprises little with Cambodia. While Cambodia was a French colony for many years, Thailand has always been free, which is also the meaning of the word "Thai." This is clearly reflected in the culture on just about all levels. There are none of the subservient attitudes toward Westerners that are so prevalent in nations and people who have lived under colonial rule for decades or centuries. So their attitude towards foreigners is always courteous and respectful, but there is an underlying current that spells out quite clearly, "We value your input, presence and money, but don't tell us what to do!" This is even evident in the churches where the role of the missionary is more that of a friend and colleague with the resources and ability to help and contribute. Personally, I found this quite refreshing and closer to the way I had always understood missions, but we heard from other missionaries that they often felt used without the opportunity to exercise true leadership.

* * *

For our family the years in Thailand became a season of many changes. We started out with six children, and left with only two. Nils had graduated from high school in Penang, and was ready to move on to the U.S. to study, but things turned out to be quite difficult for him. Since our older children did not qualify for American citizenship, they needed a Green Card to live and study in the U.S. For Björn, the process had been quite straightforward, and took around six months. There was the issue with us not making enough money to be financially responsible for him, so Cathy's brother Paul stepped in as a co-sponsor for him. By the time we applied for Nils' card, the September 11 disaster had taken place, and increased national security had changed all the rules. We were required to get police reports for him from both Cambodia and Malaysia, which took months to obtain. Everything was questioned and double- and triple-checked, and the whole process took 18 months. In the meantime, Nils could neither work nor study. We had bought him a small motor cycle so that he could be out with his friends, but that resulted in an accident which required shoulder surgery. This was a tough time for him and us, and it was overshadowed by another tragic event.

One evening I had driven Nils to Grace International School to work out at the fitness club. After he had stepped out of the car, I was about to make a U-turn on the residential road. Looking in my mirror and over my shoulder I saw that the road was clear, and made a slow turn. The expression, "He did not know what hit him," began to take on a whole new meaning for me that night. Halfway through my turn, my car was hit by a projectile that caused it to jump sideways while both side windows exploded. With my peripheral vision I saw a shadow fly over the car, while some tangible object flew through the side window, missing my face by an inch and then exiting through the opposite window. The engine stalled and I looked out my right window. All I could see was a pile of twisted metal that had once been a motor cycle. About ten meters on the left of my car laid the body of the driver. While I tried to open my bashed-in door, Nils come back and pointed to the body in the road saying, "Dad, I think he's dead!"

With great dread in my heart, we walked over to the body, and even before we got there we could smell the alcohol cloud surrounding him. Then we heard him moan — he was still alive! We did not dare to move him, since there was a big chance that either his neck or back were broken, so all we could do was pray. None of the neighbors came out to help or check, but someone must have called the police, for they were on site within ten minutes, with an ambulance following.

They picked the poor guy up without checking for fractures and told me to follow the ambulance with my car, which thankfully was still drivable. My right forearm was bleeding where a chunk of glass was embedded, but I was in a state of shock and hardly noticed it. They took us both to a small clinic, where they discovered that the motorcycle driver had no broken bones, but was obviously bleeding in his brain, since he landed on his head, not wearing a helmet. They sent him on to a big hospital in town and quickly patched up my arm. My car was impounded; I was asked to give an account of what happened, and then the police drove me home. The passing words from the officer were, "If he dies we come and arrest you!"

I had no idea what to expect next, and so I called a friend who asked me to contact a Thai pastor who had some experience with accidents involving foreigners. We met, and he went with me to the police station the following day where there was a large group of people waiting for us. Very soon it became obvious that this was not going to be treated as a matter of justice, but of convenience. The fact that the motorcycle driver was driving an unregistered vehicle without any lights whatsoever was of no importance. That I could not have possibly seen him since his bike was black, and he was wearing camouflage fatigues was irrelevant. And when I pointed out that he was obviously drunk they all laughed at me, and one of them pointed out the obvious: It was after nine o clock, implying that around that time all Thai men are drunk. The police chief, who also came to the accident scene thought I must have been drunk myself, since I was so calm and quiet through it all.

According to their cultural thinking, this was a clear-cut case. Since I had insurance on my car, and the poor victim did not, I had to be guilty, otherwise there was no money for his hospital bill. Before we left the station, I was advised to settle with the family of the young man, so that we all could avoid a court case.

In talking with my new pastor friend, it became obvious that I did not have a choice. Since the victim was one of the bread winners in the family, they would all suffer now, so a compensation of $2,000 was in order. If I did not pay, they could make my life miserable by pressing charges. So I scraped together the money, and together we went to the hut of the family. I apologized for my careless driving and handed over the cash, while they signed a written statement that they would not press charges. It was then we heard part of the background of this tragic story.

The young man's name was Nookon, and he had been home all evening drinking, when he got a phone call that his cousin had been in a road accident. He had rushed off with his bike to find out what had happened and could not stop when he saw my car turning. For the next ten days things were touch and go for Nookon who was in a coma. Twice his skull had to be opened to drain the blood and other fluids. I visited him several times in the hospital, where he was in an acute ward with at least twenty other road accident cases. There was such an atmosphere of pain, suffering and desperation in that hall that I dreaded to go back. After ten days he awoke, but nobody could predict if he would ever recover fully from the damage to his brain.

In the meantime I was wrestling with the obvious questions, and more than once I asked God the same question, "Why did you allow this to happen; what am I supposed to learn through this?" Eventually I heard an answer that was very clear, and it went something like this: "I want you to get a feeling for what it is like to live without justice, as so many people around you". Much later I found out that the City of Chiang Mai is full of hundreds of thousands of illegal immigrants and refugees without papers, receiving little if any justice. They are ruthlessly exploited by everyone around them, and they have neither a voice nor a listening ear. While I was processing all of this came the next blow.

Nookon was released from hospital after 22 days and went home to rest and convalesce. The next day, the police came to our house dropping off a document I could not read. Again, I needed the help of my new friend, and I was shocked to find out that now the state was suing me for attempted manslaughter! Apparently, there is a law that says that if an accident victim is in the hospital for more than 21 days, the case changes from "civil" to "criminal." It was obvious they kept Nookon just long enough, but the police made it quite clear they would be willing to drop the case if I was willing to make a sizable donation to the local station.

No way was I going to play along with this kind of corruption. That very same police chief lived in our neighborhood in a nice house with several luxury cars in the driveway. His official salary was less than five hundred dollars per month, and everyone was aware of his sideline income.

Then I heard the story of another German missionary who had been in a similar situation a few years earlier. He had decided to fight his case in court, which took more than two years. During that time he was not allowed to leave the country. The result was that he was sentenced to two years jail on probation, plus had to pay a fortune in court fees. When I heard that I was no longer sure if I could, or even wanted to go that route, since it was obvious that I was never going to get any justice, no matter what I did. My heart began to fill with compassion for the oppressed people all around me.

In my desperation, I asked for advice and counsel from some of our friends, and I called Martin in Switzerland explaining the situation to him. His answer was very clear and directive: "Don't waste your time on this. Give them some money, and do your job!"

So we got back to the police and haggled about the size of the contribution. They started at one thousand dollars, but in the end we negotiated a sum of three-hundred, and they promised to drop the case.

By the time I got our car fixed I spent over $3,000 on something I never felt guilty about. It was not a nice feeling, but that was the lesson God wanted me to learn, and I will never forget it.

All of this took place just before Christmas and it looked like it was going to be a rather bleak one. But then we got news from our eldest son Björn that he would come to visit over Christmas together with Charles and Dianna's daughter Laura. So it turned out that we had a wonderful Christmas together with all our children, and our future daughter-in-law.

For Carina the move had been quite easy, for a very simple reason. Her boyfriend Josh, who was in her class at Dalat School in Penang, had also moved with his parents to Chiang Mai, and they were together again. Josh had also grown up as an "MK" (missionary kid) in various nations in Asia, and the two had much in common, and spent more and more time together. Carina graduated from high school, and Josh went with his folks back to Oklahoma for a season.

* * *

Life in Thailand was wonderful in so many ways. We loved the rich natural beauty of the rolling hills covered with rainforest, the ever-blooming trees, bushes and flowers. It did not take us long to fall in love with the famous Thai cuisine, and our tolerance for spicy food grew steadily, and even our youngest enjoyed spicy food that many Westerners would deem inedible.

Favorite places to go with friends and visitors were the various elephant camps, where you could see the mammoth animals in a totally different environment than the zoo or circus. Not only can one ride them through the jungle, but they had been trained to do things that would seem impossible for such large mammals. You could watch them paint amazing pictures with their trunks, throw darts with astonishing accuracy, or play soccer with giant balls. After each show the visitors could feed them bananas and sugarcane and have their pictures taken with them while they performed more tricks and clowned around.

Lars and Leif went to Grace International School which offered a strong program and allowed them to make new friends quickly, while Eja and Lena studied at home with a Christian curriculum. The only big hurdle for all of us was the language which we found extremely hard to learn, and so we lived in this "expat bubble" where everyone spoke English. We started attending one of the large International churches, and soon we found ourselves involved in leading worship and teaching as well as leadership.

In the spring of 2002, we all travelled to Oklahoma to take part in Björn and Laura's wedding, which turned out to be a beautiful outdoor celebration with many guests. Charles and I shared the ceremony and it was a very precious time. After that we visited Cathy's parents and some of her siblings in New Jersey. Little did I know that this would be the last time for me to see my in-laws. Later that year Nils finally got his Green Card and left home for the U.S.

Only one and a half years later, Carina and Josh were married at a beautiful hill resort not far from our home. The next day, they left for their honeymoon and then on to Oklahoma. Six months later, Lars left home for California after graduating from Grace. My friend Don was helping to get him settled with friends from the church there. Only two years later, it was Leif's turn to graduate and join his brothers in the U.S. Our nest was being emptied rapidly, and it never got easier to see our children leave, especially since we knew it would be years before we would see them again.

* * *

From the very beginning in Chiang Mai, I worked hard to get our training schools started up again. Martin had delegated that particular area to one of the young and upcoming leaders in the Vineyard Bern. He had many new ideas, and initiated a joined training program with another training school called "Factory," because it had started up in Switzerland in a converted factory. I did not really buy into the idea, but I trusted their wisdom and needed their help to promote the schools back in Europe. Together we had three schools, and things went quite well, but the numbers were much smaller than formerly in Penang.

Then, one day I got a phone call from that young leader, and he let me know that they had decided to scrap the schools. That decision had been made completely without me, and at first I thought I had not understood clearly, but things had been decided and that was that. I was devastated to say the least. The schools were the only reason why we had moved to Thailand, and they had become a significant part of our income. There was no alternate plan or offer for us, neither in Asia, nor back in Germany, nor Switzerland. At this point I would have considered leaving Asia if there had been any indication that we were needed or wanted anywhere else. As it was, we were dumped and left to find our own reason for staying in Thailand.

We invested more and more into our roles in the international church, and I was soon asked to become one of the elders. Of course this was on a voluntary basis with no pay or compensation. Thankfully, we still had the financial support of most of our friends, and we were somehow able to survive financially.

Working in this church was both exciting and challenging. Since most of the members were missionaries, there was a constant coming and going, and it was hard to determine who actually belonged. For most of the people, meeting on Sundays was really all they wanted, and often it was more for the reason of networking than worshipping God together. Cathy and I were part of the worship team and led quite often. With people being as diverse as Mennonites to Pentecostals this also proved to be a real challenge. Some wanted hymns, some not, and we discovered very soon that it was impossible to make everybody happy. Everyone was so busy that there was no true fellowship, except among those from the same network or organization. There was very little desire for ministry and prayer, and I started to feel increasingly out of place.

* * *

There were some real highlights during that season, and one was a refugee family from Burma. Because of the sensitive nature of this whole situation I feel it is better for me to withhold their real names. The family was from one of the largest ethnic groups in the region, the Shan. The father, let's just call him Aung, was a lawyer involved in the human-rights-movement, which placed him on the black list of the Burmese military junta. Things got so bad that he had to flee together with his wife and teenage son and daughter. They made it safely across the border into Thailand, and a missionary family took them in and arranged a small house for them not far from us.

Their teenage children received Jesus in their lives, and shortly afterwards the mother came to faith as well. But not Aung. He was a devout Buddhist who took his faith very seriously. He used to spend many hours meditating in the Lotus position while staring into the sun. Not only did he not get blinded, but at several occasions he actually levitated in a state of demonic trance. Many from the church began to pray for him, and shortly afterwards Jesus appeared to him during one of his meditations. While staring into the sun he saw the Son of God and surrendered his life to him. Soon the whole family started coming to church and we had the privilege of seeing them baptized in the swimming pool of the hotel were we had our meetings.

I do not think that I have ever seen any new convert grow as fast as Aung. His hunger for God and his Word was insatiable, and he joined one of our training schools. During our times of worship he would initially sit in the Lotus position and worship Jesus with tears running down his face. Since he rode with me each day to the classes we had much time to talk. One morning he seemed quite troubled, and I knew that there was something he wanted to say, but felt embarrassed to do so. Eventually I got him to open up, and he explained to me that every time he read about the Kingdom of God in the book we were studying that week, he would begin to tremble and shake. He was so relieved when I explained to him that he was just experiencing a touch from his Father in heaven, and that he should simply enjoy it with a grateful heart.

Since Aung had been an influential leader among his people, someone soon tracked him down, and he received numerous calls and invitations to secret political meetings. One day he confided in me that he had been asked to become the president in exile of the Shan people, a tribe of over ten million people without a homeland. His love and burden for his own people were evident, but we felt that he needed to grow more in his new-found faith before giving in to such an enormous request. He agreed, and instead started writing psalms and songs in their dialect, and sent them back into Burma. Coming from him, they must have been a considerable influence and testimony for Jesus. Since they were political refugees registered with the UN they were in a long line of refugees waiting to be repatriated in a Western country. When the call finally came, we were all surprised at the favor Aung carried, even with Western diplomats. The UN made him a deal totally unheard of. They would send them to New York City where he was offered a position at the human-rights division of the United Nations. If he would serve them for three years, the whole family would receive American citizenship, and they would be free to come and go as they pleased. And that is exactly what happened. We connected them with a Vineyard church in New York City, and they are now U.S. citizens. I would not be surprised to hear his name one day in the media as a major political leader for the minorities in Myanmar. I will always be grateful for the privilege to guide him a bit on his journey with Jesus.

✳ ✳ ✳

On December 26, 2004, we were on our way to a church service, when the whole region suffered one of the deadliest natural disasters in modern times. Had we not been riding in our ancient, noisy and a bit wobbly Isuzu station wagon, we would have felt the 9.3 earthquake that shook the island of Sumatra that morning, triggering a massive tsunami that ended up killing 230,000 people in fourteen nations.

It took quite some time for the news of what actually happened to filter through, but it became clear that no one had ever witnessed a tragedy of these proportions before, and every organization and mission scrambled to get involved in the relief operations. In Thailand, there would be over 8,000 casualties with over 2,800 people missing whose remains would never be discovered. Among the casualties was one of the Thai King's grandsons, adding to the nation's utter devastation. Over 1,000 German and Swedish tourists were among the victims, and the economy would suffer for years to come.

Unlike after the volcanic eruption in 1991, I did not feel an urge to get personally involved in the relief operations. The reason for that was quite simple. Every organization was heavily involved with huge amounts of money and personnel made available, and already stories came back of some areas being flooded with relief workers, and fights breaking out among organizations, as well as grave misuse of funds, and the ever present corruption. In addition I really was not trained in the areas that needed most attention.

Amazing stories became known of missionaries being spared because their booking was messed up and they ended up in a hotel higher up than the one they had booked originally. For weeks no one spoke of anything else than tsunami stories, most of which were tragic stories of death and suffering.

About six weeks later, I got a phone call from Martin in Bern. He said that they were flooded with gifts and offerings for the tsunami victims, and that he would send me 16,000 dollars to go and do something. So much for me trying to stay out of the picture.

Thankfully, some folks from the Vineyard in Bangkok had taken a scouting trip down south and explored the areas affected by the disaster. Just as we had heard, they reported that most organizations were active in the area of Phuket and Khao Lakh which were hard hit. Then they discovered that only very few had gone to help further south. They connected me with a Baptist pastor who was reaching out to an unreached people group called the Sea Gypsies, or "Chao Leh."

I flew down to Krabi and met up with the pastor. The next day he took me on a trip with his pickup truck. After a long drive and two ferry boats, we arrived on the island called "Koh Lanta". There, on the southern tip, was a village of this particular tribe, also referred to as "The People of the Sea." Their history is a bit sketchy, but most anthropologists believe that they had come from the Malaysian peninsula over 500 years ago. They built their huts on stilts over the water and live almost entirely off what the sea supplies. They have their own language and culture, and though some have converted to Islam, most of them still today are animists. At the time I met them, there was no believer in Christ among them, and obviously no church.

The Baptist pastor had begun to meet with some of them for Bible study, but he was not able to bring much material help. The tsunami had been powerful enough to wipe out their huts and fishing boats. The Thai government had helped them to rebuild their simple homes, and some of them had either repaired or bought new boats. The particular boats they favor are wooden longboats that need a special type of outboard motor. When we walked through the village, we saw that most men were sitting around fixing their fishing nets, or drying a few fish. It was obvious that they were in great despair, for most of them did not have functioning boats to go out to sea. After talking with the villages elders, it became obvious that their greatest needs were engines for their boats.

Previously, I had heard the story of an organization helping an impoverished tribe in South America by setting up what they called a "pig bank". The idea was to give each family one or several female piglets that they were to raise. Only the headman had a hog, a male pig of breeding age, and the villagers had to go to him to get their pigs impregnated. When the litter was born, they would return one piglet to the pig bank who would use that to help other families in need.

I simply told them that story as an example of a functioning micro -business. They were so excited that they asked if we could help them in the same way. Unknown to me, they had a real fondness for pork as an alternative to the seafood which was their staple. The few pigs they owned had drowned in the tsunami. Since they lived in the midst of Muslim territory, pork was scarce and expensive.

In the weeks to come, we supplied fifteen Diesel engines for their boats, as well as 168 piglets that were divided among 74 families. The piglets were vaccinated, and each family received special feed for three months as well as training on how to raise them. One piglet from each litter would be given to the pastor and the emerging church. After several months, there were over twenty believers among them who met regularly in homes.

When I visited the village a few months later there was great joy, and they proudly showed me the pens they had built for their newest family members. With lots of laughter and giggles, they recounted the story, of how the squeaking and smelly piglets had been transported in trucks through Muslim territory.

My pastor friend had also visited a smaller Sea Gypsy village that was mostly Muslim. He brought them some food and four of our boat engines. When the Imam reprimanded the villagers for associating with a

Christian they answered, "You have not done anything to help us in our time of need, but this Christian pastor has shown us great love."

After a few months, I received a message with the testimony of one of the new converts, who said this: "Every evening when I drive my boat out to sea I thank the God who loves me and provides for me." Mission accomplished.

* * *

Four years had gone by in Thailand, and it felt like we had accomplished what we had come for. We had a few good schools, and served a local church to the best of our ability. In the back of my mind was the question what would come next. After all, in the past we had moved every four to five years, and it seemed like it was time to move on.

One day I was driving back home on the highway to Hangdong, and, as so often, I used these times to talk to the Lord. As I was raising the issue regarding our future, I heard his voice loud and clear in my heart, and the words totally surprised me when I heard, "Would you be willing to invest ten years of your life into this city?"

I was so shocked by these words that I almost drove into the car beside me, and then I started thinking about what that would be like. Immediately all the advantages came to mind of how great it would be to actually sink roots in one place and break this nomad life-style of ours. But I could not figure out why on earth we should stay on in Chiang Mai with no clear objective and goal ahead. I figured if God would speak to Cathy as well then just maybe I had heard correctly.

When I came home, I asked Cathy if the number "ten" meant anything to her, but she said it didn't. Of course she wanted to know what I was talking about, and so I told her what I thought the Lord had spoken to me on the way home. To my surprise she expressed the same relief at the thought of actually staying longer in one place than our customary four to five years. So all that was lacking was for the Lord to show us the reason for staying on, but, as always, He was well ahead of us.

* * *

Some months later, we had another one of our Vineyard Asia Summits, and since this one was in Bangkok it was easy for me to attend. The meetings were great, and especially during the worship times I realized how much I had missed that particular style of intimate worship. While there, a man by the name of Don Sciortino approached me and wanted to talk. He was one of the leaders at the Anaheim Vineyard, the very church started and led by the late John Wimber. Don told me that he had felt for quite some time that God put Thailand on their hearts, and that he would like to come with teams to help and support. Initially, I was not too excited about his offer, though it warmed my heart to hear that someone from the Vineyard actually cared about us there in Thailand. But so many had made similar promises in the past, and I did not want to raise my hopes and expectations, for fear of being let down again. But Don proved to be a man of his word, and over the years that followed he became one of my closest friends and kept visiting at least once a year.

At that same conference, I met another couple from California by the names of David and Sheila Johnson. They had spent the last three years helping to plant the Vineyard in Singapore, and they were now moving to Chiang Mai. When they first came they stayed at a guest house while they were looking for a house. We met there and talked, and of course one of my first questions was, "So, what are you planning to do here in Chiang Mai?"

David's answer took me by surprise, when he said they had come to plant a Vineyard church. Totally intrigued, I asked the next logical question: "So how long are you planning to stay?"

"Oh, about one year...," was his serious reply, while in my heart all warning lights came on at the same time. Everyone knows that it takes more than one year to plant a church from scratch, and his reply almost made me angry.

As it turned out, they found a house not very far from where we lived and we started seeing each other more and more. They were just a few years older than Cathy and I, and we had a lot in common. It did not take long for us to become best friends, and when they started a small group on Tuesday evenings, it was just natural for us to attend. David was a worship leader as well as an awesome drummer. We had great times of worship and sweet fellowship together, and soon there were others who joined us. We started early morning prayer times, as well as worship times beside some of the Buddhist temples in town.

In the meantime, we continued to serve at the international church, but now the contrast between what we were doing, and what we really wanted to do and see had become even more visible to me, and I knew the time had come to work ourselves out of our responsibilities there. One by one we turned things over to others, and it was obvious that we were not really needed there anymore.

Don came to visit with a team, and with him came Mark Fields, the leader of the missions task force for all the Vineyards in the U.S. Riding in the car together after visiting the elephant camp, they asked me if we could see ourselves taking on the church planting project in Chiang Mai. After the disaster many years ago back in Germany, I had never really seen myself as a church planter, but at the same time I knew that what David and Sheila had begun was really what I had wanted all along. When they expressed their confidence in our leadership, it had a very healing effect on my soul, and I felt like God had given me another chance. With our involvement at the other church slowly being phased out, the time seemed perfect.

We continued to work under David and Sheila, and then one day David asked the question, "So, you wanna take it now?"

Thankfully, they stayed on for another year. They stayed six months longer than promised, and by the time they left for home in California, we had become so close that it turned out to be a very painful farewell. David is a biker and had bought himself an old 750 Honda, which became his parting gift to me.

Before they left, we had many challenging and wonderful experiences together. We saw a Buddhist monk come to faith in Jesus and experienced the ups and downs of discipling him. But what I really missed after they left were the wonderful times of worship we had together.

At one point we felt we should take our worship out into a small park in the city. We knew we would need a special permit for that, so we went to the city hall to apply for it. The clerk there did not give us much hope but said we would hear from them one way or another. Just a few days later, we got a call from city hall, and they asked for a special meeting with some of their representatives. They made us an offer we could not resist. They were planning a special celebration at the park, to inaugurate a new program called "Night Park." The idea was to open up the park until midnight to keep the youth from the streets and troubled areas. Police patrols on bicycles would ensure everyone's safety. For the opening night there would be a special celebration, but the band they had hired backed out, and could we take their place? If we would do that for them then we could use the park whenever we wanted! We tried to explain to them that we were not an ordinary band that played for entertainment, but they said that did not matter.

On the evening of the program we went there early to set up and practice and were shocked to see all the preparations they had made. There was a stage with lots of decorations and balloons, and a large sign with the name of our "band". They had called the day before asking for it, and being put on the spot we had to come up with some name right away, so we said, "New Vine." The sign they had made announced "New Wine" which made us all laugh.

We really were not prepared for what happened next. A convoy of luxury cars started pulling up, and the mayor, the police chief, and the governor of the district, plus a TV station came to listen to us worship Jesus! After a few songs, there were the obligatory speeches by some of the big wigs, and then something totally unexpected happened. Instead of the usual blessing of a Buddhist priest, they asked us to pray and bless the park, which we gladly did. Then they called us up to help cut the ribbon.

After all the balloons had been released the dignitaries got ready to leave. The governor thanked us and told us to keep playing until midnight — it was barely nine o'clock!

News of this event spread quickly throughout the churches, and we got messages of congratulations from believers all over Thailand. No one had ever heard of anything like that happening before, and we received instant recognition and respect. For the next year, we met there for worship one Sunday a month and had many wonderful conversations afterwards with both local folks as well as tourists from many different places.

* * *

During the time when we contemplated getting involved in another church plant I had a very special encounter with the Holy Spirit. Every morning I walked our Yellow Labrador "Abby" around our neighborhood, and these walks had become regular prayer times for me. One morning we passed by an empty lot when God spoke to me very clearly, "If you build a house for yourself then I will show you how to build mine." Just a few days earlier we had found out that we could no longer extend the lease on the house we had been renting for five years. That had been a big blow for us, for we loved living in that house and the whole neighborhood. There were no other houses available for rent, and it looked like we would have to search elsewhere. Our landlord felt bad about having to kick us out, and since he was a contractor he offered to build us a house for a special price. At first the idea had seemed too absurd to even consider, but after that morning walk we met with him to inquire what exactly would be required.

As anywhere else in the world, we would have to come up with a 20% downpayment, and then finance the rest through a bank. Since the construction of the house would take eight months, we could pay off the downpayment in eight parts, and then get a mortgage that would be similar to the monthly rent we had paid so far. Since foreigners are not allowed to own land in Thailand the deed would have to be registered in the name of a Thai citizen, and our contractor offered to do that in the name of his wife. We were aware that this was a huge risk, and we had heard several stories of foreigners being conned into financing a building, just to be kicked out a few years later without a chance to get any kind of justice. On top of it all, we were dealing with non-Christians, and in the natural realm, the whole plan seemed like one bad idea.

But God had spoken, and then provided a way to make it all possible, so we decided to trust that family, and signed the contract for him to build us a house. For the first time we were able to plan and design a home for ourselves, and since we lived just around the corner we could watch the daily progress. In financial terms that meant we had to double our income for the next eight months, and with much prayer and the help of dear friends we managed to do just that.

The whole thing was an amazing experience, and all the time the Lord kept showing me how the different phases of the project corresponded with what was happening at the church plant. Building a house in Asia must be quite different from doing it in the Western world. Though we had proper blueprints from an architect, the workers changed things as they went along. One day I checked out the progress of one of the bathrooms, and saw to my surprise that the workers were building a wall in the middle of the room. I quickly called the contractor who also lived nearby. When he asked them what they thought they were doing they replied they thought it would be better that way. He set them straight and the next day the wall was gone again. Working with that man turned out to be a very pleasant surprise. He was truly a man of his word and could be counted on to keep his part of the bargain. End even years later when something went wrong at the house he would take care of it.

Before Cathy and I married I had told her that we most likely would never have a home of our own, and it had truly never been a value or dream for us. Here we were thirty years later moving into a brand-new house with a lovely garden. One of my standard jokes at that time was, "Honey, I never promised you a rose garden, but I'll build you one anyway." And that is what I did, together with a fishpond and many other trees and bushes.

There is that scene in the movie "Far and Away" with Tom Cruise where his character's father in Ireland said to him, "A man's land is a man's own soul." I can't say I agree with that sentiment, but there is something special about walking through your garden and tending it. There is a sense of pride and ownership, and it releases creativity, the very thing that God gave Adam when He breathed life into him. This was a totally new experience that reminded me of the goodness of God every day. It was like being spoiled by your dad, not for what you did, but simply because of who you are.

* * *

One of the biggest challenges of living in Thailand was the whole visa situation. Many years ago, when the missionary organizations came to Thailand, they were given a certain amount of visa slots according to their size and involvement in the country. These figures were never updated, and by the time we got there it was virtually impossible to get one of the coveted and official missionary visas. For the first six years, we got by with volunteer visas which required a letter of invitation from a registered charity. These visas were never issued within the country, but had to be obtained at a Thai embassy outside the country. Depending where you applied, you could get a one-year visa, or only three months. That decision was totally up to the local officials, and it soon became quite a science to find out who was offering longer visas, and who only gave three months. Even if you were lucky to get a twelve-month visa, you were still required to leave the country every three months in order to activate the next part of your visa. The whole situation required most foreigners to do "visa runs."

Chiang Mai is less than three hours from the Burmese border, and we took countless trips there. That meant leaving by car, bus, or hired van early in the morning to the border, walk across the bridge into Myanmar, get a one-day visa there, and turn around to get your next three months' stamp at the Thai border. In order to get another one-year visa you had to go further, like Singapore or Malaysia. One time we even went to Kunming in China, but ended up getting only three months. The amount of money and time invested in getting visas for Thailand was a huge part of our living expense. But the Lord had a solution for us.

I had heard that our friend Charles in Oklahoma had worked on and received a master's degree, and somehow that challenged me to take another look at my education. My three years at Faith School of Theology were not even enough for a bachelor's, though I had studied off and on unofficially without getting any credit. Having a degree had never been a priority for me, but all of a sudden I felt stirred to look into doing some more postgraduate studies.

A good friend sent me a book unlocking some of the secrets of entering a degree program through an accredited institution, versus a more nontraditional approach. The whole thing seemed quite confusing, and I had to find a program that would allow me to stay in Thailand and continue what we were doing.

I heard from a friend in Germany that there was a Christian university in Florida that offered a more nontraditional, long-distance education, and so I contacted them to inquire what my options were. They replied with an offer that seemed too good to be true. Not only were they willing to give me credit for all my previous studies, plus work experience, but they offered me a position to train the national leadership of the Assemblies of God in Vietnam over a period of three years, and, in return, I would get a Master' in Cross-cultural Communication. Since this would require numerous trips to Ho Chi Minh City, I would get a 50% discount on the tuition.

I took a trip to Vietnam to meet my future students as well as my mentor, a pastor in the U.S. and a Vietnam veteran. As of this writing, Vietnam is one of the last few communist nations in the world, and the moment I landed in former Saigon I recognized that spirit of fear and oppression from our trips behind the Iron Curtain many years ago.

Most of the churches in Vietnam were still underground, with only the Catholic Church and one other denomination officially recognized by the government. The Vietnamese Assemblies of God had applied for official recognition years ago. The government had made it as hard as possible for them to comply with their requirements, persisting that all of their top leaders have at least a master's degree in Theology, which could not be obtained in Vietnam. The Florida university stepped in to provide that opportunity for them, and I was to be one of their main teachers and the overseer of the program. Ironically, I was to help them get their master's degree to get my own, but they did not care, and neither did I.

I got to do what I love best, and get a degree for it besides. But I worked very hard. My job consisted of reading numerous books on the topics of theology, church planting and world religions, then condensing each book in simplified English. I would then send my version of the original book to them in Vietnam where it was translated into Vietnamese. Then I would spend one week there teaching it to them. They in turn had to write essays on each topic that I had to read and grade. Since several of them could not write in English there had to be translations back and forth which made the whole program a very tedious affair. I finished my part in three years and then wrote a final thesis evaluating the program.

Working with these pastors was a great privilege for me and increased my respect for this part of the church. These men were sacrificing so much, and many of them had been in prison, or suffered abuse by the police and authorities. When they told me their stories, they did so with joy and a sense of pride for having suffered for Christ. One story in particular stood out to me. Every year they would hold a youth conference which they knew was illegal. So they would always have two leadership teams. One team would let itself get arrested by the police to be beaten, abused, and fined, while the other team would continue the youth camp. Every year they would change the teams, so that everyone eventually got their turn on either one of the teams. They would joke about whose turn it was to get beaten up by the police this year. To them it was the normal Christian life, and they were willing to pay that price.

The place where I taught was an official English school. The building had three stories, and on the first two levels they offered English courses. The classroom on the top floor was their "secret Bible school." There was a button under the counter of the reception desk by the entrance which the receptionist would press in cases when the secret police came to pay them a visit. By the time they would reach the third floor all Bibles were gone and a normal English class was in session. As far as the police were concerned I was only there to help them teach English.

Shortly after their graduation, I got news that the government had granted the Assemblies of God in Vietnam official status as a recognized church movement in the country. I don't think that this eliminated all forms of persecution for them, but certainly made things easier. It felt good to have played a small part in that development.

The greatest payback came just a few weeks after I had received my diploma in the mail. A Swedish missionary friend asked me if I would be interested in an official missionary visa. There was a Scandinavian mission that had a slot available that I could get. But there was one snag. The requirement was a masters degree. We got that visa slot and enjoyed official missionary status without expensive "visa runs" in the years that followed.

✳ ✳ ✳

Our international Vineyard church had evolved, and we began regular Sunday services, first in homes, and then in several halls. As much as I enjoyed the fellowship and times of worship, there was something regarding our setup that left me with a sense of want. Just like the larger international church, our people were mainly missionaries and foreigners who would come and go, and there was no sense of permanence.

Even from the first few years in the Philippines I realized that our role as foreigners should never be to pastor a local church, except, of course, in extreme pioneer situations where there was no local leadership. I had seen too many missionaries come and "plant" new churches that would collapse or disappear as soon as they left or the money from the West dried up.

After so many years, I was quite familiar with Asian culture, yet time and time again I was confronted with cultural issues where I had to admit I had no answer for certain deeper points. Culture is 100% learned, and unless you are born and raised in a particular culture it takes many years to fully understand how people "click." The part of culture that we see in the way people look, talk, dress, and act is only the tip of the iceberg, and there is an immensely complicated structure underneath that one cannot simply learn from books and charts. Our main calling is to make disciples, but how can I disciple someone if I do not understand why they act and feel the way they do?

For that very reason I would have never agreed to lead a Thai church, Vineyard or not. So the first big question we faced was, what is our calling as a church, and who do we want to target? There were several international churches in town and we felt there really was no need for another one. However, there was one particular people group that neither they, nor the local Thai churches were targeting, and that was the many mixed couples and families. Even in our neighborhood we had met several European or American men married to Thai women, and we soon found out that they did not really fit in anywhere. Even the Thai wives, or husbands, were no longer accepted within their own culture, but had become strangers in their own land, and many of these marriages did not last. Over the years we were able to serve a number of these couples, but we also attracted a fair amount of missionaries looking for a home away from home.

All of that left me unfulfilled because deep down I was longing to see a local expression of our Vineyard, like there was in Bangkok, where our friend Sukit had planted a church in the heart of one of the biggest slums. I prayed earnestly that God would supply a local leader who would enable us to plant a Thai expression of the church. There was one mixed couple who had joined from the very beginning. The husband was Thai, and I was certain that he was our man, but they had so many struggles in their relationship that it became obvious that I had misjudged the situation. Eventually they left the church and I was becoming increasingly desperate in my search for our Thai leader.

One day as I was praying and reminding the Lord about this need, he spoke quite clearly and said that he had answered that prayer a long time ago. At the same time I saw the face of a Thai lady by the name of Poommarin, which means butterfly in Thai.

I had met Poommarin several years earlier, when we had one of our first schools. She had joined one week of our training, the week on church planting, and then she served us as an interpreter and Thai teacher.

One day in class I taught on God's heart for the poor, referring to my story and experience. As an assignment I told our students to go into the city two by two and find the poor. The next day one team reported with great excitement, "We have found them!" They discovered a slum area in Chiang Mai that few missionaries knew about. The old city is surrounded by a square moat and a wall with gates on each side. Today, large parts of the wall are gone, but the moat is still there, and the gates have been rebuilt. In olden days, there was an area outside the Southeast corner of the wall that was designated for the outcasts. The lepers, gamblers and drug addicts lived there for hundreds of years. Nowadays that area is part of the new city, but is indeed a slum area with great poverty. Many illegal immigrants as well as tribal people live there in huts and try to make a living by making handicrafts they sell to tourists at the famous nearby Night Market.

Our students went in several times a week to pray for people and play with the children. Poommarin joined them as a guide and interpreter, and when the school was over, she continued to go there with her husband Somchai. For years they had worked there among the poor, organized English classes as well as finding sponsors for the children who were too poor to go to school. Though schooling is free in Thailand, the students need to buy their own uniforms and books which are too expensive for many.

I knew that Poommarin and Somchai had a call for church planting, and that was why she had joined our training on the subject. So I wrote her a message and told her what God had shown me in prayer, and asked if she was still interested in planting a church. She said she cried when she saw my message, for she knew she had been running from that calling.

It all made so much sense. They had gained the respect and trust of the people in that area, and had not kept it a secret that they were Christians. So they began with Bible studies in different homes, and since they had no worship leader, Cathy and I joined them once a month to teach them worship songs and stories from the Bible.

So now we had a two-track church, and though I thoroughly enjoyed our international family, I knew that it was the local expression that had a real chance to represent God's Kingdom among the Thai people.

✳ ✳ ✳

We met a couple from South Africa, Dave and Sandra Macmillan, who were heavily involved in a prayer ministry in town. They had rented a small prayer room where they met regularly for intercession and worship, following the model of the International House of Prayer in Kansas City. We were invited to join their meetings, and at first I was a bit resistant to giving myself to something new and different. Deep down I knew that what they stood for was right and necessary. Just the simple fact that missionaries had come to Thailand for over 200 years, and yet, there were no more than one-half percent Christians in the country, made it obvious that the very thing lacking was ongoing prayer. I don't want to imply that the early missionaries did not know how to pray, but I know from my own experience how easy it is to get caught up in the business of ministry, so that prayer and devotions take a back seat.

Just driving through the city and seeing the thousands of temples, altars and spirit houses should be a constant reminder that this is a spiritual battle. Victory can only be won by spiritual authority which we have access to in prayer, as well as in keeping an intimate relationship with God. So I felt myself drawn back to these prayer sessions, and soon we were invited to lead some of them. When the Macmillans had to go home because of family reasons, they asked us to consider taking over that prayer ministry, and we did that parallel to building the church.

Though it was not always easy to generate interest and commitment for that type of ministry, we were met powerfully by God and I received a growing hunger for more. We had rented a large house for meetings with the international Vineyard, as well as for our ongoing training schools, and it became too much of a financial burden to also rent the small prayer room. We gave it up and moved the prayer meetings into the same house. I was so convinced that we needed to step up our prayer efforts that we started the "Chiang Mai House or Prayer," and tried to marry it with the church. When reading again that Jesus said His house should be a house of prayer for all nations, I felt we should set an example by demonstrating we could be both church, as well as a house of prayer.

For the opening night I invited many friends to help us dedicate the place, and it so happened that Dave and Sandra were in town. Unknown to us, there was a team from IHOP in Kansas City visiting Chiang Mai, and they dropped in and blessed us as well.

That is when the real battle began. Within the next few weeks we lost about half of our people in church who felt they were not called to that type of commitment in prayer. With the help of the "remnant," and an intern from Germany, we tried to have some expression of prayer and worship every day.

When we lost that house because of renovations we found a bigger and better one in a great location, but I had to realize soon that it was not as simple as I had thought. The activities of the church and the house of prayer attracted two different groups of people, with very little overlap, but we faithfully kept praying and worshipping in our prayer room without windows and fresh air.

During this season we walked with a great number of wonderful people from many nations and church backgrounds. From Pakistani refugees to high caliber leaders from Northern Ireland, New Zealand, the United States as well as other countries, we gave them the best we had. Visitors from many Asian nations would show up for our gatherings. Some had come for practical reasons, like applying for a new visa, or celebrating a birth, and many came simply for a break and some spiritual refreshment. Somehow they found us, and we always made sure that they felt welcome in our midst. We spent quality time ministering to them in prayer and with words from the Lord. In that way our ministry extended far beyond the reach of our small group in Chiang Mai.

* * *

Besides our growing burden and love for prayer, the Lord had yet another treat for us. The Vineyards in the U.S. had begun to pay more attention to, and take better care of their workers in foreign fields, and began inviting smaller groups to what they called, "leader care retreats." Because of our relationship with several US leaders we were graciously invited to take part in a number of these.

We were introduced to the whole topic of "spiritual formation." Instead of receiving extensive teaching, we were led in simple exercises of prayer and meditation on God's Word that were based on ancient practices of the Desert Fathers and other monastic movements of long past.

At first I found it hard to connect with this mystical side of Christianity, and I complained to the Lord that I thought it to be mere milk, to which He replied quite clearly,

"Yes it is, but this is a milk you never had!" So I opened my heart to ways of connecting with God that were very old, but quite new to me.

These retreats turned out to be absolute highlights during that season, and I found myself introducing spiritual formation exercises in various contexts. I began to understand that some of the difficult times in my life could have been much easier if I had been taught to take better care of my soul.

* * *

Back in Chiang Mai, we were confronted again with the variety of tastes and styles within God's family. Since we were Vineyard after all, I felt quite protective of our values and DNA. Somehow I felt that we had no right to exist if we were becoming like everyone else. Fully aware that we were not better than any other expression of the Church, I did not want to give up what took us so long to rediscover. That caused some misunderstandings from others who had come to us from outside the Vineyard, and deep down I realized that this church really had no future. Considering our lost church plant many years ago in Germany, I was not ready to acknowledge that to myself, but God had such an ingenious way to shake up our nest once again.

It began with an invitation from our friend Anders in Sweden, when he called all the members of our former youth group to a 40-year reunion in June of 2011. Oh, how I wanted to go, but it just did not feel right for me to leave Cathy and the two girls behind while I would go off to enjoy myself in Sweden. So we decided that either we would all go, or not at all. We had prayed hard for the funds, but about a month before the event we realized we just did not have the money, and so I wrote to our friends in Norrtälje and told them I would not be able to come.

The very next day I received an email from a couple in South Korea, whom I had met a few years earlier when I attended a conference with Don and the wedding of our common friend Song-Hee Bae. In their message, they relayed how they had been prompted by the Lord to send us some money for a trip, but they had delayed in doing so. They were wondering if we still needed money for a trip, and how much? They paid for all of us to go to Sweden for the reunion!

What a gift and wonderful experience! We thoroughly enjoyed our time with most of my old friends in Norrtälje, and even got to take a road trip to visit with my heroes, Karin, Bosse, and Stina. I thoroughly enjoyed showing Eja and Lena all the places where memorable things happened during my short time there, such as the old restaurant boat where I had poured out twenty eggs while working in the kitchen. The Swedish words for cleaning dishes and beating eggs sound vaguely similar, and instead of beating the eggs in the bowl the cook had handed me, I poured them down the drain and washed the bowl.

On the way back to Stockholm, we decided to visit the Stockholm Vineyard, something I had wanted to do for many years. We had such a great time worshipping with them and hanging out together with their leaders, Ted and Siw Jeans, as well as a group of their young people.

On our last evening in Sweden, we had walked to watch the very late sunset at a lake. It was there I found myself wishing God would call us to live in Sweden, but I almost felt guilty for asking, and pushed this desire deep down in my heart. When we sat on the plane to Germany the next day, to spend a few days with my Mom before going back to Thailand, I was overcome with such an immense sadness as we left the southern tip of Sweden, that I began to wonder what was really going on. But after a short visit in Nuremberg, we returned to Chiang Mai and continued our lives and ministry just as before.

* * *

Over the next few months, things were shaking up in our international Vineyard. One day I had to admit to myself that the church had become something I never wanted it to be. Giving in to pressures and demands to have a youth ministry as well as to cater to the younger kids, we had become so program oriented that all our energies were swallowed up serving the needs and demands of people who were reluctant to get involved themselves. Given the fact that they all had their own ministries throughout the week that was understandable, but this was a track that was so inward focused that I felt I had lost the grace to continue.

The following Sunday I explained to everyone how we had side-slipped from our values and our calling to build Him an altar of worship in the city. I then suspended all regular activities and simply invited everyone to come on Sundays for a time of seeking the Lord and simply soaking in His presence. To borrow the language of Graham Cooke, "This went over like a rat sandwich," and we lost a good amount of our regulars. These Sunday soaking times became something very precious for those who attended, but I realized I had lost the vision for another reboot of the church.

* * *

In the very beginning of 2012, I made arrangements to attend the Vineyard Leaders Conference in Berlin, and then I had an inspired idea. What if I quickly popped over to Stockholm, just to evaluate these intense emotions I felt when we were there just six months earlier? A quick check with a budget airline confirmed that I could get a flight for less than twenty Euros. When I asked Ted Jeans if it was okay for me to visit that particular weekend, he not only encouraged me to come, but even extended an invitation to speak that Sunday.

While in Berlin I had a talk with Martin, hoping he could help me to make sense of these strange and new longings in my heart. When I mentioned Sweden he became thoughtful, and said, "I think you would fit well there."

The Sunday at the Stockholm Vineyard became a mark stone for the future in a very powerful way. While sharing my heart with the church there was a profound sense of convergence, like everything that ever happened in my life until now pointed to this place. The following day, while riding in his car, Ted told me the story of the salmon always returning to the place where it was spawned, and it was like a tap from the Holy Spirit right between the eyes! Exactly forty years ago I was reborn in this very city, and the time had come for me to return home. When I checked the voyage of the salmon later on the internet, I noticed that Ted had failed to mention a rather important detail: After overcoming numerous obstacles and retuning to its place of birth, the salmon dies, but not before giving life to many, thus making it the most fruitful time of its life. But then I never had issues about dying. I went to Cambodia willing to lay down my life and always treated every assignment like it was my last. Besides, there are a lot worse places to die than Sweden.

THE SALMON RETURNS

When I told Cathy what had happened during my visit to Stockholm, she did not seem very surprised and let me know that she had always felt we would be living in Sweden someday. That totally surprised me, since she had never mentioned it, but at the time I was relieved that this did not come as a complete shock to her. However, we did wonder about the timing. Were we running ahead of God? What about the "ten years" I had heard the Lord talk about? When exactly had they started? By the time we were planning to move it would have been eleven years.

Then we took a closer look at the situation of our family as well as our work in Thailand. Eja would graduate soon from high school and had already decided that she wanted to live and study in Oklahoma, so she would be leaving home either way. The prospect of leaving was really hard for Lena. Born in Malaysia and growing up in Thailand, Lena only knew Asia as home.

When we mentioned our plans to our closest friends, they were sad, but most of them confirmed that the timing seemed right, and that God was definitely in all of this.

Once again we were caught up in a whirlwind of preparations for a major move. This one was different however. Somehow this did not feel like another chapter in the book of our lives, but rather the closing of a book, and the start of a totally new one — a sequel.

We put our house on the market, but the climate for real estate was down, and we only had a few nibbles. Our other belongings, however, sold like hot cakes. On the Saturday of our big garage sale, we had people waiting at the gate thirty minutes before we opened, and after three hours we had sold most of our belongings.

Flights were booked, and we started looking for apartments in Stockholm. That is when another realization hit us: We were about to move from one of the cheapest countries in the world to one of the most expensive.

* * *

We officially closed down the international Vineyard with a celebration. This time I did not feel that I had failed, for I knew we had given our best, but it was only meant to be for a season. The Vineyard would live on in Chiang Mai through the church in the slums, and we had full confidence in Poommarin and Somchai to guide the little flock into the future. For the remaining weeks before our departure we met with friends in a home group. Another ministry with similar values took over the lease of our church building, and it would continue to serve as a place of training, prayer and meeting with God.

Time came close to our departure date, and we still had not sold the house. We had hoped that after paying off the mortgage we would have a small profit to help us move and get established in our new home. But God had different plans.

A friend had given me the calling card of a real estate agent, and I gave him a call to see if he could help us. He came a few days later to look at the house, and introduced himself as "John." As we talked more, we realized we had several friends in common, and then an incredible story emerged. During the beginning of our church plant, we had been asked to pray for a Thai man by the name of John and his wife and son, who had some family problems and were open for the Christian faith. For several months we prayed for them but never met, nor heard what had become of them. Here before us stood the same John and told us how he and his family had become believers two years ago, and he would be more than pleased to help us sell our house.

We found homes for our pets and made the rounds saying goodbye to many friends. It was a very emotional time for all of us, but for me it was more than just leaving a home and friends. Forty years earlier, God had put Asia on my heart, and now we were about to leave for good. There were times of doubt, and a sense of betrayal tried to overshadow the joy and expectation of what was to come. I had been quite sure that I would spend the rest of my life on this vast continent, and now we were about to leave. Deep down I knew that my work in Asia was not yet done, but God was repositioning me, giving me a louder voice to speak on behalf of the multitudes waiting to hear the good news of the Kingdom. In the midst of it all, the Great Comforter calmed my heart with the assurance, "The best is yet to come!"

∗ ∗ ∗

On July 10, 2012, after twenty-four years of living in Asia, we boarded a Finnair flight from Bangkok to Helsinki, and then onward to Stockholm, Sweden. The salmon was returning to the place where it all began — the voyage of grace.

"But I don't place any value on my own life. I want to finish the race I'm running. I want to carry out the mission I received from the Lord Jesus— the mission of testifying to the Good News of God's kindness (grace)."[6]

Go to www.voyageofgrace.com for pictures corresponding to each chapter in this book.

---

[6] Acts 20:24 (NLTse)

Made in the USA
Charleston, SC
24 April 2015